Australian Sport

Australia is only a small player in the world's political and economic landscapes, yet, for many decades it has been considered to be a global powerhouse in terms of its sporting successes. In conjunction with this notion, the nation has long been portrayed as having a preoccupation with sport. This labelling has been seen as both a blessing and a curse. Those who value a Bourdieuian view of culture bemoan sport's centrality to the national imagination and the consequent lack of media coverage, funding and prestige accorded to the arts. Other scholars question whether the popular stereotype of the Australian sportsperson is, in fact, a myth and that instead Australians are predominantly passive sport consumers rather than active sport participants.

Australian sport, through its successes on the field of play and in advancing sport coaching and management, has undergone a revolution, as both an enabler of global processes and as subject to its influences (economic, political, migratory etc.). This book will examine the shifting place of Australian sports in current global and local environs, from the perspective of spectators, players and administrators.

This book was previously published as a special issue of *Sport in Society*.

Kristine Toohey is Professor in Sport Management at Griffith University, Australia.

Tracy Taylor is Professor of Sport Management for the Faculty of Business, University of Technology, Sydney, Australia.

Australian Sport

Antipodean Waves of Change

Edited by
Kristine Toohey and Tracy Taylor

Routledge
Taylor & Francis Group

LONDON AND NEW YORK

First published 2011
by Routledge
2 Park Square, Milton Park, Abingdon, Oxon, OX14 4RN

Simultaneously published in the USA and Canada
by Routledge
711 Third Avenue, New York, NY 10017, USA

Routledge is an imprint of the Taylor & Francis Group, an informa business

This book is a reproduction of *Sport in Society*, vol. 12, issue 7. The Publisher requests to those authors who may be citing this book to state, also, the bibliographical details of the special issue on which the book was based.

Typeset in Times New Roman by Taylor & Francis Books

British Library Cataloguing in Publication Data
A catalogue record for this book is available from the British Library

ISBN13: 978-0-415-44745-4

Disclaimer
The publisher would like to make readers aware that the chapters in this book are referred to as articles as they had been in the special issue. The publisher accepts responsibility for any inconsistencies that may have arisen in the course of preparing this volume for print.

Contents

SPORT IN GLOBAL SOCIETY - CONTEMPORARY PERSPECTIVES

Series Editor: Boria Majumdar

AUSTRALIAN SPORT

Antipodean Waves of Change

Sport in the Global Society – Contemporary Perspectives
Series Editor: Boria Majumdar

The social, cultural (including media) and political study of sport is an expanding area of scholarship and related research. While this area has been well served by the Sport in the Global Society Series, the surge in quality scholarship over the last few years has necessitated the creation of *Sport in the Global Society: Contemporary Perspectives*. The series will publish the work of leading scholars in fields as diverse as sociology, cultural studies, media studies, gender studies, cultural geography and history, political science and political economy. If the social and cultural study of sport is to receive the scholarly attention and readership it warrants, a cross-disciplinary series dedicated to taking sport beyond the narrow confines of physical education and sport science academic domains is necessary. Sport in the Global Society: Contemporary Perspectives will answer this need.

Titles in the Series

Australian Sport
Antipodean Waves of Change
Edited by Kristine Toohey and Tracy Taylor

Australia's Asian Sporting Context
1920s and 1930s
Edited by Sean Brawley and Nick Guoth

'Critical Support' for Sport
Bruce Kidd

Disability in the Global Sport Arena
A Sporting Chance
Edited by Jill M. Clair

Diversity and Division – Race, Ethnicity and Sport in Australia
Christopher J. Hallinan

Documenting the Beijing Olympics
Edited by D. P. Martinez

Football in Brazil
Edited by Martin Curi
Football's Relationship with Art: The Beautiful Game?
John E. Hughson

Forty Years of Sport and Social Change, 1968-2008
"To Remember is to Resist"
Edited by Russell Field and Bruce Kidd

Global Perspectives on Football in Africa
Visualising the Game
Edited by Susann Baller, Giorgio Miescher and Raffaele Poli

Sport in Australia: 'worth a shout'

Kristine Toohey[a] and Tracy Taylor[b]

[a]Department of Tourism, Leisure, Hotel and Sport Management, Griffith University, Queensland, Australia; [b]School of Leisure, Sport and Tourism, University of Technology, Sydney, Australia

With just over 21 million people[1] Australia has a vast land mass and a relatively small population. Despite the latter, Australia has been lauded, rightly or wrongly, as a successful, obsessive and cocky sporting nation that consistently 'punches above its weight'.

Australia's sporting success and dominance across a number of sports has been attributed to a variety of factors, including: inheritance of the British sport ethic in the early years of white settlement and colonization; dominance of a masculine and competitive culture; a paucity of cultural alternatives; a temperate climate; and availability of open spaces.[2] Whatever the explanation, the centrality of sport to the Australian psyche has been a subject that has fascinated both sport studies scholars and a small number of academics from other disciplines. For example, the social commentator Donald Horne, writing in *The Lucky Country*, in the 1960s, believed that, 'sport to many Australians is life and the rest is a shadow. Sport has been the one national institution that has had no knockers. To many it is considered a sign of degeneracy not to be interested in it. To play sport, or watch others play and to read and talk about it is to uphold the nation and build its character.'[3] Despite such populist observations, it is germane to question whether or not this preoccupation with sport is unique to Australia. Furthermore, is the nation really a haven for an unquestioning, sport-crazed populous that obsessively hold sporting victories above all else, irrespective of sportspersonship and ethical responsibility? Richard Cashman, writing some 30 years after Horne, in *Paradise of Sport*, legitimately questions if this scenario was ever really the case and, if so, has the trend continued?

National sport participation data, if selectively applied, does give some credibility to this 'sporting Aussie' image. The Australian Bureau of Statistics (ABS) reported that in 2004–05 'nearly two-thirds (66% or 10.5 million people) of the Australian population aged 15 years and over reported that they had participated in sports and physical recreation' at least once during the 12 months prior to interview in 2005–06.[4] However, these figures are somewhat misleading as 'participation' means engaging in physical activity (not necessarily sport) only once in the previous 12 months, rather than on a weekly, or even monthly basis. As the most popular activity was walking and the overall number of people participating in non-organized activities (54%) was almost double that for participation in organized activities (28%)[5] then the picture of a nation obsessed with bats, balls, Speedos and other sporting paraphernalia does not appear to be the reality. Nevertheless, the sporting image that the nation has presented to the world has produced a backlash from some intelligentsia, including Bourdieu-inspired critical analysts who lament sport's place in the national psyche at the expense of more cultured pursuits. One social commentator, Keith Dunstan, who wrote *Sports*, one of the first serious studies of sport in Australia, also infamously founded the Anti-Football League (AFL) in 1967. The organization once boasted 7,000 members and in one year even recorded a profit of A\$28,000, which was donated to charity,[6] further suggesting that not all who inhabit the 'Great South Land' are 'Aussie Aussie Aussie, Oi Oi Oi' robotons.[7]

An informed middle ground, between the sporting utopians and the cynics, may better reflect the reality of the nation's sporting landscape as well as the oft promulgated and similarly questioned Australian ethos of giving everyone a 'fair go'. Cashman invites Australian academics to 'criticise and scrutinise our sporting culture' to provide a way of making sport 'more accessible, equitable and fair to all Australian who wish to participate in it, and less corrupt, racist and sexist'.[8] This volume of *Sport and Society* heeds this *cri de coeur*. In light of the 2008 cricket 'Bollyline Tour' imbroglio, when the Indian team threatened to cancel its tour after a series of controversial and maligned actions by players and decisions by officials at the Second Test in Sydney, his decade-old call to shoulder academic arms could easily be extended to investigate how Australian international relations in the twenty-first century shape our international sporting identity and influence our relations.

In the main, contemporary mainstream Australian media continue to present the nation's success in sport as taken for granted and rarely acknowledge that there are barriers to sport participation faced by a number of segments of the population that, *ipso facto*, exclude many Australians from dipping their toes in this seemingly inexhaustible 'pool of talent'.[9] It was a far different story just 30 years ago when the golden era of Australian sport was thought to have well and truly ended with a whimper. In 1976 Australia did not win any gold medals at the Montreal Olympic Games, a far cry from their successes at the Games and other arenas in the 1950s and 1960s. Even before the final strains of the Olympic Closing Ceremony had sounded, the Australian Federal Government announced a review of the nation's sport as a means to redress a situation which to some Australians was tantamount to a national disaster. Although other countries were implementing systemic government sport systems, at this time there was very limited Australian federal government involvement in sport. The first federal government department with a specific remit for sport (the Department of Tourism and Recreation) had only been established in 1972 and federal funding was insignificant.

Yet, the suggestion to review sport policy did not meet with unanimous approval from either sport administrators or citizens in general. Articles and letters to editors questioned past aspects of the nation's international sporting achievements, especially an undue emphasis on winning; the lack of funding for sport at the grass-roots (sport for all) level; the Australian media's unrealistic expectations of sporting success; and the consequences of emulating the sporting infrastructure of Eastern European countries, which was seen as the antithesis to the Australian sporting culture and its espoused egalitarian ethos. Others, willingly or simply coming to terms with the realities of the necessity to invest dollars to win medals, countered these objections and argued that Australians were readily accepting failure by regarding it as less distasteful than the risk of diluting the purity of the amateur system that dominated sport delivery philosophy.[10]

Since that very public blip on the radar of Australia's sporting supremacy, the involvement of government in high performance sport has increased and the nation's record has once again been in the ascendancy, culminating in the sporting juggernaut that was the Sydney 2000 Olympic Games. These Games were an organizational success

(Marion Jones and other drug cheats aside) and the nation took pride in its achievement in producing what International Olympic Committee President, Juan Antonio Samaranch described as 'the best ever Games'.[11]

Recently, though (especially since Australia placed behind Great Britain on the Beijing 2008 medal count), there is growing concern that a second slide into sport oblivion may be on the horizon and scholars and sports administrators have begun to analyse the reasons for the post-1976 resurgence of Australian international sporting success, suggesting various strategies designed to continue this global sport domination into the future.[12] Such commentaries include discussions of how to remain at the top of the sporting ladder without the aid of performance-enhancing substances, genetic manipulation or resorting to 'sledging' opponents into submission.

In this volume of *Sport in Society* the contributions take a somewhat different approach to analysing Australia's current sport environment and offer a range of atypical insights. The changing social context of sport, highlighted by the expanded role and pressures of commercialization, professionalism, the media and globalization, is of particular relevance here. In exploring the contemporary sporting landscape, the essays in this volume go beyond just scrutinizing the sports for which the nation is usually identified, such as Australian Rules Football (or indeed any football code), cricket, swimming, yachting or netball. Encompassing a variety of theoretical frameworks, none of which has been privileged above another, the essays in this volume present the reader with a range of perspectives. Sport's place is also questioned in relation to its relevant markets and stakeholders, such as participants, spectators, sponsors and regulators. The roles of colonization, immigration and government's responsibility in the development of these processes are also scrutinized. Sports' relationship with stratification matters, especially ethnicity, class and gender which are key themes in the material presented.

Popi Sotiriadou's essay, 'The Australian sport system and its stakeholders' opens the batting by using stakeholder theory to examine the nation's past and present sport policy relationships. Her argument centres on the position faced by many Australian sports, forced to seek new sources of income in response to crucial financial imperatives. Sotiriadou concludes that these pressures drove change and the subsequent actions that revitalized the Australian sport system.

'The Janus face of diversity in Australian sport' by Tracy Taylor, Daniel Lock and Simon Darcy examines the changing face of cultural diversity in Australian sport. Through a case study of football, or soccer as it is more commonly known in Australia, the cultural context and the relative diversity of sport in Australia historically is discussed.

Carole M. Cusack and Justine Digance in 'The Melbourne Cup: Australian identity and secular pilgrimage' explore how the nation's best-known sport event takes on religio-spiritual significance. They believe that 'the Cup' functions both as a medium for the experience of the sacred, which involves vindication of both individual, personal identity, and *communitas*, which reinforces Australian national and cultural identity. In exploring the themes of the Cup the defining parameters of *secular pilgrimage* are articulated.

Matthew Burke and Geoffrey Woolcock are urban geographers. In 'Getting to the game: travel to sports stadia in the era of transit-oriented development' they examine the conditions influencing the travel behaviour of Australian sports patrons going to large sport events. They contend that new Australian sports stadiums are returning to the core of cities and to sites supported by high-capacity public transport infrastructure. Their research adds to our understanding of travel to and from stadiums as part of the sport patron experience, which, to date has been given lesser attention in the academic literature than the experience in the stadium itself. Burke and Woolcock argue that the return of sports fans to public transport is creating new opportunities for experience-based sociality in public spaces. They contend that the docile behaviour of Australian stadium goers is reinforced by the use of public transport, which by its nature requires attitudes of reciprocity and self-discipline. In light of this, they explore the siting of a proposed stadium on Queensland's Gold Coast and question the veracity of the current decision on where it is to be located.

Gender representation and power in the management of Australian cricket during a period of governance change provides the framework for '"Brave new world" or "sticky wicket"?: Women, management and organizational power in Cricket Australia', by Megan Stronach and Daryl Adair. The authors outline the key aspects behind the amalgamation of the men's and women's governing bodies and conclude that while the strategy to integrate was one based on good intentions, the reality has been quite different.

Richard Cashman's contribution looks beyond Australian shores to her neighbours to the North West in 'Asia's place in the imaging of Australian sport'. Cashman notes that since 1945 Asia has become a powerful factor in Australian life in general and that the Australian-Asian sports nexus has been transformed as a result. He attributes Asia's increasing role in Australian sport as a by-product of sport globalization.

Steve Frawley and Kristine Toohey use a figurational framework to investigate the intended and unintended consequences of the Australian Olympic Committee's (AOC) strategic and operational involvement in the Sydney 2000 Olympic Games. They conclude that the AOC leveraged its prior experience and extensive Olympic figurations in order to gain a strategic advantage over the other Australian Olympic stakeholders.

The place of rugby union football from its inception to professionalization in Australian society has presented a rich context for Peter Horton to critically investigate social issues, such as identity formations and contestations. Horton concludes that even though Australian rugby operates in a globalized context, it remains culturally distinct, thus rejecting the notion that globalization completely engulfs local sport cultures.

Dwight Zakus, James Skinner and Allan Edwards provide the anchor leg for the volume by exploring pertinent and contemporary debates about the contribution that sport makes to social capital. By drawing on recent empirical research the authors investigate how sport in Australia has contributed to social capital in both urban and rural settings.

It is virtually impossible to be all-encompassing in presenting commentaries on Australia's sporting fabric. So we accept that this volume's 'design' will resonate with some and not others, just as the unveiling of a new Wallaby jersey or Australian Olympic team uniform divides opinion. The viewpoints presented by the authors in this collection convey their position on the respective topics, and we do not suggest that these are the only or the 'correct' perspectives. In selecting the contributions for this volume we have followed the advice given in a pre-games warm-up talk by Australia's most popular contemporary sports announcers, the dynamic duo of H.G. Nelson and Rampaging Roy Slaven. 'Go in hard, early and often. Win the stink and win the match! And remember: in or out ... it is always worth a shout!'[13]

Notes

[1] Australian Bureau of Statistics, 'Population Clock'.
[2] Toohey, 'The Politics of Australian Elite Sport', 6–7.
[3] Horne, *The Lucky Country*, 22.
[4] Australian Bureau of Statistics, 'Participation in Sports'.
[5] Ibid.
[6] Barrett, 'Smoking Ball is Back', 1.

[7] This is a chant popular amongst Australians when supporting their national side or athletes both at home and abroad.

[8] Cashman, *Paradise of Sport*, 208.

[9] See also Taylor and Toohey, 'Sport, Gender and Cultural Diversity'; Taylor and Toohey, 'Behind the Veil'; Booth and Tatz, *One-eyed*.

[10] Toohey, 'The Politics of Australian Elite Sport'.

[11] Toohey, *Official Report of the XXVII Olympiad*, Vol. 2, 137.

[12] See Ferguson, *More than Sunshine & Vegemite*; Stewart *et al.*, *Australian Sport*; and Bloomfield, *Australia's Sporting Success*.

[13] RGM, 'Roy Slaven & HG Nelson biography', 1.

References

Australian Bureau of Statistics. 'Participation in Sports and Physical Recreation, Australia'. 2007. http://www.abs.gov.au/AUSSTATS/abs@.nsf/Latestproducts/4177.0Main%20Features22005-06?opendocument&tabname=Summary&prodno=4177.0&issue=2005-06&num=&view=.

Australian Bureau of Statistics. 'Population Clock'. 2007. http://www.abs.gov.au/ausstats/abs@nsf/94713ad445ff1425ca25682000192af2/1647509ef7e25faaca2568a900154b63?OpenDocument.

Barrett, D. 'Smoking Ball is Back'. *Herald-Sun.com*. http://www.news.com.au/heraldsun/story/0,21985,21714629-2862,00.html.

Bloomfield, J. *Australia's Sporting Success: The Inside Story*. Sydney: University of New South Wales Press, 2003.

Booth, D., and C. Tatz. *One-eyed: A View of Australian Sport*. Sydney: Allen & Unwin, 2000.

Cashman, R. *Paradise of Sport*. Oxford: Oxford University Press, 1995.

Dunstan, K. *Sports*. Melbourne: Sun Books, 1981.

Ferguson, J. *More than Sunshine & Vegemite: Success the Australian Way*. Broadway, NSW: Halstead Press, 2006.

Horne, D. *The Lucky Country*. 2nd ed. Sydney: Angus and Robertson, 1965.

RGM. 'Roy Slaven & HG Nelson Biography'. http://www.rgm.com.au/C_royhg.html.

Stewart, B., M. Nicholson, A. Smith, and H. Westerbeek. *Australian Sport: Better by Design? The Evolution of Australian Sport Policy*. London: Routledge, 2004.

Taylor, T., and K. Toohey. 'Sport, Gender and Cultural Diversity: Exploring the Nexus'. *Journal of Sport Management* 13, no. 1 (1999): 1–17.

Taylor, T., and K. Toohey. 'Behind the Veil: Exploring the Recreation Needs of Muslim Women'. *Leisure* 26, no. 1/2 (2002): 85–105.

Toohey, K. 'The Politics of Australian Elite Sport: 1949–1983'. PhD diss., Pennsylvania State University, 1990.

Toohey, K. *Official Report of the XXVII Olympiad*. Sydney: SOCOG, 2001.

The Australian sport system and its stakeholders: development of cooperative relationships

Kalliopi (Popi) Sotiriadou

Sport Management Program, Faculty of Health Sciences and Medicine, Bond University, Queensland, Australia

The way the Australian sport system arrested its unrelenting decline in the 1970s to become a model of best practice perplexes many countries. This essay aims to give an insight into the way the system was transformed and became successful. The essay reviews the decline, and then the evolution and devolution of the system, and analyses the stakeholders involved, and the inter relationships developed to achieve success. The study is based on a document analysis examining 74 annual reports from 35 national sporting organizations over a period of four years, before and after the Sydney Olympic Games. The results of the study show that in the face of financial instability and an over-reliance on government funding, sport stakeholders sought alternative sources of income, amalgamated or worked in collaboration with other stakeholders, and/or opted for intra-organizational cooperation. The sport system in Australia has proven resilient and able to adapt to an ever-changing environment via the cooperation of its stakeholders and their willingness to work together towards a common goal.

Introduction

Success in sport in Australia is epitomized by an effective national sports system that offers improved participation in quality sports activities by all Australians and helps those who are talented and motivated to reach their potential excellence in sports performance.[1] This success is measured by the medals won on the international stage by elite athletes and by the number of people participating in sport at a community level. Continuing elite success and increasing community participation demonstrate the effectiveness of the sport system in Australia. The way Australia has recently achieved results is the envy of many sport systems globally.[2] However, to reach its current phase of development, the sport system in Australia underwent – and is still experiencing – critical transformation.

The way the Australian sport system recovered from its inability to win a gold medal in the 1976 Olympics to win an all time high of 17 gold medals in 2004 perplexes countries worldwide. Previous efforts to explain this success have concentrated on the contribution of sport science and sport medicine to the development of the system.[3] Other studies[4] have examined the importance of retaining volunteers for a sustainable system. There is no study that analyses the stakeholders, their roles, relationships, involvement and impact on sport. The aim of this essay is to elucidate the way Australia has created a model of best practice in sport through examining sport stakeholder relationships.

First, this essay addresses the developmental changes of the Australian sport system since the 1950s as reflected through three distinct stages: the slow decline, the evolution and the devolution of the Australian sport system. The classification of these stages is based on significant sporting events (e.g. Olympic Games) and the government policies/actions they prompted. An understanding of the transformations the system underwent is important to understand how Australia has adapted to a changing global sport environment.

This essay analyses the stakeholders involved with the system, their roles and interrelationships. In doing so, it explains the way stakeholders cooperate and interact to achieve a sustainable sport system in Australia to deliver quality programmes equally for mass participants and elite athletes. The second section is important in demonstrating the impact that each developmental stage has had on sport stakeholders and the ways they managed different pressures. This section reports the results of a study that used 74 annual reports collected from 35 participating national sporting organizations (NSOs) covering the years from 1999 to 2002 as its primary source of data generation. The annual reports constitute the formal written source of information that reflects NSOs' operations with regard to sport, and interactions with the federal government and other key stakeholders. Additionally, these reports provide the annual contributions of all state sporting associations (SSAs), staff and members of the board of directors collectively in a reliable, publicly available form on which to develop an understanding of stakeholder roles and interrelationships for a successful sport system. Data analyses revealed themes of internal changes and governance level approaches to management and these are used to discuss the Australian sport system and its key stakeholders.

Finally, the essay presents the future issues and trends that stakeholders may be faced with and concludes that a critical ingredient for the sustainability of the Australian sport system is its capacity to adapt to a complex environment. In this respect Australia has learned from its past and has become proactive with a long-term vision and strategies to sustain a successful sport system.

The changes of the Australian sport system

The way sports integrate into social life varies from society to society, and the way they are organized differs from place to place and time to time. These different approaches to developing sport depend largely on the ideological position of governments at different levels. Leach suggested that the two contesting major ideologies are liberalism and socialism.[5] Liberalistic ideology advocates minimum government, as well as individual and market freedom. In this view, extensive state welfare provision is generally seen as undesirable. In contrast, socialist states view state welfare provision (hence involvement with grassroots sport) as a form of collective intervention which is designed to meet a range of social needs and solve important social problems in the general interest. Political ideologies help interpret governments' approach to manage sports.

In a comprehensive study on sport systems and their approaches to success, Green and Oakley point out that, amongst a number of select countries, Australia has demonstrated the most notable sustained improvement in efficiency regarding output of Olympic medals.[6] They identify two factors as political and financial catalysts for developing Australia's sport system: first, the poor performance at the Olympic Games of 1976 and the second was the bidding for, and hosting of, the 2000 Olympic Games in Sydney. These two factors are used here as the basis for distinguishing the modern Australian sport system into three developmental stages: the 'slow decline', the 'evolution' and the 'partial devolution' that the system has been, and is still, experiencing (see Table 1).

Table 1. Policy stages of the modern Australian sport system.

Characteristic	1950s to mid-1970s	Mid-1970s to 2000	From 2001
Dominant ideology/ies	Slow decline Conservative/liberal approach: Australia seen as a naturally superior sporting nation	Evolution Social democratic policy and Neo-liberalism: Sport as a legitimate public policy issue of concern	Partial devolution Neo-liberalism: Decentralization and devolution of sports organizations – increasing independence as a necessity for financial survival
Role of government	Lack of systematic government involvement	An increasing government investment and involvement	ASC extended NSOs' power to increase their administrative and financial efficiency and carry out functions independent of the commission
Approach to management	Highly volunteer based, amateur/unorganized and uncoordinated approach to sport management	Introduction of numerous sport agencies and organizations, a trend toward professionalism and commercialized sports, and subsequent fall in volunteer numbers	Sport organizations seen as more autonomous entities to strive for their financial survival
Performance	Hands-off approach – Limited support for travelling	Frazer (liberal) government (1975–83), saw a re-focus on elite	Howard (liberal) government (1998–current) targets elite sports with greater potential for medals, elite sport still a policy priority – Emphasis on talent identification
Participation	Participation based on infrastructure created during 1930s and 1940s – Creation of the National Fitness Council and Fitness Australia Campaign in the late 1960s	Whitlam (labour) government (1972–75), saw sport as a vehicle to improve peoples well being – Fraser (liberal) government (1975–83), 'Life. Be in it' programme. Expectation for grassroots participation to be simulated by elite success	Howard (liberal) government (1998–current) sees a cause of concern in dropping participation numbers and places a new emphasis on grassroots participation.

The seminal characteristics of the first era of the modern Australian sport system that lasted until about 1976 were a lack of government involvement with, and finance of, sport, and an amateur, unorganized and uncoordinated approach to administering sport. During the 1950s and 1960s, sport was ideologically and financially an issue of free choice for the individual, hence considered outside the realm of federal government responsibility.[7] Some assistance for team travel and accommodation to Commonwealth and Olympic Games and for costs associated with hosting such events was available but overall financial support was meagre.[8] Sport was almost exclusively controlled and implemented by volunteers and voluntary organizations which, along with sport participants, were the main stakeholders within the sport system.

The traditional ideological position of conservative/liberal approaches to involvement in sport coupled with the relative success of Australian Olympic performances prior to the 1976 Olympic Games in Montreal reinforced conservative thinking that Australia was naturally a superior sporting nation.[9] However, the 'hands-off' approach to sport was slowly taking its toll on the system.[10] Elite athletes' international performances could not match the success of athletes from countries such as former East Germany and the former Soviet Union. These countries were investing vast resources to promote research and used sport sciences and technology to identify and prepare athletes for competition.

The second era of the modern Australian sport system, 'the evolution', began after 1976 and was characterized by the introduction of numerous sport agencies and organizations, the move toward professionalism and commercialized sports and, more importantly, an increasing investment and involvement from the federal government. That involvement changed the way sport was delivered in Australia.[11]

The Whitlam Labor government, elected in December 1972, recognized sport as a legitimate area of involvement and expenditure.[12] The then Minister of Sport, Frank Stewart, commissioned John Bloomfield of the University of Western Australia to prepare the first detailed report on sport – *The Role, Scope and Development of Recreation in Australia*.[13] For the first time in the history of Australia, sport was politically recognized as an integral part of Australians' lives and received federal government attention.[14] The importance of the report was the framework it established for federal government support and assistance to national sporting organizations (NSOs). (These bodies are known as sports federations or national sports government bodies in other sports systems.)

Whitlam's democratic social policies that introduced sport and recreation were significantly different to the subsequent Fraser Liberal government (1975–83). The Fraser government gave a distinct emphasis on developing elite athletes. The then government was hoping Australians would simulate elite success.[15] However, following pressures to improve Australians' health, Fraser initiated the 'Life. Be in it' programme to create incentives and encourage physical activity.

The most influential development during the system's evolution were the establishment of the Australian Institute of Sport (AIS) in Canberra and the Australian Sports Commission (ASC), Australia's primary national sports administration and advisory agency during the 1980s.[16] The ASC was established with the objectives to: (a) 'sustain and improve Australia's level of achievement in international sporting competition', (b) 'increase the level of participation in sport by all Australians', and (c) 'increase the level of assistance from [the] private sector'.[17] The institutional base of federal support changed in May 1989, with the amalgamation of the AIS and the ASC, to form a new commission under the ASC Act 1989.[18]

Also, in the 1980s a number of NSOs became well established and started work in partnership with their SSAs. At this stage, Australian sport was managed by volunteers under the 'delegate system'. Under this system, nominated representatives of clubs, regions, or states were appointed to the governing body. With sport rapidly changing in nature and demands, this system, however democratic, became inflexible and unable to deliver results.[19] Increased government funding, together with the pressures of commercialization, forced a cultural change within sporting organizations that historically existed under systems of 'institutionalised amateurism'.[20]

Another characteristic of the evolution of the system was the move towards professionalism.[21] In particular, government funding marked the growing recognition of the importance of professionally played sport in Australian society.[22] Consequently, high levels of government funding contributed to the professionalism of Australian sports organizations and increased involvement of stakeholders, such as sponsors, and helped shape the multifaceted industry of sport.

The move towards commercialization and professionalism contributed to unprecedented success on the international stage. During this period, sport organizations questioned the effectiveness of their relationships with the government and other stakeholders in the industry, and the ramifications of an increased reliance on government finance in the system. For example, sports, in anticipation of funding reductions,[23] expressed the need to restructure and increase their membership numbers.[24]

Since 1989, the federal government has allocated money in discrete packages to the development of elite sport every four years. Examples include the *Next Step* initiative from 1989 to 1992, which poured $217 million into sport over the four-year cycle.[25] The *Maintain the Momentum* programme from 1992 to 1996 injected another $293 million over its four-year cycle and handed more power to NSOs.[26]

Whilst sport was restructuring to adapt to the new environment, Australia's elite success at an international level during the 1990s was improving. Australia won 27 medals at the 1992 Barcelona Olympics including seven gold, and 41 medals at the 1996 Atlanta Olympics with nine gold. Sponsors saw the potential gains of associating their names and products with that success and, as they invested in sports, there was a need for sports to adjust to an even more complex landscape.

Until the mid 1980s, at the junior and youth levels (i.e. until the age of 18 years), the Australian sport system predominantly focussed on identifying elite performers.[27] The early 1980s did not give rise to any significant programmes to promote mass participation or develop an integrated approach involving NSOs and state authorities.[28] Hence, while elite sport was reaping the rewards of increased stakeholder focus, mass participation numbers started to decline. One of the outcomes of the focus on elite was a high dropout rate in the adolescent age groups.[29]

Under normal circumstances, the four-year funding cycle would have run its course in 1996, the year of the Atlanta Olympic Games. However, circumstances changed on 23 September 1993, when the International Olympic Committee awarded the 2000 Olympic Games to Sydney.[30] In response the federal government, through the ASC, decided to continue with the *Maintain the Momentum* funding cycle and, in 1994, announced the *Olympic Athlete Program* (OAP), a A$135 million six-year package. In addition, in 1995, the ASC formally established a Sport Development Division.

According to the Sport 2000 Task Force, while Australia's results in international sporting competitions were exceptionally good and showed that 'elite sport has been served well by the ASC',[31] the lack of real growth in the membership levels of sporting organizations and the decline of numbers participating in organized sport during the previous 25 years suggested that 'strategies have not achieved increased participation in organised sport'.[32]

This lead to the third phase of development of the Australian system. It began after the 2000 Olympic Games and is still in effect. This phase is characterized by an emphasis on additional programmes for community participation in sports,[33] less central control by the ASC and an effort to maximize the input of the stakeholders within the system. The anticipated success of the various programmes and resources supporting the development of Australian athletes at the Sydney Games was expected to help sports increase their mass participation numbers. However, appropriate infrastructure to capitalize on that success was lacking. On 24 April 2001, the Australian government announced the 10-year *Backing Australia's Sporting Ability – A More Active Australia* plan. This plan included funding of A$408 million for the new *Sport Excellence Program*, which was introduced to build upon the achievements of the elite athletes at the international and national levels.[34] There was also provision for an A$82 million infusion of funding (over a four-year period starting 2001–02) through *Active Australia* to increase mass participation in sport at the club level.[35] Putting additional resources into sport did not necessarily fit the prevailing ideology of neo-liberalism; however, supporting sport was seen to have a strong electoral appeal.[36]

According to the Department of Industry, Science and Resources,[37] there has been a slight policy shift towards participation programmes, and in particular talent identification initiatives, with the ultimate aim of increasing the pool of elite athletes. So, while catering for the elite level remained a policy priority, the four-year plan announced in 2001 saw participation as a means of increasing the pool of talented athletes and not as an end itself. Smith perceived this attempt to increase community sport as a possible response to one of the key findings of the Sport 2000 Taskforce's *Shaping Up* report: that too many Australians were inactive and that more resources needed to be directed to participation programmes and campaigns.[38]

Stewart-Weeks predicted that the Australian sport system would face a third phase of development in the post-2000 Olympic Games era, with the main trend towards less public funding at all levels of sport.[39] However, after the Games, the Australian government continued to provide unprecedented levels of funding to sport. For example, in its 2006–07 budget it allocated A$204 million to the ASC, trying to tackle head-on the challenge from other countries seeking to emulate Australia's Olympic success as well as to invest in initiatives that offer improved participation in quality sports activities by all Australians.[40]

Nevertheless, a new direction emerged post 2000. In his discussion on changes to the sport system, Bloomfield outlined a new era of sport, where the ASC extended NSOs' power to increase their administrative and financial efficiency and carry out functions independent of the commission.[41] The aim was to maximize NSOs' ability to function at full capacity and deliver sports in a more efficient and self-sufficient way. For this to take place, NSOs needed to reduce their reliance on federal government funding and establish greater independence as a necessity for financial survival. By implication, an assumption drawn from Bloomfield is that NSOs are no longer seen as instruments of sport policy, but rather as organizations able to shape power relations.[42]

The ASC provides leadership in all facets of sport from the elite level through to the wider sporting community. To achieve its goals, it works with a number of stakeholders ranging from governments and organizations at all levels to corporations and individuals. These stakeholders interact closely to achieve success in sport. The following section discusses the different roles of these stakeholders and describes the interrelationships they have established in order to achieve that success.

Stakeholder relationships

Stakeholder theory suggests that an organization has relationships with many constituent groups, or 'stakeholders',[43] that affect and are affected by its decisions.[44] A stakeholder is defined as a group or an individual who can affect and is affected by the actions, decisions, policies, practices or goals of the organization.[45] According to Mitchell, Agle and Wood,[46] stakeholder theory seeks to systematically address the question of which stakeholders do or do not require or deserve management attention through evaluation of relationships between organizations and stakeholders. In that sense, stakeholder theory is useful in understanding and evaluating the sport industry stakeholders and their relationships that this study reports.

The results support Jones' assertion that the organizations that develop cooperative relationships with stakeholders will have a competitive advantage over other organizations.[47] NSOs argued that success in sport is inconceivable without the cooperation and the coordinated input of stakeholders for the delivery of strategies, policies and programmes. Stakeholder coordination is more commonly problematic within federal systems (e.g. Canada, Australia, Spain) where different states/regions have a degree of political autonomy.[48] The roles different stakeholders hold within the Australian sport system is a reflection of the Australian federated model. This model includes governments at the national (e.g. federal government), state (e.g. state departments) and local levels (e.g. local councils). Sport organizations are structured similarly and are represented by national sporting organizations (NSOs), state sporting associations (SSAs) and local clubs.

NSOs form the primary link to the ASC and implement the strategies the commission formulates. Hence, NSOs, as sports' national representatives, manage and coordinate the participation and development aspects of their sports. At the same time, as Farmer and Arnaudon noted,[49] NSOs are involved in organizing and conducting national champion-ships, liaising with the international parent body, marketing and promoting national events, fund-raising for national teams, selecting and developing talent, selecting national teams for international events and liaising with the federal government. Over time, the ASC and the NSOs have developed a close working relationship, a partnership, to achieve sport goals. Interaction between the ASC and NSOs often takes place through sports consultants.

While the primary responsibility for developing and directing individual sports lies within the NSOs, it is the ASC that delivers the government's policies to (a) promote and encourage community participation in sports, and (b) significantly improve Australia's sporting performance at the elite level. In addition, the ASC offers leadership, coordination of funding and other support to individual sports and the organizations that represent them. The NSOs work closely with their state and territory associations, academies and institutes of sport, schools, community groups and local clubs to deliver sport programmes. Governments and these organizations collectively have either an interest in, or the power to affect, the sport system through shaping sport strategies or instigating programmes.

Stakeholders within the sport system have different responsibilities and roles, varying from shaping to implementing policies, strategies and programmes. As stakeholders perform their tasks they interact with each other and form relationships that assist them to achieve their goals. The necessity for stakeholders to work with each other to fulfil their objectives has been documented by a number of researchers in organizational theory.[50] These relationships are under constant review as stakeholders aim to maximize their contribution to the system and minimize federal government reliance. As a result, sports tend to lobby or search for alternative sources of income, change their structure to streamline their organization, amalgamate to strengthen their sport, and shape intra-organizational relationships to advance their governance style.

The relationships various stakeholders have within the system, in particular those of governments and organizations, are largely driven by the federal government through the ASC. Consequently, the operations of many organizations and governments are influenced by the ASC's policy direction, priorities and resource distribution. Due to the centrally controlled sport system through the ASC, during the evolution phase of the system, many sporting organizations and governments operating at different levels were, and still are, not self-sufficient. This economic and strategic reliance (as well as other external factors such as professionalism) has put pressure on many sports organizations. The nature of ASC funding has important implications for the sport system as it affects operations, especially of NSOs, and influences sports organizations' governance strategies and structure.

The theoretical perspective of resource dependency helps explain inter-organizational links and power relationships.[51] More specifically, resources dependency theory is characterized by interdependencies created between organizations or stakeholders because of the stakeholders needs to acquire resources. As a result, some stakeholders exert more power over others as they have control over the needed resources.[52] The ASC provides resources (financial and human) and programmes for both the elite athlete and membership/participation ends of the sport system. In return for this investment, the commission requires that sports increase 'their popularity', public profile, awareness and growth in participation numbers, and international success and medals at the elite level. In essence, the commission's involvement allows the government to establish success criteria at all levels and implement performance benchmarks in return for allocating grants. A critical ASC policy requires NSOs to report to the statutory authority on the ways they intend to, or have, implemented the policies/programmes through strategic plans and annual reports. Plans and reports are forms of formal communication; an important element in successful partnerships[53] that enables common understanding of terms and conditions, agreements and decisions.[54]

The ASC grant allocations have fluctuated over time and the nature of that funding has been somehow provisional and uncertain. Bourne and Walker explain that some stakeholders (the ASC in this instance) that have a stake in the entity (i.e. sports), have certain expectations and, consequently, engage in certain types of behaviour, sometimes supportive and some times unsupportive.[55] As noted earlier, Stewart-Weeks[56] speculated that post-2000 Australia's sport policy would be a combination of less public funding (in relative terms) at all levels and growing expectations for service and performance. Shilbury recognized the need for NSOs to reduce their dependence on government funding in the post-2000 policy agenda and explained that this 'is not an argument to reduce overall Government funding, but recognition that such funding will not continue'.[57]

Grant fluctuation and financial uncertainty compels NSOs to lobby the government through the Confederation of Australian Sports or search for alternative funding. Thibault and Harvey[58] argued that in order to deal with uncertainty, sport organizations establish strong links with various stakeholders to coordinate their efforts and increase their resources. Shilbury's[59] cluster model emphasized and drew attention to the need to be less reliant on government funds. Depending on the sport, the most common source of income for NSOs' financial viability derives from either intensified effort to increase members/participants and adjust membership fees, or financial assistance from sponsors.

Although sports recognize sponsorship as an important source of revenue, not all manage to attract corporate funds. Australian Canoeing, for example, found the post-2000 Olympic sponsorship market very difficult and as a result, they remained reliant on government funding for the majority of their programmes.

Implications to the sport system

The results of this study showed that, depending on the NSOs' elite and mass participation outputs, the commission's funding continued, increased, was reduced or was withdrawn. These funding patterns directly affect NSOs' operational choices. For example, continuous or increased funding has positive results on maintaining elite success but it does increase the NSOs' funding reliance and accountability to the commission. Government funding fluctuations and in particular reduction or withdrawal of grants negatively can affect elite athletes and their ultimate success.

In addition, these fluctuations raise concerns about overall operations and provision of services in sports. Many sports recognize their substantial dependence upon government funding to maintain their level of operations. When low funding or withdrawal of grants to NSOs leads to the termination of staff employment contracts, the workload of remaining staff increases. Therefore, some have difficulty in hiring and keeping the number of staff necessary to meet operational needs. In response, NSOs report that sport organizations often develop higher levels of teamwork and realize the potential that joint efforts have to offer to their future survival.[60]

Shilbury[61] recognized the need for sporting organizations to consider alternative forms of structure and management procedures to ensure best practice. His concern was that the immaturity on the part of some sporting organizations in Australia limited their ability to be financially autonomous. Increasingly, though, many organizations appear more prepared to develop/alter their structures. Internal restructuring, with the flexibility to restructure as required, is becoming common practice within sporting organizations to ensure they are well placed to meet the challenges and demands of their sport.

Organizational structuring presents a challenging and powerful tool to ensure that sporting organizations can adapt to the environment in which they operate.[62] Athletics Australia provides a good example. Ryan claimed that, after its initial unsuccessful effort to amalgamate, eventually Athletics Australia's organizational restructuring boosted its organizational performance.[63] He suggested that small NSOs, seeking to run their sport like a business, 'could do well to follow the governance overhaul example set by Athletics Australia'.[64] Flexible structures enable NSOs to work in collaboration, advance their communication and reduce duplication, develop networks and shape effective linkages with each other. It is commonly accepted by the ASC that the development of structures that promote appropriate financial controls, unity of purpose and successful risk management practices, has a 'significant impact on the performance of a sporting organisation'.[65]

At a governance level, the two major patterns emerged involving organizational partnerships of intra-organizational cooperation or amalgamations. Intra-organizational cooperation is evident between NSOs and SSAs. NSOs delegate membership/participation strategies and programme implementation, support and funding to SSAs. NSOs have an indirect involvement with mass participation rather than a sole focus on elite success, and share responsibilities for mass participation and junior and talent identification programmes with their SSAs. The sphere of the NSOs' support to SSAs appeared to be extensive. The central areas of provision to SSAs are programmes to attract/retain members and participants, and identify/develop talented players. In addition, NSOs assist their state associations with management/administration needs and provide SSAs initiatives to develop coaches/umpires at the community level. Hence, it could be argued that through growing intra-organizational cooperation, a balanced approach within the sport system, catering for all participation levels, is achieved.

These results are in accord with Elias, Cavana and Jackson's stakeholder analysis that recognized that 'stakeholders exist beyond the boundary of a single organisation into a partnership infrastructure'.[66] Notably, the NSOs support SSAs in actively increasing membership and participation. Therefore, intra-organizational cooperation between NSOs and SSAs, as well as the flexibility for organizational restructuring, assists sporting organizations at the national level in filtering down funding, support and sport development responsibilities to the state level, which provides a balanced approach to sport within Australia.

NSOs also receive funds from the ASC to assist clubs/associations at the local level in areas such as club development, attracting young people, and encouraging clubs to appoint junior development officers. SSAs and clubs/associations are responsible for the delivery of programmes developed and funded by the NSOs. As well as NSOs, state governments, through their diverse offices for sport and recreation, such as the Office for Recreation, Sport and Racing of South Australia, Sport and Recreation Victoria and the NSW Department of Sport and Recreation, financially support many of the SSAs' activities. Also, local clubs join together to construct common facilities for training and playing; clubs, schools and communities share resources and build facilities; and local governments in regional areas establish sporting hubs in their communities to centralize resources.

In their study examining tourism development and stakeholders, Sauter and Leisen noted that collaboration 'among key players is a fundamental ingredient in sustainable development efforts'.[67] The various sporting associations across Australia look to work together on a range of long-overdue initiatives for strengthening and expanding sport into the future. Basketball Australia[68] provides an example of how cooperation in the governance of sport can work. The vision and agenda for the future of the sport developed is the result of the cumulative efforts of those in the basketball community. The 'One Basketball' programme highlighted the need for integration and unification in all that they did, and the need for consistency in branding and programme delivery. Overall, intra-organizational cooperation enhances the ability to share responsibilities, effectively communicate and assist each other to achieve goals, and implement national initiatives.

In addition to intra-organizational cooperation, other collaborative patterns at the governance level involve amalgamations. Amalgamation is the unification process that brings selected sporting organizations under one national umbrella. Brown argued that in the recreation and sport industry amalgamation generally takes one of two forms: a merger that brings two or more organizations together in a new entity; and a takeover 'when one or more organisations cease to exist in their own right and their resources, assets and roles are consolidated into an existing entity'.[69] Mahony and Howard referred to the synergy between sporting organizations and the merging of teams, leagues and organizations in the same industry as horizontal integration.[70]

Soccer (football) provides a case in point, where amalgamations were achieved for the good of the game. In its effort to unify the game, New South Wales Soccer Federation and New South Wales Amateurs formed Soccer New South Wales in 2002. The same year, the South Australian Soccer Federation, the South Australian Amateur Soccer League, the South Australian Junior Soccer Association and South Australia Women's Soccer

Association formed a new body – Soccer SA. Brown observed that even though soccer reaped the benefits of reduced duplication of activity and resources and gained sponsorship, 'it has taken time to build trust amongst the group',[71] share information and put aside many past difficulties.

Other examples of sport amalgamations, such as that of the Women's Hockey Australia and the Australian Hockey Association's (men's hockey), to form Hockey Australia, have also led to initial disadvantages, such as loss of volunteers and members, loss of jobs and clashes of cultures. Phillips explained that 'amalgamating sporting associations often faces financial barriers and inequalities, clashes over facilities and debates over board representation – all flavoured by egos both strong and fragile'.[72] For example, following the recommendation from hockey's international body in 1998 for Women's Hockey Australia (WHA) and the Australian Hockey Association to amalgamate, gender issues made the process very complex. Specifically, WHA felt their independence was in jeopardy, while Australian Hockey was more open to the change because their role was unchallenged and they saw the amalgamation as an opportunity to capitalize on the strong profile of the women's hockey team.

Schraeder and Self demonstrated that mergers and acquisitions are becoming a strategy of choice for organizations attempting to maintain a competitive advantage.[73] While two or more organizations may work well together, when merged they have the potential to complement each other in the future. For instance, the amalgamation of the two national bodies of hockey provided 'a window of opportunity for hockey to be seen as a sport that is producing world class athletes, coaches, administrators, and facilities. There must be positive long-term goals to provide a legacy for the sport.'[74]

Significant other stakeholders

So far, this essay has discussed governments' and organizations' roles and relationships, and the implication of these relationships to the sport system and the way it operates. In addition to the sport organizations and governments at all levels that primarily initiate strategies and programmes and provide resources, other significant stakeholders are actively involved with sport in Australia. This group of stakeholders includes volunteers (e.g. umpires, administrators), paid staff (e.g. coaches, sport development officers), participants/members at various levels of skill, including athletes, spectators and supporters, and sponsors. These stakeholders contribute towards the implementation of the sport strategies, programmes and events that governments and organizations provide (e.g. sport development officers and coaches implementing programmes, volunteers involved with running of events). These stakeholders may also participate in those programmes, work for these organizations/governments, or attend/watch sporting events and have a stake in the achievement of sport policy objectives.

Professional and effective management of sport organizations is important for the sustainability of operations in a complex and volatile national and international environment. Environmental conditions place increasing demands on management/administration staff and the boards of directors. As the professional end of the sporting spectrum becomes more commercial, NSOs are exposed to a range of new pressures. It is becoming very challenging to ensure that sport is 'appropriately stewarded, governed, and nurtured in an increasingly aggressive, litigious environment'.[75] Hence, the professional management of sports by administration staff and board of directors and a commercialized approach to sport have the potential to ensure growth. Corporate contributions can reduce sports' financial problems. It enables sports to achieve development and growth goals through the implementation of development programmes, competitions across all levels and in due course elite success.

Despite this increasingly commercialized and professional environment, volunteers are still the most valuable asset to sports. Volunteers, whether active participants or not, may include members of the board, club members, field and court operators, family and friends. They may be involved in player development, coaching, refereeing and officiating in programmes at all levels, administering sporting organizations, and making decisions of strategic importance as members of boards. The variety of tasks that volunteers undertake, from website services, to officiating, promotions to development work and the smooth running of programmes and events, shows how important they are. Cuskelly, McIntyre and Boag[76] claim that despite the trend towards hiring paid staff to follow professional sport management procedures, volunteers remain important to the operation of many sports organizations. They maintain that the nexus between volunteers and sports organizations is important because the delivery of community-based sport 'is reliant upon the willingness of a large number of volunteers to commit their time and energy'.[77] Significantly, this time and energy is translated by almost all sports into considerable fiscal savings and ultimately the future viability and health of sports.

The contributions of paid officers and personnel are also important. Paid staff positions may vary from contracted officers and support staff to coaches, umpires and administrators or members of the board, and provide the human resources infrastructure of sport.

At the elite level, the results achieved by athletes would not be possible without the support and hard work of coaches, and in today's competitive and professional sporting environment, coaching resources are vital in making sure Australia continues to groom stars of the future. Previous research[78] describes coaches as co-pilots lending their experiences and enabling and guiding athletes to navigate and reach desired goals. The coaches' role is also recognized at a community participation level. In addition to coaches, sport development officers (SDOs) play a significant role in achieving the objectives of growth of sport by promoting it and increasing its public profile.

Finally, active participants and the people who follow, support or watch sports give meaning and purpose to all the other stakeholders and act as the ultimate stakeholders that shape the future of sport in Australia through their changing needs, wants, skills and requirements. This group of significant stakeholders is the lifeblood of the Australian sport system. Part of their contribution can be estimated in economic terms. For instance, the total expenditure by Australian households on sport and recreation products in 2003–04 was A\$6.332.50 million. This includes the expenditures of 7.1 million people aged 15 years and over who exercised three times per week or more[79] and of the 7 million people aged 18 years and over who attended at least one sport event in 2005.[80]

The challenges ahead

Stakeholder theorists suggest that all stakeholder interests must be attended to for an organization to be successful.[81] Stakeholders in the sport industry will need to consider strategies and modifications of the way sport is played if they want to keep it relevant to the changing society. This way, the decline in Australian children's physical activity and increasing obesity coupled with the declining birth rate and an ageing population could lead to opportunities to create innovative and effective programmes rather than threaten the system. The Active After-Schools Communities programme is an example of the ASC's involvement in addressing the problem of childhood obesity and decreasing motor skill development. Also, rather than just relying on elite athlete performances alone to encourage the community to take up exercise, existing or retired elite athletes have actively become involved as role models through coaching/training camps and sponsorships (carefully designed and mindful of athletes' busy schedules). The Australian Government Healthy Active Ambassador Program, announced in July 2006, brought together current and former champions from a variety of sports as ambassadors to motivate and educate Australian children. The programme's aim was to raise awareness among Australians, particularly young people, of the importance of healthy eating, physical activity and maintaining a healthy weight.

Another issue is the sport delivery structure, traditional versus contemporary pathways, and the emergence of less organized participation patterns amongst young adults who wish to push themselves to the limits of their physical ability and fear through extreme sports. Extreme sports, such as ice climbing, often involve speed, height or highly specialized gear. These sports are usually individual rather than team sports and push the limits and boundaries of the way current sports are 'played' and delivered to the public on an ad-hoc individual basis rather than through clubs.

Several countries, including the United Kingdom, South Africa, France and Canada, hire Australian sporting personnel in their efforts to learn from the Australian sport system. Australia is also hiring personnel from overseas, in particular coaches in sports such as table tennis. This inflow-outflow of expertise is an example of good business and is positive for the Australian economy. However, losing knowledgeable and capable coaches, sport managers, sport scientists and athletes to rival countries may present a threat to Australia as it leaves the country with less talent and perhaps necessitates the overseas quest for quality staff.

Australia will have to invest more money in science/technology advancements and innovative talent identification programmes if it wants to match current overseas groundbreaking talent identification initiatives. Benefiting from its lottery system, the United Kingdom is offering a programme by which they recruit young athletes of different ethnic/racial background, who possess certain physical characteristics that give them a performance advantage in several sports over athletes of Anglo-Celtic origin.[82]

Conclusion

The aim of this essay was to elucidate the way Australia has created a model of best practice in sport through examining sport stakeholder relationships. The identification and evaluation of stakeholders and stakeholder relationships helps organizations better respond to the environment they operate in and formulate more informed strategies.[83] The economic environment the Australian sport delivery system experienced leading into 2000, and possibly afterwards, is very similar to the circumstances and economic context of the 1990s in Canada, with fiscal restraints exercised by the government and a period of uncertainty. Thibault and Harvey[84] examined the nature and extent of inter-organizational linkages between the partners involved in Canada's sport delivery system during this economic environment. Results from this study reinforced the argument that in order to deal with uncertainty, links between stakeholders need to be established, fostered and maintained. Linkages between stakeholders will assist in sharing resources, in the coordination of work-related activities and to fulfil their objectives.

The concept of resource dependence does not mean that sporting organizations are totally at the mercy of their environment. Rather, 'it means that they must develop strategies for managing both resource dependence and environment uncertainty'.[85] This essay has argued that sporting organizations should tailor their structure as a strategy to cope with the environment. These results support contentions in the literature on organizations' responses to uncertainty that demonstrate a close connection among environment, structures and effectiveness.[86]

In the immediate future, the Australian sport system will be faced with challenges. To ensure sustainable success in sport, the right strategies, actions, practices and relationships need to be in place. There is evidence that Australia is working towards its sporting future. The ASC 2007 annual forum addressed what needs to be done in sport at all levels to ensure that the Australian sports system is a relevant, robust, sustainable, progressive and contemporary industry in the twenty-first century. In addition, in 2007, the ASC reviewed the *Australian Sports Commission Act 1989* for appropriateness and adequacy of the provision of ASC Act. This has enabled the ASC to reflect and respond to the availability of emerging technologies, shifts in lifestyles and societal trends in order to deliver outcomes that give effect to the Government's sport policy.

A critical ingredient for the sustainability of the Australian sport system is its capacity to adapt to a complex environment and be prepared to deal with future trends and challenges. To do that, NSOs still need to reduce their reliance on federal government funding and establish greater independence to be financially viable. Organizational theory literature relating to non-professional sport suggests that such organizations operate in a volatile environment.[87] In response, sporting organizations amalgamate, tailor their structure or strive for inter-organizational cooperation. Galaskiewicz noted that no organization or stakeholder is totally self-sufficient.[88] The results of this study illustrate that stakeholders enter into inter-organizational relationships with other stakeholders to secure resources, and they create or develop linkages between them for the achievement of their goals.[89]

Although stakeholders strive for functional and financial autonomy, this state is hardly ever fully realized. Considering that not all NSOs are ready for that move, and in recognition of the need for NSO support towards that transition, the ASC offered a new wave of assistance through the Governance and Management Improvement Program (GMIP). Freeman's seminal book on stakeholder theory posits that successful organizations must systematically attend to the interests of various stakeholder groups.[90] Indeed, this program helps NSOs in relation to their structure, governance, management and strategic direction. This assistance is focussed on increasing the capacity and capability to work towards their strategic objectives. In efficient and effective sport systems, 'links are in place between funding agents and those leading programmes; roles and relationships are clearly defined and understood'.[91] In Australia, a National Elite Sport Council (NESC) has been established for this very purpose. NESC, in its role as the national coordinating group, is committed to fostering enhanced collaboration and coordination among the AIS, state institutes and academies of sport and the national high performance sport network, as well as across sports. An integral component of this programme is a continued commitment to foster cross- and multi-disciplinary exchange, ensuring that Australia remains at the forefront of high performance sport development.[92]

It is reasonable to suggest that the power to sustain a successful sport system lies within the cooperation and relationships of governments, sporting organizations, sport managers, sport management academia and significant others. This study argued that stakeholder theory is an appropriate method of building inter-organizational relationships. These results are in congruence with previous research that used stakeholder theory to study the stakeholder relations within the sporting industry.[93] The relationships this essay presents are the outcome of a dynamic and competitive industry that demands results and continuing re-evaluation of sport strategies.

The Australian sport system is resilient and has adapted to its ever-changing environment. It has delivered successful elite performances at an international level and catered for the masses of the Australian population and their needs. The system has the foundations and the pathways in place to deliver future participation opportunities. However, the stakeholders involved within the sport system in Australia will have to work with diligence in order to adapt to a complex, constantly evolving and uncertain environment, prepare to deal with future challenges and become financially strong.

Notes

[1] Australian Sports Commission, *Annual Report 2005–2006*.

[2] Australian Sports Commission, *Strategic Plan 2006–2009*, Department of Communications Information Technology and the Arts Funding Boost for Australian Sports, Senator Rhn Rod Kemp.

[3] Bloomfield, 'The Contribution of Sports Science'.

[4] Cuskelly, 'Volunteer Retention in Community Sport Organisations'.

[5] Leach, *Political Ideologies*.

[6] Green and Oakley, 'Elite Sport Development Systems'.

[7] Semiotuk, 'Theoretical and Methodological Considerations'.

[8] Jobling, *Sport and the State*.

[9] Stewart *et al.*, *Australian Sport*.

[10] Pyke, 'Science in Australian Sport'.

[11] Bloomfield, 'The Contribution of Sports Science'; Westerbeek, Shilbury and Deane, *The Australian Sport System*.

[12] Webb, Rowland and Fasano, 'Development of Sport Policy'; Confederation of Australian Sport, *A Whole New Ball Game*.

[13] Woodman, 'Sport Development: Systems, Trends and Issues'.

[14] Jobling, 'Sport and the State'.

[15] Stewart *et al.*, *Australian Sport*.

[16] Vamplew *et al.*, *The Oxford Companion to Australian Sport*.

[17] Quoted in Jobling, *Sport and the State*, 254.

[18] Farmer and Arnaudon, 'Australian Sport Policy'; Jobling, 'Sport and the State'; Shilbury, *Sport Management in Australia*.

[19] Shilbury, Deane and Kellett, *Sport Management in Australia*.

[20] O'Brien and Slack, 'Deinstitutionalising the Amateur Ethic'.

[21] Cashman, *Paradise of Sport*.

[22] Westerbeek, Shilbury and Deane, *The Australian Sport System*.

[23] Sweaney, 'Where Do We Go From Here?'.

[24] Sotiriadou, Quick and Shilbury, 'Sport for "Some"'. Lorsch and Morse, *Organizations and their Members*.

[25] Cooke, 'Sport and Politics'.

[26] Ibid.

[27] Westerbeek, Shilbury and Deane, *The Australian Sport System*.

[28] Farmer and Arnaudon, 'Australian Sport Policy'.

[29] Hogan and Norton, 'The "Price" of Olympic Gold'. Sotiriadou, 'Sport for "Some"'.

[30] Confederation of Australian Sport, *A Whole New Ball Game*.

[31] Quoted in Department of Industry, Science and Resources, *Shaping Up*, 73.

[32] Ibid.

[33] M. Grattan, 'Grassroots Sport Targeted as $547m Kicked into Play'. *Sydney Morning Herald*, 2001.

[34] Department of Industry, Science and Resources, *Backing Australia's Sporting Ability*.

[35] Grattan, 'Grassroots Sport Targeted as $547m Kicked into Play'.

[36] Stewart *et al.*, *Australian Sport*.

[37] Department of Industry, Science and Resources, *Backing Australia's Sporting Ability*.

38 Smith, 'Active Australia'.
39 Stewart-Weeks, 'The Third Wave'.
40 Nihill, 'Funding Boost for Beijing Challenge'.
41 Bloomfield, *Australia's Sporting Success*.
42 Ibid.
43 Covell, 'Attachment, Allegiance'.
44 Freeman, *Strategic Management*.
45 Carroll, *Business & Society*.
46 Mitchell, Agle and Wood, 'Toward a Theory of Stakeholder Identification'.
47 Jones, 'Instrumental Stakeholder Theory'.
48 Green and Oakley, 'Elite Sport Development Systems'.
49 Farmer and Arnaudon, 'Australian Sport Policy'.
50 Miles and Snow, *Organizational Strategy*. Pfeffer and Salancik, *The External Control of Organizations*.
51 Pfeffer and Salancik, *The External Control of Organizations*. Quoted in Johns and Saks, *Organizational Behaviour*, 489.
52 Johns and Saks, *Organizational Behaviour*.
53 Huxham and Vangen, 'Working Together'.
54 McQueen, 'Us and Them'.
55 Bourne and Walker, 'Visualizing Stakeholder Influence, 17–25.
56 Stewart-Weeks, 'The Third Wave'.
57 Shilbury, 'Considering Future Sport Delivery Systems', 217.
58 Thibault and Harvey, 'Fostering Interorganizational Linkages'.
59 Shilbury, 'Considering Future Sport Delivery Systems'.
60 Paulson, 'A Paradigm for the Analysis of Interorganizational Networks'; Pennings, 'Strategically Interdependent Organizations'.
61 Shilbury, 'Considering Future Sport Delivery Systems'.
62 Sotiriadou and Quick, 'Management Processes'.
63 Ryan, *Athletics Australia Overhaul Boosts Performance*.
64 Ibid., 1.
65 Quoted in Australian Sports Commission, *National Sporting Organisations Governance*, 1.
66 Elias, Cavana and Jackson, 'Stakeholder Analysis', 301.
67 Sauter and Leisen, 'Managing Stakeholders', 312.
68 Basketball Australia, *2000 Annual Report*.
69 Brown, *Amalgamation*, 1.
70 Mahony and Howard, 'Sport Business in the Next Decade'.
71 Brown, *Amalgamation*, 3.
72 Phillips, *How Hockey Avoided Merger Meltdown*, 1.
73 Schraeder and Self, 'Enhancing the Success of Mergers and Acquisitions'.
74 Quoted in Women's Hockey Australia, *2000 Annual Report*, 1.
75 Quoted in Confederation of Australian Motor Sport, *2000 Annual Report*, 2.
76 Cuskelly, McIntyre and Boag, 'A Longitudinal Study'.
77 Ibid., 181.
78 Heah, 'Tips on Being a Good Coach'.
79 Department of Communications Information Technology and the Arts, *Participation in Exercise*.
80 Australian Bureau of Statistics, *Sport and Recreation*.
81 Covell, 'Attachment, Allegiance and a Convergent Application of Stakeholder Theory: Assessing the Impact'.
82 Bloomfield, 'The Contribution of Sports Science'.
83 Cummings and Doh, 'Identifying Who Matters'.
84 Thibault and Harvey, 'Fostering Interorganizational Linkages'.
85 Quoted in Johns and Saks, *Organizational Behaviour*, 489.
86 Lorsch and Morse, *Organizations and their Members*.
87 Sotiriadou and Quick, 'Management Processes'.
88 Galaskiewicz, *Exchange Networks and Community Politics*.
89 Paulson, 'A Paradigm for the Analysis of Interorganizational Networks'; Pennings, 'Strategically Interdependent Organizations'.
90 Freeman, *Strategic Management*.

[91] Quoted in Green and Oakley, 'Elite Sport Development Systems', 258.
[92] Australian Sports Commission, *National Elite Council Strategic Plan 2006–2008*.
[93] Merrilees, Getz and O'Brien, 'Marketing Stakeholder Analysis'.

References

Australian Bureau of Statistics. *Sport and Recreation: A Statistical Overview*. Catalogue no. 4156.0, Edition 2. Canberra: ABS, 2006.

Australian Motor Sport. *2000 Annual Report*. Malvern East, VIC: Confederation of Australian Motor Sport, 2000.

Australian Sports Commission. *National Elite Council Strategic Plan 2006–2008*. Canberra: Author, 2006.

Australian Sports Commission. *National Sporting Organisations Governance: Principles of Best Practice*. Canberra: Author, 2002.

Australian Sports Commission. *Strategic Plan 2006–2009*. Canberra: Author, 2005.

Basketball Australia. *2000 Annual Report*. Bondi Junction, NSW: Author, 2000.

Bloomfield, J. *Australia's Sporting Success: The Inside Story*. Sydney: UNSW, 2001.

Bloomfield, J. 'The Contribution of Sports Science and Sports Medicine to the Development of the Australian Sports System'. *Journal of Science & Medicine in Sport* 5, no. 1 (2002): 1–8.

Bourne, L., and D.H.T. Walker. 'Visualizing Stakeholder Influence – Two Australian Examples'. *Project Management Journal* 12, no. 4 (2006): 17–25.

Brown, S. *Amalgamation: A Guide for Recreation and Sporting Organisations*. South Australia: Office for Recreation & Sport, 2003.

Carroll, A.B. *Business & Society: Ethics and Stakeholder Management*. 3rd ed. Cincinnati, OH: Southwestern, 1996.

Cashman, R. *Paradise of Sport: The rise of Organised Sport in Australia*. Melbourne: Oxford University Press, 1995.

Confederation of Australian Sport. *A Whole New Ball Game*: Sports 2000 Task Force. ACT: Author, 1999.

Cooke, G. 'Sport and Politics: A History of Government Funding'. *Sport* 16, no. 1 (1996): 17.

Covell, D. 'Attachment, Allegiance, and a Convergent Application of Stakeholder Theory to Ivy League Athletics'. *International Sports Journal* 8, no. 1 (Winter 2004): 14–26.

Covell, D. 'Attachment, Allegiance and a Convergent Application of Stakeholder Theory: Assessing the Impact of Winning on Athletic Donations in the Ivy League'. *Sport Marketing Quarterly* 14 (2005): 168–76.

Cummings, J.L., and J.P. Doh. 'Identifying Who Matters: Mapping Key Players in Multiple Environments'. *California Management Review* 42, no. 2 (2000): 83–104.

Cuskelly, G. 'Volunteer Retention in Community Sport Organisations'. *European Sport Management Quarterly* 4, no. 2 (2004): 59–76.

Cuskelly, G., N. McIntyre, and A. Boag. 'A Longitudinal Study of the Development of Organizational Commitment amongst Volunteer Sport Administrators'. *Journal of Sport Management* 12, no. 3 (1998): 181–202.

Department of Industry, Science and Resources. *Backing Australia's Sporting Ability: A More Active Australia*. Canberra: Author, 2001.

Department of Communications Information Technology and the Arts. *Participation in Exercise, Recreation and Sport. Annual Report*. Standing Committee on Recreation and Sport. Canberra: Department of Communications, Information Technology and the Arts, 2006.

Department of Industry, Science and Resources. *Shaping Up: A Review of Commonwealth Involvement in Sport and Recreation in Australia*. Canberra: Author, 1999.

Elias, A.A., R.Y. Cavana, and L.S. Jackson. 'Stakeholder Analysis for the R&D Project Management'. *R&D Management* 32, no. 4 (2002): 301–10.

Farmer, P., and S. Arnaudon. 'Australian Sport Policy'. In *National Sport Policies: An International Handbook*, edited by L. Chalip, A. Johnson, and L. Stachura, 1–22. Westport, CT: Greenwood Press, 1996.

Freeman, R.E. *Strategic Management: A Stakeholder Approach*. Englewood Cliffs, NJ: Prentice-Hall, 1984.

Galaskiewicz, J. *Exchange Networks and Community Politics*. Beverly Hill, CA: Sage Publications, 1979.

Green, M., and B. Oakley. 'Elite Sport Development Systems and Playing to Win: Uniformity and Diversity in International Approaches'. *Leisure Studies* 20 (2001): 247–67.

Heah, M. 'Tips on Being a Good Coach'. *Malaysian New Straits Time-Management* Times, May 7, 2003.

Hogan, K., and K. Norton. 'The "Price" of Olympic Gold'. *Journal of Science & Medicine in Sport* 3, no. 2 (2000): 203–18.

Huxham, C., and S. Vangen. 'Working Together. Key Themes in the Management of Relationships between Public and Non-Profit Organizations'. *International Journal of Public Sector Management* 9, no. 7 (1996): 5–17.

Jobling, I.F. 'Sport and the State: The Case of Australia and New Zealand'. In *Sport: The Third Millennium*, edited by F. Landry, M. Landry and M. Yerles, 251–60. Quebec: Les Presses De l'Universite Laval, 1991.

Johns, G., and A.M. Saks. *Organizational Behaviour: Understanding and Managing Life at Work*. Toronto: Pearson Prentice Hall, 2005.

Jones, T.M. 'Instrumental Stakeholder Theory: A Synthesis of Ethics and Economics'. *Academy of Management Review* 24, no. 2 (1995): 206–21.

Leach, R. *Political Ideologies: An Australian Introduction*. 2nd ed. South Melbourne: Macmillan, 1993.

Lorsch, J.W., and J.J. Morse. *Organizations and their Members: A Contingency Approach*. New York: Harper & Row, 1974.

McQueen, M. 'Us and Them. Decoding the Language of Nonprofit-Business Partnerships'. *Non-profit World* 22, no. 1 (2004): 21–22.

Mahony, D.F., and D.R. Howard. 'Sport Business in the Next Decade: A General Overview of Expected Trends'. *Journal of Sport Management* 15, no. 4 (2001): 275–96.

Merrilees, B., D. Getz, and D. O'Brien. 'Marketing Stakeholder Analysis – Branding the Brisbane Goodwill Games'. *European Journal of Marketing* 39, no. 9/10 (2005): 1060–77.

Miles, R.E., and C.C. Snow. *Organizational Strategy, Structure and Process*. New York: McGraw-Hill, 1978.

Mitchell, R.K., B.R. Agle, and D.J. Wood. 'Toward a Theory of Stakeholder Identification and Salience: Defining the Principle of Who and What Really Counts'. *Academy of Management Review* 22 (1997): 853–86.

Nihill, G. 'Funding Boost for Beijing Challenge'. *Ausport* 3 (2006): 3–4.

O'Brien, and T. Slack. 'Deinsitutionalising the Amateur Ethic: An Empirical Examination of Change in Rugby Union Football Club'. *Sport Management Review*, 2 (1999): 24–42.

Paulson, S.K. 'A Paradigm for the Analysis of Interorganizational Networks'. *Social Networks* 7 (1985): 105–26.

Pennings, J.M. 'Strategically Interdependent Organizations'. In *Handbook of Organizational Design*, edited by P.C. Nystrom and W.H. Starbuck, Vol. 1, 433–55. New York: Oxford University Press, 1981.

Pfeffer, J., and G.R. Salancik. *The External Control of Organizations: A Resource Dependence Perspective*. New York: Harper & Row, 1978.

Phillips, S. *How Hockey Avoided Merger Meltdown*. Canberra: Australian Sport Commission, 2002.

Pyke, F. 'Science in Australian Sport: Its Origins and Challenges'. *Sport Health* 25, no. 2 (2007): 26–30.

Ryan, C. *Athletics Australia Overhaul Boosts Performance*. Canberra: Australian Sport Commission, 2002.

Sauter, E.T., and B. Leisen. 'Managing Stakeholders'. *Annals of Tourism Research* 26, no. 2 (1999): 312–28.

Schraeder, M., and D.R. Self. Enhancing the Success of Mergers and Acquisitions: An Organizational Culture Perspective. *Management Decision* 41, no. 5 (2003): 511–22.

Semiotuk, D. 'Theoretical and Methodological Considerations for Comparative and International Sport and Physical Education'. In *Methodology in Comparative Physical Education and Sport*, edited by R. Howell, 41–59. Champaign, IL: Stipes, 1979.

Shilbury, D. 'Considering Future Sport Delivery Systems'. *Sport Management Review*, 3, no. 2 (2000): 199–221.

Shilbury, D., J. Deane, and P. Kellett. *Sport Management in Australia: An Organizational Overview*. Melbourne: Strategic Sport Management Publishers, 2001.

Smith, A. 'Active Australia?' *The Sports Factor*. Radio National. Sydney: ABC, 2000.

Sotiriadou, K. 'Sport for "Some"'. In *Leisure Futures, Leisure Cultures: Selection of Papers from the 5th Anzals and 3rd Women in Leisure International Conferences, 2001*, edited by S. Colyer and F. Lobo, 105–16. Perth: Praxis Education, 2003.

Sotiriadou, K., and S.P. Quick. 'Management Processes, Organisational Structures and Contexts in Greek Yachting Organisations'. *International Journal of Sport Management* 3, no. 4 (2002): 290–307.

Sotiriadou, K., S. Quick, and D. Shilbury. 'Sport for "Some": Elite Versus Mass Participation'. *International Journal of Sport Management* 7, no. 1 (2006): 50–66.

Stewart, B., M. Nicholson, A. Smith, and H. Westerbeek. *Australian Sport: Better by Design? The Evolution of Australian Sport Policy*. New York: Routledge Taylor & Francis Group, 2004.

Stewart-Weeks, M. 'The Third Wave: Developing a Post-2000 Sport Policy Framework'. *Sport* 17, no. 1 (1997): 6–12.

Sweaney, K. 'Where Do We Go From Here?' *Australian Leisure Management* 25, no. 4 (2001).

Thibault, L., and J. Harvey. 'Fostering Interorganizational Linkages in the Canadian Sport Delivery System'. *Journal of Sport Management* 11 (1997): 45–68.

Vamplew, W., K. Moore, J. O'Hara, R. Cashman, and I. Jobling. *The Oxford Companion to Australian Sport*. Melbourne: Oxford University Press, 1997.

Webb, P., G. Rowland and C. Fasano. 'Development of Sport Policy and Programs in Sporting Organisations: Theoretical and Practical Considerations'. *The ACHPER National Journal* 129 (1990): 5–8.

Westerbeek, H., D. Shilbury, and J. Deane. 'The Australian Sport System, Its History and an Organisational Overview'. *European Journal for Sport Management* 2, no. 1 (1995): 42–58.

Women's Hockey Australia. *2000 Annual Report*. Surry Hills, NSW: Author, 2000.

Woodman, L. 'Sport Development: Systems, Trends and Issues'. *Sports Coach* 11, no. 4 (1988): 29–38.

The Janus face of diversity in Australian sport

Tracy Taylor, Daniel Lock and Simon Darcy

School of Leisure, Sport & Tourism, University of Technology, Sydney, Australia

In this essay, Janus is used as a metaphor for examining the nature of cultural diversity in Australian sport. It does so by firstly presenting a historical context for sport in Australia and the relative lack of cultural diversity found in sport. Within a country dominated by the running codes of football and cricket, the position of soccer in Australia was somewhat unique as it became a bastion for many non-Anglo migrant groups. However, in the 1980s and 1990s soccer's lack of organizational success at the state and national level was negatively ascribed to the tensions between the ethnically affiliated clubs, the same clubs that were ironically the stalwarts driving the growing popularity of the sport. We examine the initiatives used to restructure the game in Australia to make football more appealing to mainstream (i.e. non-ethnically aligned) spectators. The contemporary situation is explored through secondary documentation and the results of a survey of 3,056 spectators undertaken during the first season of the new A-League are presented. The essay concludes with a discussion about the relative success of the restructure in terms of changing the face of Australian soccer.

Introduction

The dual face of Janus, the Roman god, was historically used to symbolize change and transition. Janus was also known to represent time because he could see into the past with one face and into the future with the other. Janus also stood for being two faced, that is, not always being what it seemed on the face of it. In this essay, Janus, as depicted in Figure 1, is used as a metaphor for examining the nature of cultural diversity in Australian sport. Specifically, the discussion presented here draws on soccer (football) as a site of the changing faces of cultural diversity as waves of migrants arrive, acculturate and forge new identities in this southern island.

The original settlement of Australia by Aborigines occurred at least 40 millennia ago and the indigenous population remained relatively undisturbed until the eighteenth century[1] After this time substantial numbers of mainly European arrivals fundamentally changed the country's composition.[2] Australia became a settler nation, one which 'Europeans have settled, where their descendants have remained politically dominant over indigenous people, and where a diverse, gendered society has developed in class, ethnic and racial terms'.[3] Contemporary Australian national identity has been conspicuously forged by continuing migration that has occurred since the initial colonization. However, it was not until a 1972 pronouncement of policy change by the Federal Labor government that the country officially was deemed to support multiculturalism.[4]

Historically, visible minority ethnic communities in Australia were subject to widespread systemic discrimination perpetrated under the banner of government policies promoting cultural purity, assimilation, integration and even multiculturalism.[5] While

Figure 1. Janus. Source: http://www.meridiangraphics.net/janus.htm.

most Australians agree that people should not be subject to prejudice due to their ethnic background, equally 'most Australians also expect migrants to embrace their new home and to do in Rome as the Romans do'.[6] The presence of cultural pluralism due to the immigration of people from diverse ethnic backgrounds has appeared threatening to hosts who 'often express the fear that they are being "swamped" by foreigners'.[7] To some, multiculturalism implies that the face of Australian national identity will be reshaped and lose its unique and quintessential 'Aussieness'. Nevertheless, multiculturalism was put 'at the heart of Australia's developing nationhood and national identity' by 1982,[8] and as history has shown, writing the valuing of different cultures and ethnicities into policy did not always directly translate directly into putting it into practice.

Sport is a particularly useful site for examining the changing and complex interplay of race, nation, culture and identity in very public contexts.[9] The role that sport has played in Australian society with respect to both creating and alleviating cultural tensions, particularly with regard to minority ethnic involvement in the sport of soccer has been widely discussed and debated.[10] Notably, celebrations of national identity as expressed through support of an ethnically aligned soccer team have been viewed by some sections of the Australian community as a direct challenge to any notion of a culturally inclusive community or multiculturalism. That is to say, the expressions of support and nationalistic pride in countries other than Australia, by groups of individuals living in Australia, has often times been construed as non-Australian and certainly non-assimilationist.

The face that one presents to the outside world is comprised of a complex set of identifiers. In this essay we look at the 'Janus face' of soccer as an allegorical representation of the fragmented and seemingly contradictory nature of cultural identity in Australian society. The Janus face of soccer is explored by examining the sport's cultural history in Australia. The discussion then outlines the strategic changes that the Football Federation Australia has implemented in soccer in Australia since 2003. The relative effect of these changes is assessed through the results of an FFA survey of non-members gathered during the first season of the A-League competition. The online survey participants were recruited by each A-League club during home matches in the first season of the competition. The survey was completed by 3,056 A-League non-member spectators. The analysis of the survey included frequencies and cross tabulations of age, gender and cultural affiliation of the non-member spectators of the seven Australian A-League clubs. This study aims to provide empirical data to compliment the qualitative studies of

Hallinan, Hughson and Burke[11] and Hay[12] conducted with fans of Melbourne Victory since the A-League was launched in 2005.

Sport and cultural diversity

In this section, we briefly address sport and cultural diversity to provide a basis to discuss the role soccer has played in Australia's migrant communities. In the first decades of the nineteenth century, the migrant arrivals consisted largely of convicts, free settlers and colonial gentry,[13] bringing with them British social, political, ideological and educational discourse. Links to England were maintained through various institutions, including sport.[14] British arrivals influenced the type of sports that were popular into the middle to latter part of the nineteenth century, namely horseracing, prize fighting and cricket. Each of these sports established exclusive clubs for its middle- and upper-class members and membership was highly selective. 'Nostalgia no doubt led to the adoption of many British sporting activities, but others were the result of deliberate attempts by the colonial wealthy and educated classes to replicate English social life, including its social structure.'.[15] There was noted resistance to the cultural domination of the English by the predominantly Irish convict and working class, and women's sport opportunities were limited to a few 'suitably feminine' sports.[16] Scottish and English working-class migrants who set up soccer clubs in Australia at this time began a tradition of naming clubs after their homelands or existing clubs overseas, such as the Caledonians, Northumberland and Durhams, Rangers, Celtics and Fifers.[17]

While the government tried to encourage more migrants from Britain in the early part of the twentieth century by offering them financial assistance, immigration from the UK was in decline by the early 1930s and it became apparent that the dream of a self-supporting British Empire was unattainable. Consequently, Australia was forced to start looking beyond the British Isles to sustain its commitment to a large immigration intake.[18] Although not targeted, and arriving mainly unassisted, mainland European immigrants began to significantly contribute to the growth of the early twentieth-century Australian population. In the aftermath of the Second World War, Australia's immigration policy gave British immigrants predominance, and tried to uphold a White Australia intake.[19] However, over 170,000 displaced persons from the refugee camps of Europe arrived in Australia between 1947 and 1954.[20] The arrivals were encouraged to assimilate into the Australian way of life as quickly as possible and become inconspicuous in their new land.[21] There was a strongly expressed public expectation that, 'everyone would learn English, everyone would look alike, and everyone would share values, beliefs and practices'.[22]

Despite this assimilation expectation, ethnic affiliated clubs, newspapers, cultural, religious and sporting bodies expanded,[23] but newly arrived ethnic minority groups did not fully embrace the established Australian sports of cricket, rugby or rowing.[24] Instead, soccer flourished as the newly arrived males from Europe swelled the player ranks and quickly made the game their own. Soccer subsequently went from an English-controlled game to a sport administered and played by large numbers of European Australians. As noted in a government report (on Croatians in Australia), 'perhaps the sphere that has come closest to uniting the Croatian-born is sport, and especially soccer, in which many Croatian teams and players have competed with great distinction in the top grades'.[25] In many ethnic communities, sport participation was a counter balance for government and community expectations of cultural assimilation as it provided the participants with an avenue to express their cultural identity.[26] By the 1970s the federal government finally bowed to pressure and replaced its assimilation focus with a policy of supporting multiculturalism and valuing cultural diversity;[27] however, soccer continued to be supported by ethnically based community clubs, and consequently the sport was not fully embraced as Australian.[28] As soccer grew globally, the prevailing perception of soccer as a migrant sport was problematic and seen as a hindrance to its development as an Australian sport. However, it was not until the later part of the century that the sport was forced to undergo a 'major facelift' and purge the game of its ethnic appearance.

The changing face of soccer

There is a significant body of research on sport and ethnicity which discusses the role of soccer/football in multi-cultural Australian society during the second half of the twentieth century.[29] However, the changed face of soccer in Australia, represented by its name change to football, followed a structural overhaul of the sport which commenced in 2003. The restructure of football was designed to provide an avenue for the expression and appropriation of cultural distinctiveness and change through the renaming, repositioning and re-conceptualization of the game in Australia. Notably, the new face of football was to reflect the national competition and national federation's (the FFA's) strategic agenda of de-ethnicization and the development of a 'new' football culture in Australia.

The sport of soccer was introduced to the country by British migrants in the nineteenth century. While soccer originally had British roots, as noted earlier in this essay, its popularity with post-war migrants shifted its participant base to encompass non-English-speaking ethnic communities, and this orientation earned soccer the derogatory colloquial title of 'Wogball'. The ethnic orientation of football and its use in maintaining specific cultural identities has been widely acknowledged.[30] Socio-historical narratives of ethnic involvement in the game have chronicled the sport's role in the lives of selected migrant communities[31] and sociological studies on football hooliganism and expressive nationality have investigated the darker side of this allegiance.[32]

Mainland European involvement in football grew enormously in the mid 1940s[33] when migrants were brought to Australia to fill gaps in the antipodean labour market.[34] Many migrants lacked competency in the English language and culture, and unsurprisingly friendships formed on the boat trip to Australia or in the migrant camps with others who spoke the same language, had the same cultural background or were of the same religion. These relationships were carried into settlement, and enclaves of migrants formed in 'inner-city locations, long abandoned by the middle classes'.[35] These patterns of development were similar in Sydney and Melbourne with significant inner-city enclaves of Italians (Leichhardt and Carlton), Greeks (Marrickville and Lonsdale St, Melbourne), Chinese (respective Chinatowns), while other immigrants decided to settle in the middle suburbs in Asian 'ethic precincts' (Bankstown and Richmond) and outer suburbs (Cabramatta and Springvale) due to the advantages of space and price.[36]

The role of the soccer club in migrant acculturation in Victoria has been extensively reviewed in relation to the plethora of ethnically aligned clubs in and around Melbourne.[37] As Hay argued, soccer provided an avenue into mutual support systems, invaluable to new migrants.[38] Ethnically aligned communities formed around soccer clubs in Perth, although these communities became fragmented as migration rates reduced.[39] Soccer was presented as a game for lower-class migrants, just as the upper classes lay claim to the sport rugby union through its prevalence in the private school system.[40]

Ethnically based football clubs developed and served to reinforce settlement patterns, as the sport became a focal role in many migrant communities.[41] These football clubs established a point of common ground for migrants, and provided opportunities to socialize and converse with their compatriots. Such clubs attracted members from their constituent countries or religion (e.g. Hakoah Football Club – Jewish) but there was limited appeal outside of the cultural and religious boundaries. Playing, watching and participating in football was a pastime which was familiar and the space provided a transition avenue between their former home country and the new Australian environment.[42] Soccer was henceforth known as a 'multicultural affair'.[43] However, as many of these clubs conducted their business and social activities in languages other than English, a stereotype emerged that football clubs 'were creating barriers for Australians of long standing, who were not prepared to work at overcoming their initial feelings of strangeness when they came into contact ... there was a fear of the foreigner'.[44] In other words, the public face of soccer was decidedly non-Anglo and these clubs were seen as unwelcoming and non inclusive of cultures other than their own.

The question of de-ethnicization

Attempts to remove the ethnic names, symbols and linkages present in many football clubs were driven by imperatives to develop football's following beyond specific ethnic communities and to disassociate the sport with ethnic rivalries. The notion of de-ethnicization was first mooted in Canberra in 1960, when local football officials raised it as a means to curb the violence associated with ethnic rivalries.[45] Despite three attempts to de-ethnicize the NSL, in 1977, 1992 and 1997[46] the process failed to eventuate as clubs with strong cultural ties and values were not about to simply renege on long-established traditions.[47]

The outcome of forcibly removing explicit demonstrations of ethnicity (such as a club name, through de-ethnicization legislation), merely led clubs to espouse their cultural heritage and pride in alternate ways. Expressive forms of culture have endured; Sydney United (formerly Sydney Croatia), Marconi Stallions (Italian heritage), and Sydney Olympic (Greek heritage) all compete in the NSW state league with clearly visible allusions to their historical nationalities in kit and insignia. The unsavoury side of maintenance of expressive identities was evidenced in the 2005 season when fans of Sydney United (Croatian) and Bonnyrigg White Eagles (Serbian) rioted during a NSW Premier League fixture. The events of 13 March 2005 prompted an independent enquiry report, which heavily criticized Soccer NSW and both clubs,[48] while also proposing measures for improving the implementation and management of football in Australia. Hughson[49] has provided a tempered argument on the de-ethnicization agenda, discussing its paradoxical standing with Australian multicultural policy which espouses the value of cultural diversity.[50]

The various incarnations of football governance (Australian Soccer Federation [ASF], Soccer Australia [SA], Australian Soccer Association [ASA], and Football Federation Australia [FFA]) have viewed ethnicity as a divisive factor, which limited the appeal of the game to a broader audience. More specifically, de-ethnicization, from a governance perspective, is based around the notion that anyone should be able to play, support or work in any football club, regardless of their ethnic heritage. Such considerations of inclusiveness and the necessity to engage football's huge participation base at a youth level (the popularity of football as a participant sport is second to only swimming in Australia)[51] underpinned the radical overhaul of football in Australia, initiated by the intervention of the Australian federal government.

Two documents outlined the proposed changes to the structure of football governance[52] and the constitution of the National Soccer League (NSL).[53] The recommendations of *The Crawford Report* and *The Report of the NSL Task Force* provided the basis for a dramatic change to soccer governance. Australian business tycoon, Frank Lowy, who brought with him strong connections to soccer/football, was recruited to provide a new approach to leadership and drive change in Australian football. The appointment of John O'Neill as Chief Executive Officer signalled a break from tradition and an ushering in of a new era for the sport. O'Neill was the driving force behind the development of the Australian Rugby Union and the 2003 Rugby World Cup, and had not been previously associated with soccer. This was followed by a name change for the governing body of soccer, to the Football Federation of Australia (FFA). O'Neill's mandate was to replace the old face of soccer with a new face for football[54] from 'wogball' to 'football for all Australians'.

The new image was championed though the introduction of the national competition, the A-League, comprised of city-based franchises, without any links to specific ethnic communities.[55] The strategy to completely disconnect the League from its ethnic heritage was designed to create a completely new public face for football as represented in the A-League slogan, 'It's football, but not as you know it'.[56] The newly created A-League clubs[57] were disassociated from previous traditions and had no identifiable existing fan base, making the creation of a new identity paramount. Or can there be two faces of football in Australia?

Ethnically oriented clubs are still strongly represented in the state premier league and other divisions.[58] Hallinan, Hughson and Burke suggest that, despite acceptance of the corporate de-ethnicized model, suburban teams with non-Anglo ethnic derivatives remain a vital area for both sport and their respective communities. These clubs, with their rich history and traditions, represent the grass roots face of football and the ongoing relationship that ethnic communities maintain with their football club.

The composition of the new face of the A-League teams is further examined here via features that encompass ethnic, cultural, generational and national boundaries. These features are intended to be attractive to the youth market, and specifically emphasize the commonalities between young supporters and their multi-ethnic and mainstream peers i.e. the 'sweet spot of youth culture' (ages 16–24 years).[59] While the youth market has been the prime focus of the league's marketing efforts, the retention of long-term fans of the game and mainstream support are equally essential to the success of the A-League.[60] Just how successful the A-League has been in creating a new face for football in Australia, and its key features, is discussed below.

A new supporter face for football?

The new national level football league was designed to appeal to a multi-ethnic mainstream Australian society. Notably, almost one quarter (24%) of the Australian population was born overseas in over 250 different countries[61] and of these the largest groups are the United Kingdom (5.6%), and New Zealand (2.3%).[62] Multiculturalism creates a paradox in relation to football.[63] At the grassroots level, football participation is universally popular and statistics demonstrate this clearly with football being the most played team-sport for children.[64] However, there are apparent differences to this pattern based on public and private schools, the state one resides in and geographic location (city vs. rural). Professional national and semi-professional state football competitions have traditionally attracted a limited spectator following and have not been able to capitalize on grass-roots participation and develop a strong spectator base for the sport.[65] A strong body of qualitative ethnographic research[66] has consistently found that specific ethnic communities provided the majority of NSL supporters, although supporting statistical evidence is limited.

Have the changes to the national league attracted a diverse population and is this supporter base reflective of the cultural diversity of Australia? The subject of this essay is A-League non-member supporters in the period prior to and post Socceroos' qualification for the World Cup in Germany 2006. While significant publicity was created by the Socceroos' qualification for Germany, this study covers a period prior to the World Cup where the major impact of television spectatorship had not occurred. However, it is recognized that qualification led to unprecedented media coverage and television spectatorship of soccer in Australia. This effect could be the focus of another essay. This essay focuses on non-members of the A-League clubs. In the remainder of this essay, the question of whether the A-League has been successful in attracting a culturally diverse market or, conversely, if ethnic patterns of sports spectatorship are still visible, is addressed.

In his research into A-League club Melbourne Victory, Hay provides us with a starting point and an insight into the potential cultural shift since the re-development of the A-League:

> In one respect the current boom is different from all those which have gone before. Those were precipitated and sustained by high levels of inward migration of football-cognisant people; this one is virtually entirely driven by the interest of the existing domestic population.[67]

Hay examined whether there had been a shift from ethnic to mainstream and suggested that changes made to top-level football structure have opened up football to a broader cross-section of Australians. These findings corroborate research into Sydney FC's membership base that identified Sydney FC's fan base as highly multi-cultural with the clubs members representing a myriad of ethnicities. Fans of Sydney FC were characterized by a vociferous support of football, with respondents primarily supporting globally branded football teams and, secondly, by a belief that their membership of the new A-League team is symbolic of allegiance to football in Australia.[68] The latter is indicative of the latent demand for a high profile professional league competition. Both of these studies indicated that the A-League has been successful in developing a more diverse, mainstream following, due to the removal of specific ethnic references and the associated perceptions of hooligan behaviour and deviance, which had dogged the previous National Soccer League.

Method

To test these findings on a national scale (i.e. across all Australian A-League clubs) a survey was conducted in conjunction with the Football Federation Australia (FFA) at the end of the inaugural 2005–06 A-League season. Non-member spectators of the eight A-League clubs were surveyed, with the New Zealand sample excluded for this study. This sample group represented a more transient group of supporters than club members that had committed financially to A-League clubs. The online survey participants were recruited by each A-League club during home matches in the first season of the competition. Only non-members from each A-League club were sampled, which was facilitated by an initial screening question, and then consent and an email contact was obtained for their involvement for the online survey. The survey was subsequently completed by 3,056 A-League non-member spectators. The results are now presented through frequencies and cross tabulations of cultural affiliation of A-League non-member spectators.

Results

The findings provide some insights into the characteristics of A-League fans after the first season of the competition. As Figure 2 shows, not surprisingly, supporter groups in the A-League are still highly male-dominated.[69] Despite failing to broaden their gendered following, the degree to which the A-League had been successful in attracting the youth market is striking. *Sydney Morning Herald* football writer Michael Cockerill described this previously ambivalent market as: 'football's silent majority, the hundreds of thousands of youngsters playing the game who have never felt connected to it at professional level'.[70]

Some 70% of respondents were under the age of 35 years, while the most prominent age bracket was 18–25 years, the specific group targeted by the FFA, which represented some 28% of the sample group. The engagement of this previously disenfranchised market appears to have been a significant success for the FFA. Additionally, the significant number of supporters drawn from ages 36 years and upwards demonstrates that a broad spectrum of the population has been attracted.

In relation to the question of cultural diversity, 23% of the respondents were born overseas, approximately the same proportion as found in the general Australian population.

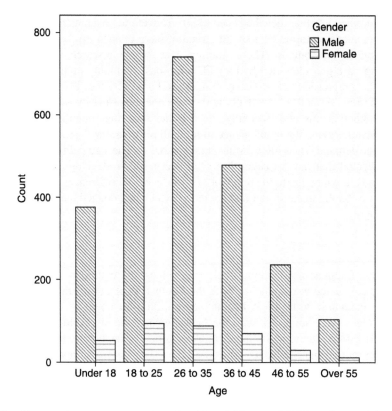

Figure 2.   Non-member survey age and gender. Note: Male n = 2708 Female n = 347.

Some 77% of respondents were born in Australia and of these, 33% were born in Australia but had one or more parents born overseas (compared with 20% in the general population). This statistic is notable as it demonstrated that the A-League has attracted a high number of Australian-born fans. In doing so, findings suggest that the FFA has been successful in attracting a market that was previously disconnected from football support in Australia.[71] The cultural diversity of the respondents parallels the general population, with a slight over-representation of second generation Australians.

The respondents, who did not identify themselves solely as 'Australian' were asked about their cultural identification. Some 51% of the sample group identified themselves solely as Australian. The remaining 49% identified with over 100 nationalities, spread across the globe. Respondents identifying with the 'United Kingdom' including England (11.4%), Scotland (2.5%), and the UK (3.5%) formed the largest cultural group outside of solely Australian.[72] In addition, a significant identification with Italian heritage (5.8%) was evident, followed by Greek (3%), Netherlands (1.4%), Croatia (1.2%), Macedonia (1.2%), Poland (1.1%), Malta (0.9%), Germany (1.1%), New Zealand (1.1%) and Ireland (see Table 1).

The cultural diversity of supporters provides evidence that A-League football clubs now appeal to Bradley's ideal of broader areas and regions.[73] However, the substantive presence of second generation Australians suggests that the sport has continued to attract a strong 'ethnically based' following. However, what is not entirely clear is whether these supporters are attending games as a continued expression of ethnicity or are simply supporting the sport of football as 'Australians'. Questions such as these are relevant to determine the extent to which soccer has retained its capacity for developing and maintaining specific cultural identities.

In examining the cultural heritage of the seven Australian A-League clubs, an interesting contrast is provided by Figure 3. Figure 3 highlights that in the majority of A-League clubs, spectators and their parents were born in Australia. However, the cities of Sydney, Melbourne and Adelaide all have a high number of first generation Australians. In fact, Sydney, Melbourne and Adelaide's non-member supporter base demonstrates that a high proportion of spectators in these cities have one or both parents born outside of Australia. While there was no dominant cultural identification in Sydney, Melbourne was more strongly identified with Italian (14%) and Adelaide with UK (20%). In contrast, the non-member spectator bases of Newcastle Jets, Central Coast Mariners and Queensland

Table 1.   Cultural identification.

Cultural identification	%
Australia	50.9
UK	17.8
Italy	5.8
Greece	3
Holland	1.4
Croatia	1.2
Macedonia	1.2
Poland	1.1
Germany	1.1
New Zealand	1.1
Ireland	1
Other	14.4*

*Only groups with a percentage higher than 1% were included

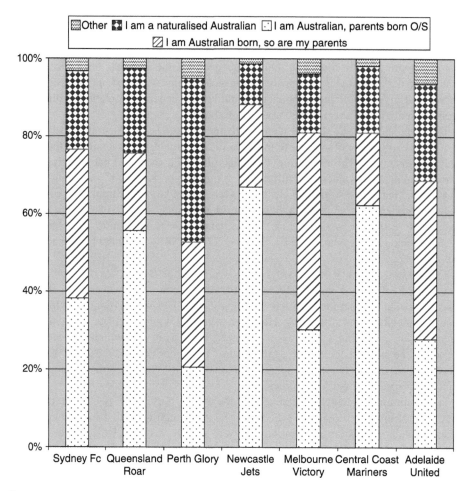

Figure 3. Cultural origin based on each A-League club. N = 3051

Roar each represent a distinctly Australian non-member support. Perth Glory was notable as its highest proportion of non-member spectator base was naturalised Australians, with 35% of its supporters identifying with UK cultural heritage. A Chi-square test for independence (p = 0.000) indicated a significant association between club supported and cultural origin. This finding has implications for the marketing and promotion of the game in the three groupings of cities/teams for non-member spectators.

Conclusion

In redefining the cultural boundaries of Australia's top-level football league, the FFA risked alienating the ethnic communities that had been the lifeblood of the game.[74] Vitriolic arguments against the removal of ethnicity from football[75] presented de-ethnicization as a return to colonial roots and the rise of the British Empire and its chauvinistic trappings.[76] Empirical research into the effects of the change since the start of the A-League outlined in this essay would lend credence to the dispute of this treatise.[77]

The Janus face of football reflects the changing supporter base and repositioning of the sport to attract a more mainstream Australian population. Dominant social groups have always had more power to (re)construct and convey particular meanings and ideologies than minority social groups. The FFA-imposed initiatives were clearly devised to alter the appearance of 'soccer', from an image that was strongly associated with ethnicity to a more diverse and culturally pluralist 'football' competition. The changes represent an ambitious strategy that required sophistication to implement, as a delicate balance was necessary to assimilate the historically based multitude of ethnic affiliations into the seemingly 'faceless' new, 'one team, one city' A-League. Evidence to date would suggest that this repositioning of football has been effective and the new face of football is attractive to a young and culturally diverse audience, and spans a broad spectrum of Australian society. The FFA was able to construct a public face that simultaneously embraced multicultural Australia.

The changes to football also reflect what is currently happening within Australian contemporary society. The federal government has recently shifted emphasis from promoting multiculturalism in favour of promoting a society which values Australian citizenship, appreciates cultural diversity and enables migrants to participate equitably. This philosophical change is not dissimilar to what has occurred in elite level football. However, the more pragmatic financial imperatives provided the prime impetus for change to football, along with the desire of those involved in the sport to position Australia on the world stage.

Football is an important social space in which shifting notions of identity and belonging can be articulated and contested; however, the degree to which the game can realistically facilitate wider transformations in social relations is limited.[78] However, the sport can make changes that will broaden its spectator appeal and at the same time embrace cultural diversity and develop culturally inclusive practices. While a dualist argument exists over the decision to implement a league without expressive ethnicity, the declining number of immigrants entering Australia[79] and the ongoing acculturation of those who preceded suggest such measures are required for the future success of the sport. It is difficult to argue from the data presented here that removing expressive ethnicity from top-level football has deprived ethnic-specific groups access to football, as the sheer diversity of the current supporter base disputes this.

Further research is required to ascertain the impact of these changes at a state league level where ethnic affiliations are still predominant. As Hallinan, Hughson and Burke clearly articulate,[80] ethnic clubs still play a role in the life of migrant communities and the impact of the governance restructure on these communities needs further attention. Have the changes alienated ethnic communities across Australia, or does the newfound accessibility of football to mainstream Australia provide migrant communities with greater acceptance, and hence, opportunities for socialization, mobility and acculturation? Whether 'soccer' is the backward-looking face of Janus and the FFA has successfully created a forward-looking diverse and inclusive face of football in Australia will be tested over the coming decade in terms of the profile of participants, spectators, volunteers, administrators and the place that football has in the Australian sporting psyche.

Notes

[1] Hanna, *Reconciliation in Olympism*.
[2] Sherington, *Australia's Immigrants 1788–1988*.
[3] Stasiulius and Yuval-Davis, *Unsettling Settler Societies*, 3.
[4] Hallinan and Krotee, 'Conceptions of Nationalism and Citizenship'.
[5] Castles, 'Nations of Immigrants'.
[6] Birrell and Betts, 'Australians' Attitudes to Migration Review', 3.

[7] Jayaraman, 'Inclusion and Exclusion', 136.

[8] Galligan and Roberts, *Australian Multiculturalism*, 7.

[9] Carrington and McDonald, *Race, Sport and British Society*.

[10] Hallinan and Krotee, 'Conceptions of Nationalism and Citizenship'; Harrison, 'What's in an Ethnic Name?'; Hay, '"Our Wicked Foreign Game"'; Hughson, Building a Brotherhood from Otherhood'; Mosely, 'Balkan Politics in Australian Soccer'.

[11] Hallinan, Hughson and Burke, 'Supporting the "World Game" in Australia'.

[12] Hay, 'Fan Culture in Australian Football (Soccer)'.

[13] Jupp, 'Waves of Migration to Australia'.

[14] Sherington, *Australia's Immigrants 1788–1988*.

[15] Vamplew, 'Violence in Australian Soccer', 3.

[16] Foley, 'Subversive Possibilities'; Lynch and Veal, *Australian Leisure*.

[17] Hay, '"Our Wicked Foreign Game"'.

[18] Sherington, *Australia's Immigrants 1788–1988*.

[19] Jupp, 'Waves of Migration to Australia'.

[20] Sherington, *Australia's Immigrants 1788–1988*.

[21] Murphy, *The Other Australia*.

[22] Jupp, 'Waves of Migration to Australia', 25

[23] Waterhouse, *Private Pleasure, Public Leisure*.

[24] Cashman, *Paradise of Sport*.

[25] Department of Immigration and Multicultural Affairs, *Croatian Born Community Profile*, 3.

[26] Mosely, *Ethnic Involvement in Australian Soccer*.

[27] Jupp, 'Waves of Migration to Australia'.

[28] Hay, '"Our Wicked Foreign Game"'.

[29] Hay, 'British Football, Wogball or the World Game?'; Mosely, *Ethnic Involvement in Australian Soccer*; Vamplew, 'Violence in Australian Soccer'.

[30] Adair and Vamplew, *Sport in Australian History*; Hay, 'British Football, Wogball or the World Game?'; Hughson, 'A Feel for the Game'; Hughson, 'Australian Soccer's "Ethnic" Tribes'; Mosely, *Ethnic Involvement in Australian Soccer*; Vamplew, 'Violence in Australian Soccer'.

[31] Ibid.

[32] Hughson, 'Australian Soccer'; Hughson, 'A Feel for the Game'; Hughson, 'The Boys Are Back in Town'.

[33] Vamplew, 'Violence in Australian Soccer'.

[34] Hay, 'British Football, Wogball or the World Game?'.

[35] Mosely, 'Soccer', 164.

[36] Ibid. Collins, 'Cultural Diversity and Entrepreneurship'.

[37] Hay, 'British Football, Wogball or the World Game?'.

[38] Ibid.

[39] Jones and Moore, 'He Only Has Eyes for Poms'.

[40] Hay, '"Our Wicked Foreign Game"'.

[41] Mosely, 'Soccer', 164.

[42] Mosely, *Ethnic Involvement in Australian Soccer*.

[43] Hughson, 'Australian Soccer', 12.

[44] Hay, '"Our Wicked Foreign Game"', 174.

[45] Mosely, 'Soccer'.

[46] Mosely, *Ethnic Involvement in Australian Soccer*.

[47] Hughson, 'A Tale of Two Tribes'.

[48] Kerkyasharian, Moss and Waller, *Report of the Independent Panel of Inquiry*.

[49] Hughson, 'A Tale of Two Tribes'.

[50] Ibid.

[51] Australian Bureau of Statistics, *Children's Participation in Cultural and Leisure Activities, Australia*.

[52] Crawford, *Report of the Independent Soccer Review Committee*.

[53] Kemeny, *Report of the NSL Task-Force*.

[54] N. Shoebridge, 'Modest A-League Faces Uphill Battle'. *Financial Review*, November 8, 2004, 50.

[55] Hay, 'British Football, Wogball or the World Game?'; Hughson, 'A Feel for the Game'; Mosely, *Ethnic Involvement in Australian Soccer*; Vamplew, 'Violence in Australian Soccer'.

[56] J. Huxley, 'Football's New Kick-start'. *Sydney Morning Herald*, August 26, 2006, 28.
[57] With the exception of Perth Glory and Adelaide United.
[58] Hallinan, Hughson and Burke, 'Supporting the "World Game" in Australia'.
[59] M. Cockerill, 'Lowy Targets Young, Welcomes Old'. *Sydney Morning Herald*, August 9, 2005, 38.
[60] Ibid.
[61] Australian Bureau of Statistics, *Migration, Australia* figures as at 30 June 2006.
[62] Ibid.
[63] Hughson, 'Australian Soccer'.
[64] Australian Bureau of Statistics, *Children's Participation in Cultural and Leisure Activities, Australia*; Australian Bureau of Statistics, *Children's Participation in Cultural and Leisure Activities*; Australian Bureau of Statistics, *Participation in Sports and Physical Recreation*.
[65] Hughson, 'Australian Soccer'.
[66] Hay, 'Fan Culture in Australian Football (Soccer)'; Hughson, 'A Feel for the Game'; Hughson, 'The Boys Are Back in Town'.
[67] Hay, 'Fan Culture in Australian Football (Soccer)', 101.
[68] Lock, Taylor and Darcy, 'Fan Identity Formation in a New Football Club'.
[69] Ibid.
[70] Cockerill, 'Lowy Targets Young, Welcomes Old', 38.
[71] Ibid.
[72] Australian Bureau of Statistics, *Migration, Australia*. The cultural background of participants was included as an open ended question. It is for this reason that the UK, England and Scotland are all included.
[73] Bradley, *Australian Soccer Federation*.
[74] Hay, '"Our Wicked Foreign Game"'.
[75] Brabazon, 'What's the Story Morning Glory?'.
[76] Ibid.
[77] Hay, 'Fan Culture in Australian Football (Soccer)'; Lock, Taylor and Darcy, 'Fan Identity Formation in a New Football Club'.
[78] Burdsey, *British Asians and Football*.
[79] Vamplew, 'Violence in Australian Soccer'.
[80] Hallinan, Hughson and Burke, 'Supporting the "World Game" in Australia'.

References

Adair, D., and W. Vamplew. *Sport in Australian History*. Australian retrospectives. Melbourne: Oxford University Press, 1997.

Australian Bureau of Statistics. *Children's Participation in Cultural and Leisure Activities, Australia*. Canberra: Australian Bureau of Statistics, 2003.

Australian Bureau of Statistics. *Migration, Australia*. Canberra: Australian Bureau of Statistics, 2005–06.

Australian Bureau of Statistics. *Children's Participation in Cultural and Leisure Activities*. Canberra: Australian Bureau of Statistics, 2007.

Australian Bureau of Statistics. *Participation in Sports and Physical Recreation*. Canberra: Australian Bureau of Statistics, 2007.

Birrell, B., and K. Betts. 'Australians' Attitudes to Migration Review'. *Institute of Public Affairs* 53, no. 4 (2001): 3–6.

Brabazon, T. 'What's the Story Morning Glory? Perth Glory and the Imagining of Englishness'. *Sporting Traditions* 14, no. 2 (1998): 53–66.

Bradley, G. *Australian Soccer Federation: Final Report*. Canberra: Australian Soccer Federation, 1990.

Burdsey, D. *British Asians and Football*. London: Routledge, 2006.

Carrington, B., and I. McDonald, eds. *Race, Sport and British Society*. London: Routledge, 2001.

Cashman, R. *Paradise of Sport: The Rise of Organised Sport in Australia*. Melbourne: Oxford University Press, 1995.

Castles, S. 'Nations of Immigrants: Australia, the United States, and International Migration'. In *Australian Multiculturalism: Social Policy and Identity in a Changing Society*, edited by G. Freeman and J. Jupp, 184–201. Melbourne: Oxford University Press, 1992.

Collins, J. 'Cultural Diversity and Entrepreneurship: Policy Responses to Immigrant Entrepreneurs in Australia.' *Entrepreneurship and Regional Development* 15, no. 2 (2003): 137–49.

Crawford, D. *Report of the Independent Soccer Review Committee: Into the Structure, Governance and Management of Soccer in Australia*, Australian Sports Commission, April, 2003.

Department of Immigration and Multicultural Affairs. *Croatian Born Community Profile*. Canberra: Australia, 1999.

Foley, C. 'Subversive Possibilities: Exploring Women's Leisure Resistance Using Historical Case Studies'. *Annals of Leisure Research* 8, no. 4 (2005): 220–41.

Galligan, B., and W. Roberts. 'Australian Multiculturalism: Its Rise and Demise'. In *Australasian Political Studies Association Conference*. Hobart: University of Tasmania, 2003.

Hallinan, C., J. Hughson, and M. Burke. 'Supporting the "World Game" in Australia: A Case Study of Fandom at National and Club Level'. *Soccer and Society* 8, no. 2 (2007): 283–97.

Hallinan, C., and M. Krotee. 'Conceptins of Nationalism and Citizenship among Non-Anglo-Celtic Soccer Clubs in an Australian City'. *Journal of Sport and Social Issues* 7, no. 2 (1993): 283–97.

Hanna, M. *Reconciliation in Olympism: Indigenous Culture in the Sydney Olympiad*. Petersham, Australia: Walla Walla Press, 1999.

Harrison, G. 'What's in an Ethnic Name? *Soccer Clubs in Australia'. Anthropology* 2 (1979): 23–35.

Hay, R. 'British Football, Wogball or the World Game? Towards a Social History of Victorian Soccer'. *Australian Society for Sports History: Studies in Sports History* 10 (1994): 44–79.

Hay, R. 'Fan Culture in Australian Football (Soccer): From Ethnic to Mainstream?' In *Football Fever: Moving the Goalposts*, edited by M. Nicholson, B. Stewart, and R. Hess, 91–96. Sydney: Maribyrnong Press, 2006.

Hay, R. '"Our Wicked Foreign Game": Why has Association Football (Soccer) not become the Main Code of Football in Australia?' *Soccer and Society* 7, no. 2–3 (2006): 165–86.

Hughson, J. 'Australian Soccer: Ethnic or Aussie? The Search for an Image'. *Current Affairs Bulletin* 68, no. 10 (1992): 12–16.

Hughson, J. 'Building a Brotherhood from Otherhood: A Case Study of Soccer, Male Identity and Ethnicity in Western Sydney'. Paper presented at the Australian Conference on Mens Issues, Sydney, 1993.

Hughson, J. 'A Feel for the Game: An Ethnographic Study of Soccer Support and Social Identity'. PhD diss., University of New South Wales, 1996.

Hughson, J. 'The Boys are Back in Town: Soccer Support and the Social Reproduction of Masculinity'. *Journal of Sport and Social Issues* 24, no. 1 (2000): 8–23.

Hughson, J. 'A Tale of Two Tribes: Expressive Fandom in Australian Soccer's A-League'. In *Football Culture: Local Contests, Global Visions*, edited by G. Finn and R. Giulianotti, 10–30. London and Portland, OR: Frank Cass, 2000.

Hughson, J. 'Australian Soccer's "Ethnic" Tribes: A New Case for the Carnivalesque'. In *Fighting Fans: Football Hooliganism as a World Phenomenon*, edited by E. Dunning, P. Murphy, I. Waddington, and A.E. Astrinakis, 37–48. Dublin: University College of Dublin Press, 2002.

Jayaraman, R. 'Inclusion and Exclusion: An Analysis of the Australian Immigration History and Ethnic Relations'. *Journal of Popular Culture* 34, no. 1 (Summer 2000): 135–55.

Jones, R., and P. Moore. 'He Only Has Eyes for Poms: Soccer, Ethnicity and Locality in Perth Wa.' *ASSH Studies in Sports History* 10 (1994): 16–32.

Jupp, J. 'Waves of Migration to Australia'. In *Stories of Australian Migration*, edited by J. Hardy, 9–32. Kensington: New South Wales University Press, 1988.

Kemeny, A. *Report of the NSL Task-Force: Into the Structure of a New National League Soccer Competition*. Sydney: Australian Soccer Association, 2003.

Kerkyasharian, S., I. Moss, and K. Waller. *Report of the Independent Panel of Inquiry into the Crowd Disturbances at the Sydney United Sports Centre on Sunday March 13th 2005*. Sydney: Soccer NSW, 2005.

Lock, D., T. Taylor, and S. Darcy. 'Fan Identity Formation in a New Football Club and a Revamped League: The A-League'. *Sport Marketing Europe* 1 (2007): 30–5.

Lynch, R. and A. Veal. *Australian Leisure*. 3rd ed. Sydney: Pearson Education, 2006.

Mosely, P. 'Balkan Politics in Australian Soccer'. *ASSH Studies in Sports History* 10 (1994): 33–43.

Mosely, P. *Ethnic Involvement in Australian Soccer: A History 1950–1990*, edited by Australian Sports Commission. Canberra: Applied Sports Research Program and National Sports Research Centre, 1995.

Mosely, P. 'Soccer'. In *Sporting Immigrants: Sport and Ethnicity in Australia*, edited by P. Mosely, R. Cashman, J. O'Hara and H. Weatherburn, 155–73. Crows Nest, NSW: Walla Walla Press, 1997.

Murphy, B. *The Other Australia: Experiences of Migration*. Melbourne: Cambridge University Press, 1993.

Sherington, G. *Australia's Immigrants 1788–1988*. Sydney: Allen & Unwin, 1990.

Stasiulius, D. and N. Yuval-Davis. *Unsettling Settler Societies*. London: Sage, 1995.

Vamplew, W. 'Violence in Australian Soccer: The Ethnic Contribution'. *ASSH Studies in Sports History* 10 (1994): 1–15.

Waterhouse, R. *Private Pleasure, Public Leisure: A History of Australian Popular Cultural since 1788*. South Melbourne: Longman, 1995.

The Melbourne Cup: Australian identity and secular pilgrimage

Carole M. Cusack[a] and Justine Digance[b]

[a]Studies in Religion, University of Sydney, Sydney, Australia; [b]Tourism, Leisure, Hotel and Sport Management, Griffith University, Queensland, Australia

Recent sociology of religion has emphasized the collapse of the sacred into the secular, and noted the shift in Western identity-formation from stable, institutional, religious sources of identity to fluid, individualist, consumerist sources of identity. One significant consequence of these changes is the sacralization of secular phenomena such as sport and shopping, and the corresponding commercialization of religious phenomena. This essay analyses the place of the Melbourne Cup, an annual horse racing event held on the first Tuesday of November, in contemporary Australian identity-formation. Further, it explores the ways in which attendance at the Cup and other modes of participation in the race, which might be viewed as 'secular' activities, have become quasi-religious or 'spiritual'. Pilgrimage best characterizes attendance at the Cup; and observance of the Cup's traditions (sweepstakes, ceasing work for the duration of the race, champagne breakfasts) are best understood as postmodern consumerist rituals for individual Australians, reinforcing personal identity.

Introduction

As a sporting event, the annually staged Melbourne Cup horse race ('the Cup') mesmerizes the entire Australian nation on the first Tuesday in November, demanding national reverence and devotion as befitting a religious festival. The Cup, which is a long-held Australian sporting tradition, provides local Melbournians, and a plethora of interstate and international tourists, with an opportunity to pay homage to many demigods. Some of these are site-specific to this Australian event (such as particular horses and individuals connected with horseracing), whilst others are more germane to postmodern consumer society. Australia is a notably secular country, its convict origins contrasting strikingly with the Pilgrim Fathers of America, and America's subsequent notable religiosity among contemporary western nations.[1] Moreover, sport, gambling and drinking, notably profane activities, have been central to Australian self-understanding since white settlement in 1788. Some have boldly suggested that, if horse racing is *actually* a religion, then it is no doubt proper 'that the day should be declared a public holiday'.[2] In the late nineteenth century, while on a visit to the antipodes, the American writer Mark Twain wrote that the Cup 'is the mitred Metropolitan of the Horse-Racing Cult. Its raceground is the Mecca of Australasia', and further:

> it is the Australasian National Day ... Cup Day is supreme – it has no rival. I can call to mind no specialized annual day, in any country, which can be named by that large name – supreme. I can call to mind no specialized annual day, in any country, whose approach fires the whole land with a conflation of conversation and preparation and anticipation and jubilation. No day save this; but this one does it.[3]

This essay explores pilgrimage to the Melbourne Cup, commencing with a brief history of the Australian horse racing industry and the Cup itself, demonstrating its importance for Australian identity. This is followed by an exploration of various themes that make the Cup a pilgrimage sporting event. The final section explores the characteristics of postmodern spirituality, and demonstrates that apparently secular events such as the Melbourne Cup can take on religio-spiritual significance for modern spiritual seekers.[4] For this argument a working definition of *secular* pilgrimage is required. This category of travel fits between traditional religious pilgrimage and purely secular tourism: this type of pilgrimage is the undertaking of a journey that is redolent with meaning, which may be associated with an individual spiritual quest, operating outside formal religion. Victor Turner's (1973) classic *schema*, although contested, has enduring relevance here. For Turner, a pilgrim is one who separates from his/her everyday situation and enters a liminal state, where *communitas* with fellows is experienced and transformation anticipated; when reintegrated into the community s/he manifests a transformed state as a result of this process. What distinguishes secular pilgrims from religious pilgrims is that the latter undertake their journey as 'an act of faith' within an established framework, whereas the former are more focused on experiencing something magical that punctuates the normal humdrum patterns of daily life.[5] This experience, when the sacred manifests amid the profane, is a memorable 'special' moment, which, for the pilgrim, is more *real* and profoundly connected to identity than everyday existence.

The history of the Melbourne Cup and its significance for Australian identity

Early colonial Australia relied upon horses for labour, transport and recreation from its foundation in 1788 through to Federation in 1901, and thus it is perhaps not surprising that horses have a special place in the Australian *ethos*. A rich tradition of bush balladeers, poets and writers have made the deeds of horses part of Australian popular legend, with Adam Lindsay Gordon, A.B. 'Banjo' Paterson and Nat Gould being some of the more notable writers who spoke of it.[6] Australian horse racing dates back to the early nineteenth century, with the establishment of a racetrack on the banks of the Hawkesbury River (on the outskirts of Sydney) in 1809,[7] and today horse racing remains an 'important sporting, social and economic event in many country towns'.[8] The initiators of racing in the colony of New South Wales were the regiments, and it functioned as a leisure activity for the emergent gentry. Governor Lachlan Macquarie permitted the first formal race-meeting 'at Hyde Park in October 1810', and in 1842 the Australian Jockey Club (AJC) was founded as a permanent institution with responsibility for organizing racing programmes and conducting meetings.[9] Yet it has been argued that, 'excessive enthusiasm among the colony's labouring classes' for racing was apparent,[10] and that men, women and children embraced racing fervently, as one of the very few opportunities available to them to escape their working lives. This attitude is expressed in a verse printed in the *Sydney Morning Herald* on 29 May 1850:

Away now from Sydney – gay Homebush the place is
I hear all around me in ecstasy say;
'Leave care till tomorrow – Let's off to the races!'
So off with the others I canter away.[11]

The 1850s gold rush in the colony of Victoria saw an increase in both the population and wealth of Melbourne. Founded in 1835, the colony's capital city grew from a sleepy town of 20,000 to a bush city of 140,000 and this rapid growth provided a demand for an increasing array of social events and entertainments.[12] Besides providing a social element for Melbourne's squattocracy, horse racing also became an outlet for the miners to spend their new-found wealth on gambling at the races. Four thousand attended the first Melbourne Cup, held at the Flemington Racecourse on Thursday 7 November 1861 (the first day of a three-day programme), which was won by Archer. Originally run as a two-mile race but converted to 3,200 metres in 1972,[13] the Cup is a handicap race which favours mature horses who are stayers, rather than younger untried horses. In 1869, the Victorian Racing Club (VRC), which leased Flemington Racecourse at a peppercorn rental of one shilling per annum, altered the Spring Carnival programme to span four days; and in 1875 again reconfigured the event, so that the Cup was now run on a Tuesday, where it has been scheduled ever since. By the end of the late nineteenth century the Cup had become Australia's most important horse race, with the distinction of also being Australia's premier gambling event. Melbourne bank staff and public servants were given a half-day holiday for the Cup in 1865,[14] and the Melbourne Cup now enjoys the unique honour of being the only horse race in the world that confers the benefit of a full-day public holiday on its city's citizens.

With Federation in 1901 the disparate state colonies united to form the nation of Australia, and horse racing, drinking and gambling took on increased significance in the quest for national identity, with the Melbourne Cup taking its place in a sequence of national 'days' (Australia Day on 26 January, and the later addition of Anzac Day on 25 April being the most significant) offering opportunities to celebrate 'Australianness'. Melbourne was the capital of Australia from 1901 to 1927 during the construction of Canberra. This intensified the Cup's nationalistic associations. In the lead-up to the Cup's centenary in 1961, the Prime Minister Robert Menzies famously stopped parliament to listen to the Cup in 1950 (initiating a tradition continuing to the present), accompanied Queen Elizabeth II to Flemington during her visit to Australia in 1954, and in 1960 authorized the issue of a commemorative stamp to mark the occasion of her visit.[15] Arguably, Melbourne Cup Day is the most important of the 'national days' for the celebration of Australian identity: Australia Day, the commemoration of the arrival of the First Fleet of white settlers in 1788, is tainted by the protests of displaced indigenous Australians who lost their land; and Anzac Day is devoted to mourning the war dead, particularly those from the First World War. Melbourne Cup Day alone celebrates the experience of being Australian in a joyous and unshadowed fashion.

Phillips and Smith's interview-based research indicates that going to the Melbourne Cup (along with barbecues, football and Anzac Day) were amongst a range of activities and events which represented core 'Australian' cultural symbols linked to national identity.[16] It is not only in the arena of sport that ritual and spectacle play an important role in society, but also in civil religion. First coined by the French philosopher Jean-Jacques Rosseau (1712–78), the American sociologist Robert Bellah has demonstrated the relevance of this concept in the post-war west.[17] Civil religion is a 'means of investing a particular set of political and social arrangements with an aura of the sacred, thereby elevating their stature and enhancing their stability ... Well established and recognised symbols, rituals, celebrations, places and values supply(ing) the society with an overarching sense of spiritual unity ... and a focal point for shared memories of struggle and survival'.[18] It is here argued that the Melbourne Cup is part of Australia's civil religion because it encapsulates 'Australianness' as noted above by Phillips and Smith. The fact that this 'Australianness' is often deliberately constructed and artificially disseminated does not affect its imaginative power, nor the conviction with which Australians hold to it.[19]

The importance of the Cup in the national psyche is also demonstrated by the fact that the first local ballet commissioned by the newly formed Australian Ballet in November 1962 was choreographer Rex Reid's 'Melbourne Cup', and in more recent years an educational video was produced in 2000 by Adult Multicultural Education Services (AMES) on the Melbourne Cup, as a 'response to the difficulties migrants face in understanding local news and current events … extending their understanding of Australian social, political and economic events'.[20] The Cup's links to national and cultural identity have also been astutely exploited by Federal politicians, such as the Liberal Party's Andrew Robb and Don Randall. Robb 'nominates the first Tuesday in November as one of the Australian cultural values that aspiring migrants might have to know to become citizens',[21] which might suggest that drinking, gambling and manifesting an interest in horse racing are the core values that newcomers to Australia must, perforce, embrace. The Cup also features in the debate as to whether Australia should become a republic, which is a sensitive issue in the definition of national identity; in a Notice Paper dated 21 June 2006, Randall moved that 'the Queen's Birthday holiday … be replaced by a truly national day and that this uniform national public holiday be observed on the first Tuesday in November each year'.[22]

The Australian horse racing industry

As noted earlier, the horse has a special place in the development of Australia as a nation. Examples of veneration of the horse in Australian culture can be found in prints featured in newspapers and magazines, and pictures of horses being displayed in hotels and public buildings. Seven horses arrived with the First Fleet in 1788, and since that time countless thoroughbreds have been imported into Australia to provide not only a bloodline for the racehorse industry but also to breed stock and troop horses.[23] Cassidy canvasses the notion that thoroughbred racehorses are the subjects of a shared history 'linking East and West in the exchange of fine horses, against a background of constantly changing power relations'. The history and mythology surrounding the thoroughbred and its Arabian bloodline goes back to ancient Mesopotamia, where the Arab horse is traced to a sacred origin story: 'The first Arabian was a mare, the black-skinned Antelope ('Kuhaylah') created by God, saved from Ishmael's arrow by Gabriel.'[24] Bloodlines and the importance of pedigree are paramount in defining today's modern racehorse as a product of selective breeding that has taken place over centuries with speed, endurance and the will to win as some of the most sought-after characteristics. It is beyond the scope of this essay to explore the history of the development of today's racing thoroughbred horse. However, horse races are events where those with an interest in horses can go to watch (and perhaps even touch) these animals who have served humanity in times of both peace and war. Accessible to the general public by purchasing an entry ticket, racecourses are thus pilgrimage sites to the development of Arabian thoroughbred horses, a living testimony to the science of horse breeding.[25]

Even with an excellent pedigree, the success of a thoroughbred racehorse is dependent on many other variables, particularly trainers and jockeys. All of the cited works on the Melbourne Cup speak of the tradition of trainers who all aim to bring a particular horse to the peak of its racing career for the four day Melbourne Cup Spring Racing Carnival. Some trainers loom larger than others as a result of the winner(s) that they have trained, like Harry Telford, who trained Phar Lap and is part of the 'Phar Lap' legend discussed below, and Lee Freedman, who trained the record-breaking mare Makybe Diva, three-time Cup winner from 2005. Other exemplary figures are strong individualists who have trained many winners (including of the Cup) in Australia, such as Bart Cummings and

T.J. Smith.[26] Many punters pledge lifelong allegiance to particular trainers, only backing horses that are trained by their favourite. Their allegiance can be due to any number of reasons, including the training methods used by the trainer, the home town of the trainer and/or the location of their training track or stables, the trainer's charisma or celebrity status, the trainer's record in 'producing' Cup winners, or other tenuous links between the punter and the trainer.

This superstitious loyalty to a trainer, and belief in his or her 'luck' is part of the modern secular pilgrimage tradition which is inherited from medieval Christian religious pilgrimage, where the cult of the individual saint (usually associated with physical remains and miracles) meant that certain shrines were more popular than others.[27] Loyalty to a particular patron saint and a horse trainer may appear worlds apart; however both offer access to power and 'luck', respectively spiritual or secular. Racehorse owners may also share in the public's attention, though they are more tenuously linked to the horses' success. Nat Gould, a well-known late-nineteenth-century novelist who wrote several popular novels centred on horse racing, noted that 'a mysterious fascination surrounds the owner of a well-backed Cup horse, and he becomes an object of unusual interest. People gaze at him as though they were blessed with second sight or thought-reading powers, and would fain make use of them to extract information from him'.[28]

First among all the heroic horses beloved by Australians is Phar Lap, whose statue, erected in Australia's Bicentenary Year 1988, is the one identifiable devotional shrine at Flemington racecourse, where images and mementos of other winners are otherwise largely lacking (in contrast to the National Tennis Centre which openly honours previous Australian Open champions). Despite being born in New Zealand in 1927, since 1930 when he won the Melbourne Cup Australians have claimed the legendary Phar Lap as one of their own. After an unsuccessful shotgun attack on the way to the racecourse on Derby Day in 1930 (the Saturday race day before the Tuesday Melbourne Cup), Phar Lap is the only racehorse to be accorded police protection immediately after being attacked until the running of the Cup on the following Tuesday.[29] His legend grew as he became 'a symbol of heroism to a country ravaged by depression … (and) … his mysterious death was nothing short of a national disaster but his name and memory remain immortal'.[30] Phar Lap's immortality is recorded in two important reliquary sites in Australia: the Melbourne Museum and the National Museum of Australia (in Canberra). The former houses his hide, which was prepared by a firm of New York taxidermists and shipped back to Australia to go on display in 1933, and the latter has his heart on display. The skeleton went home to Phar Lap's country of birth, and is on display at Te Papa National Museum in Wellington, New Zealand. Phar Lap was one of the first five horses to be inducted into the Australian Racing Hall of Fame, which is housed at the 'Champions: Australian Racing Museum and Hall of Fame' site at Federation Square (the others were Carbine, Tulloch, Bernborough and Kingston Town). The recent establishment of this museum brought the centrality of horse racing in the Australian national ethos from the periphery of the racetrack to the centre of the Melbourne. The displays are reminiscent of religious relics (body parts of champion horses, portraits of horses, trainers and jockeys, the cups and trophies won through supreme effort).[31]

Phar Lap's legend is an appropriate entrée into the discussion of the religio-spiritual aspects of the Melbourne Cup, and its function as a pilgrimage event for secular Australians. The Great Depression in Australia was a time when hope was failing, and for many their hopes became focused on Phar Lap. In the four years that he raced (1928–32) the big chestnut gelding won 37 of his 51 races; moreover, his trainer Harry Telford was neither rich nor influential, and neither was Jim Pike, the jockey who rode him to most of his victories. After winning the Agua Caliente Handicap in Mexico (at that time the American continent's richest racing prize) Phar Lap died in the United States on 5 April 1932; many Australians believed he had been poisoned. Dozens of tributes to Phar Lap poured in from the public to Harry Telford. Telford acknowledged the almost-religious power of Phar Lap in his own tribute: 'He was an angel. A human being couldn't have had more sense. He was almost human; could do anything but talk. I've never practiced idolatry, but by God I loved that horse.'[32] In 1983 his story was immortalized in the film, 'Phar Lap', the script of which was authored by iconic Australian playwright David Williamson.[33] The Australian film industry in the 1980s was mining a rich stream of history to create a national identity for an increasingly fragmented and multicultural society in the wake of 20 years of large-scale immigration; in addition to 'Phar Lap', 1981's 'Gallipoli', 1982's 'The Man from Snowy River' and 1987's 'The Lighthorsemen', all emphasized the vital role of the horse in forging the Australian identity, and linked that image to the courage and tenacity of the soldiers who fought in the First World War, drawing on the Anzac legacy.[34]

The Melbourne Cup as a secular pilgrimage event

When considering the Cup as a possible context for secular pilgrimage, issues of personal and national identity are crucial. Postmodern secularized Western society has been characterized as being consumerist in nature, with people's patterns of consumption largely determining their identity.[35] The dominant influence of film and television, the internet and the print media has resulted in celebrities becoming powerful role models for identity construction among Western people. It is interesting to note that celebrity in Australia has until recently been almost exclusively concentrated on sport. Mandle was the first to link sport and Australian nationalism commenting that: 'Australia's national heroes are largely cricketers, tennis-players, swimmers and boxers, or even race-horses ... Phar Lap would rate more highly than any politician, Don Bradman more than any artist'.[36]

In this world of image, success and fashion, what has traditionally been understood to be religious has altered profoundly. For approximately 30 years sociologists of religion have noted how the Christian churches have embraced aspects of the media-saturated, consumerist culture that surrounds them, while the experience of the 'sacred', traditionally the preserve of the churches, has floated free, and attached itself to phenomena that were traditionally regarded as 'secular'. David Chidester has convincingly demonstrated that rock music, sport and iconic products, such as Coca Cola, are powerful conduits for contemporary people to encounter the sacred.[37]

The parallel development of traditional religious pilgrimage and modern tourism is another clear case of the sacralization of the secular. Travel, far from being a shallow recreational activity, for many people is constitutive of identity; people experience themselves as more real when encountering the 'Other' through travel. But the deregulation of the sacred has also resulted in smaller-scale experiences that are avenues to the sacred, and can be repeated:

> contemporary, secularised but not de-sacralised, people undergo initiatory ritual through consumption constantly, in mini-pilgrimages to the sites of potential transformation. Selves are acquired and discarded, and *communitas*, though fragmentary, is detectable in these patterns of consumption.[38]

Holiday destinations and sporting arenas, along with shopping malls, are the sites to which these pilgrims flock. Central to pilgrimage (whether traditionally religious or secular) is a sacred site and/or event. In the case of the Cup, both the site and event are inextricably linked because, since 1861, the Melbourne Cup has been run at Flemington Racecourse.[39] However, since then the racetrack and its surrounds, including the public enclosures, stables and transportation infrastructure, have changed so much that there is little or no physical evidence of pre-Federation days. Nevertheless, Flemington on Melbourne Cup Day is a shrine to which the secular pilgrims flock.

One of the hallmarks of any pilgrimage site is the expectation of the miraculous[40] and Cup day at Flemington is no exception. Whilst the writers understand that no miracles of the kind associated with Catholic Marian shrines, for example, have been witnessed at Flemington, many minor positive occurrences are routinely hailed as 'miracles'. For example, fine temperate weather for the duration of the event is in itself considered fortuitous, given Melbourne's unpredictable spring weather (rain preceding and during the event have become almost a common occurrence). Melbourne newspaper *The Age*, reporting on the fine weather experienced at the 1981 Cup, noted that 'a more propitious day, so far as weather was concerned, it would have been difficult to realize'.[41] Similarly, a horse with long odds winning the event is a miracle for the punters who are fortunate to place a bet on it, the horse's owners and the winning jockey. Even passing the winning post in first place does not guarantee the miraculous, because the result is dependent on the course stewards verifying the photo-finish frames, correct weight and/or the results of random swabs for banned substances.[42]

Traditionally, the Cup is associated with gambling and drinking to excess. Over 80% of Australians make a wager of some form on the Cup, reinforcing the observation by Nat Gould over a century earlier that, 'it becomes natural to Cup crowds to bet upon the great race as it does to business men to buy the evening papers. They regard it as part and parcel of the day's proceedings, and it cannot, in any sense of the word, be called gambling.'[43] This essay does not probe the role of gambling in Australian society; but certainly ritualistic and/or superstition-oriented behaviour amongst punters is well documented. This includes electing to place bets only from 'auspicious' totalisator windows or bookmakers, purchasing tickets only at certain times during the programme, placing tickets in a 'lucky' pocket or purse, and only betting on certain numbers or racing colours. Historically, the casting of lots and the consulting of oracles are both religious activities, with deities presiding over the realm of chance, such as the Greek Tyche and the Roman Fortuna.[44] Gambling on Cup day extends beyond those who have made the pilgrimage to Flemington itself, as around the nation workers hold office sweepstakes and cease working, whether solely to watch the Cup on television or as part of an extended Melbourne Cup lunch, manifesting a form of fragmentary *communitas*, as mentioned earlier.

At Flemington consumption of alcohol begins with the time-honoured ritual of breakfast in the Members' and public car parks (complete with cloth-covered tables, folding chairs and champagne). This an integral part of the Cup experience for VRC Members and the public, many of whom never actually get to see the race,[45] being entirely caught up in celebrating. The quasi-religious nature of the breakfast is part-way between the tradition of meals which unite the faithful with the divine (such as the Christian eucharist) and the libations and toasts offered to the gods in ancient Greek ceremonies, including the Olympic Games, held in honour of Zeus Olympios.[46] Moreover, alcohol has a long association with the inducement of ritual altered states of consciousness, which may have religious significance. For the argument of this essay, it is most appropriate to see indulgence in alcohol on Cup Day as a gateway to liminality, relaxing the restraints of everyday existence, and the warm fellowship enjoyed by the participants as Turnerian *communitas* in a secularized setting. Further, this *communitas* radiates out from those who are actually present at Flemington (with varying degrees of sacredness observed, intensifying in the Members' Stand, diminishing in the public car park), to the lessened, but still real, shared experience of millions via television, radio and the internet, which unifies Australia for a few moments each year.

The religious and spiritual focus of contemporary Western culture

The religious life of late capitalist Western culture is dominated by the individual spiritual quest and by consumption, which has become the pre-eminent form that shapes the quest. This is a radical departure from the 2,000 year dominance of the Christian church and its teachings, and it has been noted that three radical social changes have brought about the decline of institutional religious affiliation and the growth of eclectic personal spiritualities from the period 1850 to the present. These are individualism, secularization and consumer capitalism.[47] It is difficult to separate out these three strands: secularization, famously defined by Peter Berger as 'the process whereby sectors of society are removed from the domination of religious institutions and symbols',[48] enabled individuals to make religious and lifestyle choices that moved away from the prescriptions of Christianity; and consumption became the preferred mode of self-expression once Christianity's historic distrust of this-worldly pleasure was overcome. Whereas, in the past, religion urged contemplation of the next world and the rejection of wealth and success in this world, New Age and other late capitalist self-actualization movements urge personal fulfilment in this life as the new salvation. In this heady atmosphere, wealth, celebrity and conspicuous consumption replace piety, poverty and self-denial. This type of religiosity is essentially private and personal; often people refer to themselves as 'spiritual', rather than religious.[49] Moreover, this development takes place in a space where the boundaries between high and low culture, between good taste and bad, and even between moral and ethical choices, have become blurred.

This results in a variety of incongruous phenomena: religions based on explicit fictions (such as *Star Wars* and *Star Trek*), spiritual quests that manifest through self-indulgence, and seemingly superficial phenomena (shopping, gossip, fashion) that are in fact extremely serious. David Lyon has argued that fashion, which may appear superficial, is in fact a core identity industry in the contemporary West: 'the idea is that self-esteem and recognition by others may be purchased over the counter'.[50] Mass-market capitalism has democratized the world of fashion, which was previously restricted to the wealthy. In 1861 those attending Flemington displayed a consciousness of fashion. Bernstein describes the scene thus:

> [l]adies were present at that first Cup Day in bonnets and flounces, escorted by gentlemen in tightly-buttoned frock coats and beaver hats. Cabbage-tree hats and bush bears were prominent, as were settlers in moleskin trousers and leggings, or knee boots.[51]

Since the 1960s, fashion has played an increasingly significant role in the rituals of the Cup. Australia is a very low-key, informal society where casual clothing is the norm. This emphasizes the liminal nature of Cup Day, as it is recognized as 'one of the few times when Australians celebrate looking stylish … on that first Tuesday in November, the dark clouds part and the elegant ladies come out to shine'.[52] The intersection of fashion with celebrity watching has intensified in the past two decades. Celebrities, be they actors or rock stars, or even minor figures from reality television, are the new saints and martyrs, role models for the postmodern aspirant to self-fulfilment to emulate. The beginnings of this phenomenon were observable in the 1960s when British model Jean Shrimpton ('the Shrimp') scandalized Australia with her daring appearance at the Melbourne Cup, wearing a sleeveless mini dress without a hat or gloves. Fashion has, since the 1960s, become a crucial element of the Cup, with parades known as 'Fashion on the Field' being staged annually. Fashion retailers set up tents at Flemington and invite celebrities to be associated with them. In 2005, Eva Longoria, one of the stars of the hit American series 'Desperate Housewives', was the main attraction for the fashion and celebrity-conscious.

For locals attending the race, Australian designers are favoured, and the pilgrims thus attired provide photographic material for the women's magazines and fashion magazines of that week or month. The importance of image in contemporary society has not diminished the reverence for sporting heroes in Australian hearts, but has rather extended that reverence to the wealthy, the beautiful and the famous. In 2005, *The Australian* newspaper on Cup Day (Tuesday 1 November), as part of its extensive coverage of the Cup, included a four-page Melbourne Cup special entitled 'Fashion on the Field'. With a multitude of pictures of celebrities and the 'in' social set taken on Saturday at Derby Day (the first day of the four-day Cup Carnival), professional *fashionistas* (namely the Fashion Editor and a 'stylist' assistant) informed readers of the 'dos and don'ts' of what they should be seen wearing to the Cup in order to avoid social *gaffes*. However, the reality is that almost all of the paper's female readers attending the Cup would have already decided upon their choice of outfit some time before the big day. There is also the implicit, but unstated, fact that the *cognoscenti* have no need for recourse to such sartorial instructions: the list is for the novice racegoers, the socially inept, and perhaps also aimed at tourists who would be ignorant of the *mores* of acceptable Cup dress. Peake indicates that this extension of the realm of fashion to 'ordinary' women was part of racing traditions in the late nineteenth and early twentieth centuries. He also perceptively argues that in the 'postmodern' racing era (when the race itself is no longer the primary focus) the racing industry has continued to thrive economically by marketing its events to women and those who are interested in the 'total package' rather than the race itself.[53]

It could also be argued that the Melbourne Cup forms a cultural nexus for Australia through the exploitation of technology. Baudrillard has asserted that late or postmodern society is defined by the retreat of reality in the face of increasing images and simulacra.[54] Mass media and information technologies extend the value of an experience like the Cup, by reproducing it through image and text. Being at the Cup is the primary secular experience of the sacred, but the ritual observance of the Cup in workplaces described above is more like the performance of religious devotion for the ordinary believer. Turner argued that pilgrimage involved liminality (being out of your everyday routine) and *communitas*. Both of these phenomena are observable in the breaking of work routines to gather and watch the Cup and in the buying of sweepstake tickets and celebrating wins (even of $2 or $5). Recent research by the Australian government also provides evidence supporting this contention: the report on expatriate Australians notes Cup Day as one of the crucial days for Australians abroad to congregate, for a Melbourne Cup lunch and the viewing of the race, whether live or at some later hour due to time zones. Technology also has transformed the process of betting and winning prizes, and the earlier discussion of fashion, branding and celebrity all dovetails elegantly with the Baudrillardian assertion of the retreat of the real and the gradual advance of the hyperreal.[55]

Postmodern consumer spiritualities and their secular counterparts are bombarded with media images of lottery and Lotto wins ('the big red ball that makes dreams come true', and 'spend the rest of your life' are clearly quasi-religious slogans), because this-worldly fulfilment has replaced ascetic self-denial as the desired goal. That atmosphere of expectation and the possibility of riches is a crucial aspect of the Melbourne Cup. Joy is a potent emotion and points to the Cup devotees' belief in magic and miracles;

the possibility of a big win is ever-present. Worthington's research on the 'Melbourne Cup effect' on the Australian stock market 'provides some empirical evidence to support the conjecture that Melbourne Cup Tuesday is associated with a higher mean market return than either other Tuesdays, or other days'.[56]

It is also important to note the economic importance of the Cup to the Victorian economy, particularly as Melbourne promotes itself as the 'Event Capital of Australia'. In 2005, the four-day Spring Racing Carnival (with the Cup as the jewel in the crown) returned a gross economic benefit to Victoria of $524.3 million as part of the direct and indirect economic multiplier effect. Moreover, the Spring Racing Carnival attracted 730,000 attendees, of whom 25,602 were from international destinations and 76,042 were interstate visitors. Careful examination of Racing Victoria's documents provides substantial support for the argument of this essay that the Melbourne Cup (and associated events) is crucial for Australian identity, and that the secular pilgrims that flock to it are motivated by the yearning to experience the sacred through participating in the golden world of celebrity, wealth and conspicuous consumption. Almost AU$39 million was spent on corporate packages in 2005, with more than AU$20 million being spent on fashion purchases across the four days of the Carnival.[57] This is also evidence for Wayne Peake's contention that racing in Australia has been reinvented as an entertainment spectacle, generating an effervescence among participants that is quite separate from its 'golden age' ideals.[58] Peake does not venture into the issues of identity formation or the quasi-religious nature of Cup attendance, but we would argue that the effervescence generated by entertainment events of this type is a secularized functional equivalent of the religious *communitas* found at traditional religious pilgrimage sites.

Conclusion

This essay has probed several relationships that are of crucial importance for Australian identity, as understood historically and in the contemporary context. The first of these is the generally low level of formal religiosity among Australians, from their convict beginnings to the present where approximately 9% of Australians attend church on a regular basis,[59] and their passionate interest in sport in general, and for the purposes of this essay, racing in particular. The significance of horse racing, and the Melbourne Cup as the race *par excellence* for Australians, was elucidated by using Victor Turner's (1973) model of pilgrimage to analyse the behaviours of race-goers and others participating in Cup-related activities such as champagne breakfasts, gambling and stopping work to watch the race. It was argued that Turner's *schema*, which characterizes a pilgrim as one who separates from his or her profane everyday life and enters a liminal state, was appropriate to racegoers and watchers who dress up, eat and drink to excess, place bets in the hope of 'a big win', and suspend their daily activities (primarily work) to experience *communitas*, an effervescent fellow-feeling.

Turner's *schema* was originally developed in the context of traditional religion. This essay has also explored the relationship between the sacred and the secular, religion and popular culture, in late or postmodern Western consumerist society. It has been demonstrated that the place of institutional religion in Western culture has profoundly altered since the mid-nineteenth century, with secularization, individualism and consumer capitalism eroding traditional religion and giving rise to individual 'privatised spiritualities'.[60] These are themselves consumables, and spiritual seekers are driven by the desire for self-fulfilment, a desire that usually involves this-worldly success and riches, glamour and celebrity, as traditional religion's appeal to asceticism and self-denial gradually loses its authority. What results is a radically deregulated 'sacred', which now manifests through many aspects of life that were traditionally understood to be secular, such as shopping and rock music, travel, popular culture and sport. Consequently, the Cup functions as a medium for the experience of the sacred, which we argue involves vindication of both individual, personal identity and *communitas* which reinforces Australian national and cultural identity. Turner's pilgrims returned home and were reintegrated into their community with evidence of their transformed status. For postmodern secular pilgrims, the experience is one of many such minor transformative rituals; the consumerist nature of their quest for self-fulfilment demands that such experiences be constantly repeated.[61]

Finally, horses and racing contributed substantially to Australian self-understanding in the early colonial period. It is interesting to see how that part of Australian history both reinforces and undermines modernist national understandings. Australians have a strong self-identity; but it is largely based on the mockery of, and undermining of, aspects of character that others, Americans or English people, for example, might admire. Australians have valorised drinking and gambling, being 'laid-back' and defying authority, informality and irreligiousness.[62] Their heroes include bushranger Ned Kelly, the Anzacs of Gallipoli in the First World War and Phar Lap. It could be observed that all these heroes were ultimately 'losers': heroic achievers who died before their time. Australian icons persist in being somewhat iconoclastic. It is thus to be expected that an event such as the Melbourne Cup is not only beloved by the average punter, but is actually invoked by politicians as exemplifying the values and goals that define Australia.[63] These values appear to be those of drinking, gambling and partying to excess, which are perfectly postmodern in their collapsing of high and low culture, moral taste and aesthetic sensibility.[64] The deepest values and commitments of a nation are, of necessity, quasi-religious; the Melbourne Cup as postmodern pilgrimage offers contemporary Australians a pilgrimage to the core of their identity as a nation, and an uncritical vindication of all that it comprises.

Acknowledgements

The authors would like to thank Wayne Peake (University of Technology, Sydney) and Kristine Toohey (Griffith University) for their feedback on the horse racing industry, and Alex Norman and Dominique Wilson (University of Sydney) for their invaluable research assistance.

Notes

[1] Cusack, 'Religion in Australian Society', 29–32.
[2] Dunstan, *Sports*, 49.
[3] Twain, 'Following the Equator', 161–2.
[4] Lyon, *Jesus in Disneyland*, 88.
[5] Digance, 'Religious and Secular Pilgrimage'.
[6] Cashman, *Sport in the National Imagination*, 33.
[7] Dunstan, *Sports*, 43.
[8] Cashman, *Sport in the National Imagination*, 36.
[9] Painter and Waterhouse, *The Principal Club*, 3, 17.
[10] Peake, 'Significance of Unregistered Proprietary Pony Racing', 2.
[11] Painter and Waterhouse, *The Principal Club*, 19.
[12] Bernstein, *First Tuesday in November*, 22.
[13] Shepherd, *Australian Sporting Almanac*.
[14] Bernstein, *First Tuesday in November*, 138, 284, 22.
[15] Martin, *Robert Menzies*.

[16] Phillips and Smith, 'What is "Australian"?'

[17] Bellah, 'Civil Religion in America'.

[18] McClay 'The Soul of a Nation', 9.

[19] Crouter, 'Beyond Bellah'.

[20] AMES, *Easynews*.

[21] P. Karvelas, 'Race that Stops Nation Could Stop Your Citizenship'. *The Weekend Australian*, April 29–30, 2005, 8.

[22] Hansard, No.109, June 21, 2006, at www.aph.gov.au/house/info/notpaper.

[23] Cashman, *Sport in the National Imagination*, 34; Bernstein, *First Tuesday in November*, 149.

[24] Cassidy, 'Arab Dimensions to British Racehorse Breeding', 13, 18.

[25] Edwards, *The Encyclopedia of the Horse*.

[26] Painter and Waterhouse, *The Principal Club*, 177–9.

[27] Brown, *The Cult of the Saints*.

[28] Gould, *Landed at Last*, 207.

[29] Cavanough and Davies, *The Melbourne Cup*.

[30] de Lore, *Melbourne Cup Winners*, 45.

[31] www.museum.vic.gov.au; Champions Australian Racing Museum and Hall of Fame, www.racingmuseum.com.au.

[32] www.museum.vic.gov.au.

[33] Maslin, '"Phar Lap"'.

[34] Rita Kempley. 'The Lighthorsemen'. *Washington Post*, April 30, 1988. http://www.washington post.com/wp-srv/style/longterm/movies/videos/thelighthorsemenpgkempley_a0ca13.htm. It is interesting to note that a film about the first Melbourne Cup winner was also made in the 1980s. 'Archer' (1985) was a made-for-television feature (also known as 'Archer's Adventure') directed by Denny Lawrence and starring popular Australian television actor Brett Climo. As virtually nothing is known about Archer, the story is substantially fiction, with Archer's historically-attested victory in the 1861 Cup as the climax.

[35] Lyon, *Jesus in Disneyland*, 79.

[36] Mandle, 'Cricket and Australian Nationalism', 224.

[37] Demerath, 'Varieties of Sacred Experience', 4; Chidester, 'The Church of Baseball'.

[38] Quotation from Cusack and Digance, '"Shopping for a Self"', 231.

[39] de Lore, *Melbourne Cup Winners*, 10.

[40] Digance, 'Religious and Secular Pilgrimage'.

[41] T. Bourke, 'Looking Back on a Racy Century'. *The Age*, October 2, 2004. www.theage.com.au/articles/2004/10/01/1096527928498.html?from=storylhs.

[42] 'The Track', at www.abc.net.au/thetrack/default.htm.

[43] Superstitious gambling practices have been observed first-hand over a period of many years by Justine Digance, who has worked part-time at the on-course totalisator in both Sydney and Melbourne (including in the Members' Stand on Melbourne Cup Day).

[44] Windross, 'The Luck of the Draw', 67–8; Rankin, 'The History of Probability', 484.

[45] http://www.lonelyplanet.com/journeys/feature/melbourne_cup05.cfm.

[46] Cartledge, 'The Greek Religious Festivals'.

[47] Carrette and King, *Selling Spirituality*, 19–20; Bruce, *God is Dead*, 10–26.

[48] Berger, *The Social Reality of Religion*, 107.

[49] Possamai, *Religion and Popular Culture*, 121–33; Carrette and King, *Selling Spirituality*, 53.

[50] Lyon, *Jesus in Disneyland*, 12.

[51] Bernstein, *The First Tuesday in November*, 15.

[52] 'Australian Traditions', www.convictcreations.com.culture/traditions.htm.

[53] Peake, 'The Significance of Unregistered Proprietary Pony Racing', 9, 13.

[54] Baudrillard, *Simulations*.

[55] 'They Still Call Australia Home' at www.aph.gov.au/senate/committee/legcon_ctte/expatso3/report/index.htm; Possamai, *Religion and Popular Culture*, 135–55.

[56] Carrette and King, *Selling Spirituality*, 125; Worthington, *National Exuberance*, 7.

[57] Racing Victoria Ltd, *Spring Racing Carnival Economic Benefit Report 2005*. 2006. www.springracingcarnival.com.au/media/documents/SRCexec.pdf.

[58] Peake, 'The Significance of Unregistered Proprietary Pony Racing'.

[59] Bouma and Lennon, 'Estimating the Extent of Religious and Spiritual Activity'.

[60] Carrette and King, *Selling Spirituality*, 47.

[61] Turner, 'The Center Out There'; Cusack and Digance, '"Shopping for a Self"'.
[62] White, *Inventing Australia*.
[63] Karvelas, 'Race that Stops Nation Could Stop Your Citizenship', 8.
[64] Possamai, *Religion and Popular Culture*, 19.

References

AMES (Adult Multicultural Education Services). *Easynews: The Melbourne Cup*. Video recording. AMES Central, Melbourne, 2000.

Baudrillard, Jean. *Simulations*. New York: Semiotext(e), 1983.

Bellah, R.N. 'Civil religion in America'. *Daedalus* 96 (1967): 1–21.

Berger, Peter. *The Social Reality of Religion*. London: Faber and Faber, 1967.

Bernstein, D.L. *First Tuesday in November*. London: Heinemann, 1969.

Bouma, G., and D. Lennon. 'Estimating the Extent of Religious and Spiritual Activity in Australia Using Time-Budget Data'. *Journal for the Scientific Study of Religion* 42, no. 1 (2003): 107–12.

Brown, Peter. *The Cult of the Saints: Its Rise and Function in Latin Christianity*. Chicago, IL: University of Chicago Press, 1982.

Bruce, S. *God is Dead: Secularization in the West*. Oxford: Blackwell, 2002.

Carrette, J., and R. King. *Selling Spirituality: The Silent Takeover of Religion*. London: Routledge, 2005.

Cartledge, P. 'The Greek Religious Festivals'. In *Greek Religion and Society*, edited by P.E. Easterling and J.V. Muir, 98–127. Cambridge: Cambridge University Press, 1985.

Cashman, Richard. *Sport in the National Imagination*. Sydney: Walla Walla Press, 2002.

Cassidy, R. 'Arab Dimensions to British Racehorse Breeding'. *Anthropology Today* 119, no. 3 (2003): 13–18.

Cavanough, Maurice, and Meurig Davies. *The Melbourne Cup*. Wollstonecraft: Pollard Publishing Co, 1972.

Chidester, D. 'The Church of Baseball, the Fetish of Coca-Cola, and the Potlatch of Rock'n'Roll'. In *Religion and Popular Culture in America*, edited by Bruce David Forbes and Jeffrey H. Mahan, 213–31. Berkeley, CA and London: University of California Press, 2000.

Cohen, E. 'A Phenomenology of Tourist Experiences'. *Sociology* 13 (1979): 179–201.

Crouter, Richard. 'Beyond Bellah: American Civil Religion and the Australian Experience'. *Australian Journal of Politics and History* 36, no. 2 (1990): 154–65.

Cusack, C.M. 'Religion in Australian Society: A Place for Everything and Everything in its Place'. *Modern Greek Studies* 13 (2005): 28–45.

Cusack, C.M., and J. Digance. '"Shopping for a Self": Pilgrimage, Identity-Formation and Retail Therapy'. In *Victor Turner and Cultural Performance*, edited by Graham St John, 227–41. Oxford and New York, Berghahn, 2008 in press.

De Lore, Brian. *Melbourne Cup Winners*. Sydney: View Productions Pty Ltd, 1983.

Demerath, N.J. 'The Varieties of Sacred Experience: Finding the Sacred in a Secular Grove'. *Journal for the Scientific Study of Religion* 39, no. 1 (2000): 1–11.

Digance, J. 'Religious and Secular Pilgrimage: Journeys Redolent with Meaning'. In *Tourism, Religion and Spiritual Journeys*, edited by D.J. Timothy and D.H. Olsen, 36–48. London: Routledge, 2006.

Dunstan, Keith. *Sports*. Melbourne: Sun Books Pty Ltd, 1981.

Edwards, E.H. *The Encyclopedia of the Horse: The Definitive Guide to the Horse, the Major Breeds of the World, Their History and Modern Use*. London: Dorling Kindersley, 1994.

Gould, Nat. *Landed at Last*. London: The Modern Publishing Company, n.d. (c. 1880).

Lyon, D. *Jesus in Disneyland: Religion in Postmodern Times*. Cambridge: Polity, 2002 [2000].

Mandle, Bill. 'Cricket and Australian Nationalism in the Nineteenth Century'. *Journal of the Royal Australian Historical Society* 59, no. 4 (1973): 224–46.

Martin, A.W. *Robert Menzies: A Life*. Vol. 2 1944–1978. Melbourne: Melbourne University Press, 1995.

Maslin, J. '"Phar Lap", the Tale of an Australian Race Horse'. *New York Times*, August 10, 1984. http://query.nytimes.com/gst/fullpage.html?res=9E07E2DD1438F933A2575BC0A962948 260.

McClay, W.M. 'The Soul of a Nation'. *Public Interest* 155 (2004): 4–19.

Painter, Martin, and Richard Waterhouse. *The Principal Club: A History of the Australian Jockey Club*. Sydney: Allen and Unwin, 1992.

Peake, Wayne. 'The Significance of Unregistered Proprietary Pony Racing in the Social History of Sydney Horse Racing'. *Sporting Traditions* 20, no. 2 (2004): 1–18.

Phillips, T., and P. Smith. 'What is "Australian"? Knowledge and Attitudes Among a Gallery of Contemporary Australians'. *Australian Journal of Political Science* 35, no. 2 (2000): 203–24.

Possamai, A. *Religion and Popular Culture: A Hyperreal Testament.* Brussels: Peter Lang, 2005.

Rankin, B. 'The History of Probability and the Changing Concept of the Individual'. *Journal of the History of Ideas* 27, no. 4 (1966): 483–504.

Senate Legal and Constitutional References Committee. *They Still Call Australia Home: Inquiry into Australian Expatriates.* 2005. www.aph.gov.au/senate/committee/legcon_ctte/expats03/report/index.htm.

Shepherd, Jim. *Australian Sporting Almanac.* Dee Why, NSW: Paul Hamlyn Pty Ltd, 1974.

Turner, Victor. 'The Center Out There: Pilgrim's Goal'. *History of Religions* 12, no. 1 (1973): 191–230.

Twain, Mark. 'Following the Equator'. In *Mark Twain in Australia & New Zealand.* Melbourne: Penguin Books Ltd, 1973.

White, Richard. *Inventing Australia: Images and Identity 1688–1980.* Sydney: Allen and Unwin, 1981.

Windross, Allen. 'The Luck of the Draw: Superstition in Gambling'. *Gambling Research* 15, no. 1 (2003): 63–77.

Worthington, Andrew C. *National Exuberance: A Note on the Melbourne Cup Effect in Australian Stock Returns.* Wollongong: University of Wollongong, School of Accounting & Finance Working Papers Series, 05/10, 2005.

Getting to the game: travel to sports stadia in the era of transit-oriented development

Matthew Burke and Geoffrey Woolcock

Urban Research Program, Griffith University, Brisbane, Australia

Australian sports stadia are returning to the core of cities and to sites supported by high-capacity public transport infrastructure, forming what is often termed 'transit-oriented development' (TOD). In addition, travel demand management (TDM) is being used to condition patrons into using public transport, redefining the patron transport experience. The scale of these shifts has significant implications for patrons, most of whom attend to watch the four respective football codes – Australian Rules (AFL), rugby league, rugby union and soccer – the dominant spectator sports in Australia. These shifts are exemplified in new stadiums such as Docklands in Melbourne and Lang Park in Brisbane. The rise of TDM and TOD also requires a new approach to determining stadium catchments, for which a method based on public transport accessibility is demonstrated. The research explores the prospects of possible AFL stadium locations on Queensland's Gold Coast and questions the decision to locate the future stadium at Carrara.

'… I hate AAMI Stadium its a sterile piece of concrete and plastic, and, I hate driving there, I hate parking there, I hate walking through the approaches to the ground, I hate catching the bus there …'
(bigfooty.com member 'The Flying Doormat' discussing Adelaide's Football Park – a car dominated suburban mega-stadium – 10 September 2008)[1]

Introduction

Sports landscapes in Australian cities have shifted markedly since 1990. Old stadiums have been abandoned or demolished and new ones constructed amidst a process of rationalization and nationalization in the major sporting codes. Change is also apparent due to the transit-orientation of new stadium locations and designs. Both the siting of stadia in relation to other elements of the urban area, and their relationship to transport systems, is dictating a change in both local market catchments and in patron experience. Outer suburban car-oriented stadia, such as Football Park at Westlakes in Adelaide, to which the above blogger is referring, dominated 1960s and 1970s development in Australia. As will be shown, these have been mostly swept aside by inner urban, transit-oriented developments (TODs), where motor vehicle access to the stadium is actively discouraged. The shift is having profound impacts on sports patron travel behaviour and, we will contend, the patron experience and sports culture in urban areas.

Studies on the stadium patron experience appear to focus either on the stadium and the in-ground experience of the patron or, if the studies do consider travel, they tend to take a tourism perspective focusing more on long-distance travellers (the 'road trip') and the sports event as tourist attractor.[2] Our approach is to examine the conditions influencing the travel behaviour of the majority of sports patrons (those from within the local catchment of a stadium) and to examine the changes in planning, design and management that are transforming the travel experience.

This essay focuses explicitly on the transit-oriented stadia that have emerged in Australia, and the use of travel demand management in controlling and disciplining sports patrons towards desirable travel behaviour. As a result, the changing ethnology of the travel experience, and the implications of transit-orientation for planning and assessing stadium locations and public transport infrastructure, are explored. The essay concludes with an accessibility model to identify stadium public transport catchments, that helps assess the viability of proposed sites for an Australian Football League (AFL) stadium on Queensland's Gold Coast.

Previous research on stadium location

Past studies on sports stadium location within cities have drawn mostly from a European and North American perspective.[3] However, the majority of this literature has focused on issues of sports stadium finance, returns on investment for investors, and on the debate about the potential for stadia to revitalize depressed neighbourhoods in which they might be situated.[4] Bale showed how modernization and corporatism have regularly shaped stadium planning and architecture to the will of the power-elites and explored how economics and planning underpin stadium location decisions.[5] Siegfried and Zimbalist explored the role of state and local governments in influencing location decisions, in part financing stadium developments for public-image enhancing, consumer surplus and external benefits; and noted these benefits to the city are expanded if a high proportion of patrons at the stadium come from interstate.[6] Stadium feasibility and user studies are often conducted by proponents or their consultants, but little of this material makes its way to the academic literature.[7] In addition to Bale, a number of authors have focused on location in terms of population or market catchments, including Leonard, and Buraimo, Forrest and Simmons.[8] Researchers have explored the impacts of ground and franchise relocations on fans, including Horak's work on Admira-Wacker's relocation in Vienna, and Spirou and Bennett's work on stadium development in Chicago, which each related to the problem of travel opportunity and market catchments.[9] Berry, Carson and Smyth discussed the political dimensions of deliberations over the choice of stadium site, either close to the centre of Belfast or at the Maze/Long Kesh.[10] They used detailed analysis and extensive consultation with stakeholders to raise questions about government support for the Maze option.

Both Bale and Humphreys, Mason and Pinch have found that traffic and parking issues are the most problematic for residents living near stadium developments, even greater than hooliganism or other such incivilities.[11] The means of moving pedestrians to and from stadia are also given significant attention with computer simulations used to ensure designs meet acceptable evacuation times.[12] However, despite this focus on transport concerns, there are very few studies that have explicitly analysed the travel experiences of sports fans within the city, the transport and land use relationships of modern sports stadia, and the role of these in both bolstering and being serviced by transport systems.

Modern Australian sports stadia

Bale has aptly described modern stadia as having evolved into a small number of rationalised Modernist 'concrete bowl' mega-stadiums that embody 'placelessness' in their uniform look of glass and steel and their relocation into new parts of the city.[13] Sydney Olympic Stadium at Homebush (a suburb in the geographical centre of Sydney) is an example of this placelessness, in 2008 providing home games for not one but four National Rugby League (NRL) clubs, as well as for other sporting and non-sporting events, at a site philosophically beyond the bounded territorialities of the city's earlier sports geography. The renovated Sydney Cricket Ground, est. 1876, and the Sydney Football Stadium, first opened in 1988, are co-located at Moore Park in the city's inner-east. In both Perth and Adelaide, the two most popular Australian Rules (AFL) clubs share home grounds in renovated stadia (Subiaco and Westlakes, respectively). In Melbourne, the rationalist impulse has been more severe and the city's nine AFL clubs today share two inner-city mega-stadia (the Melbourne Cricket Ground [MCG] and Docklands), having abandoned both suburban home-grounds and the outer-suburban Waverley mega-stadium, which now serve as little more than training venues. In Brisbane (a one-team town in each of the major football codes) the middle-suburban Commonwealth Games stadium at Nathan, isolated from the public transport system, was effectively abandoned in favour of a redeveloped inner-city Lang Park, to serve the city's rugby league, rugby union and soccer clubs. The Woolloongabba stadium (commonly known as the 'Gabba), also in inner-city Brisbane, has been renovated from 2001 to more than double its previous crowd capacity to service AFL and cricket. It is to these central stadia that the majority of Australian sports patrons attend games (especially the most popular code, AFL[14]) and thus they play a key role in influencing sports cultures within urban Australia.

Historically, sports stadia in Australia followed a similar trajectory to those of the US and Europe during the twentieth century – or what Urry has declared 'the century of the car'.[15] As noted by Blainey, the first major football ground in Melbourne was at Yarra Park (site of today's MCG) which in the 1870s was 'surprisingly accessible to most of Melbourne's 200,000 people' who could walk to the ground or could arrive by train at nearby Richmond station.[16] Accompanying the growth of football competitions in Adelaide, Sydney and Melbourne, were the new technologies of the tram and the suburban railway, and these developments provided better access for player participation and increasing spectator crowds. As elsewhere, the claim that the railways helped the development of football in the city has substance.[17] In Melbourne, 'suburban steam trains carried supporters to St Kilda, Port Melbourne, Williamstown, Footscray and other grounds'.[18] The enclosed and partitioned stadia were all transit-oriented and many were suburban. Australian football leagues became professional, though they mostly remained not-for-profit enterprises (unlike in the US and UK where private ownership is dominant) and the number of clubs was rationalized, and the eventual 12 Victorian Football League clubs all had home grounds accessible from Melbourne's rail and tram system (plus the short inter-city service to Geelong). In this period, the public transport catchments and the clubs that serviced them helped construct 'a representational sport' with clubs representing distinct parts of the city.[19]

The changed mobility brought by the car and, to a lesser extent, the availability of inexpensive land on the urban fringe fundamentally altered Australian sports geographies, towards outer suburban greenfields developments in the 1960s and 1970s. The nationalization of the major football codes in the 1980s and 1990s created 'super clubs' with expanded market regions, memberships and attendance and new geographies of national and international recruitment, even for Australian Rules football. Air transport has been a key part of this shift, such that professional teams generally play in expansive national competitions, with few intra-city rivalries. This approach is best exemplified by the A-League national soccer competition which was founded on the basis of 'one-team, one-town'. Of particular note is the geographical location of the rationalized mega-stadia. Adelaide's Westlakes stadium aside (built at the apogee of 1970s' auto-dominated urban planning and surrounded by car parking), the main stadia in the major metropolitan markets are all currently near a rail system (or a major busway in the case of the 'Gabba) and lie either in the core of the city or, in Homebush's case, are at least central to most of Sydney's population. The shift away from stadium locations such as Westlakes is best explored by examining one example in detail: the shift of AFL football in Melbourne from Waverley to the Docklands.

The case of Melbourne's Waverley and Docklands stadia

Australia's greatest outer suburban stadium was Waverley Park (formerly VFL Park), some 20km from the centre of Melbourne, Australia's second largest city (see Figure 1). Waverley represented the idealised motorway stadium development of the 1970s. First planned in the early 1960s, with a capacity for more than 90,000 patrons, the stadium was built by the AFL Commission on some 200 acres (86 ha) of land adjacent to one of the city's largest freeways, serving a spectator catchment much wider than just the south-eastern suburbs of Melbourne where it was located.[20] It was not the home ground for any club, at least until late in its life, and it was dislocated from the traditional territorialities of the tribal teams in the inner-city. The open fields allowed for an abundance of car parking for 25,000 cars, this being the primary means for most patrons to attend matches (see Figure 2). Though a rail extension to the stadium was mooted, none ever emerged. For 30 years competitive AFL games were held at the venue, at a time when clubs began leaving their small suburban stadia for rationalized grounds elsewhere. But Waverley suffered in

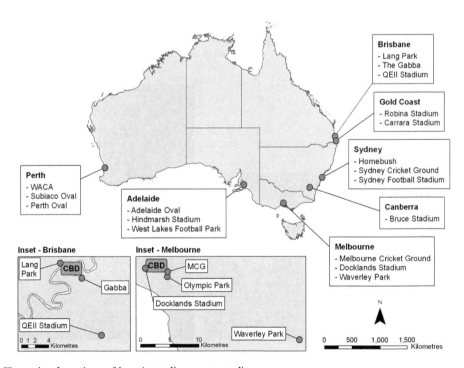

Figure 1.   Locations of key Australian sports stadia.

public opinion, at least in part because of its deficiencies of road access and public transport. Through to the end of its life (the last scheduled AFL match was played there in 1999) Waverley was generating reasonable financial surpluses to the AFL commission, and reasonably robust attendance figures, as the home ground for the Hawthorn and St Kilda teams.[21]

In the mid-1990s, an offer was put on the table by the Victorian state government that was hard for the AFL to resist: a partnership to produce a new inner-city stadium worth $300 million that would cost the Commission only $30 million with significant public infrastructure to be provided free.[22] Though highly contested, a strategic decision was taken by the AFL to construct a stadium at Docklands, only 1km from Melbourne's central business district (CBD), effectively determining Waverley's fate. In 2001, the old suburban ground was sold to the property developers Mirvac who have since turned the car-parking area into a master-planned residential community (also named Waverley Park) with the playing ground and one grandstand retained as a training facility for the Hawthorn AFL club.[23] Opened in 2000, the Docklands stadium emphasized the new ideal of the sports stadium location. Sited in the inner-city adjacent to one of Melbourne's busiest, high-capacity rail stations (Southern Cross Station) it provides easy non-car access to much of the city's population. Indeed, Docklands' capacity crowds of 55,000 cannot be provided for by car travel alone. According to ausstadiums.com, there is parking for 2,500 cars underneath the stadium and only 4,000 spaces nearby. But much of that parking also services the many office towers, restaurants, bars and other land uses clustered right around the stadium, including the AFL's head office (see Figure 2). Docklands was planned specifically as a 'stadium village'[24] similar to Stamford Bridge in Chelsea, London, clustering land uses together to ensure activities beyond just game days. This made more productive use of the land than open car parking lots would provide, given the proximity to Southern Cross Station, the Melbourne CBD and Victoria Harbour.

The Waverley to Docklands example highlights two inter-related processes. The first is that in Australia many of the refurbishments and new-build stadium developments have been returned to the core of the city. As Moriarty noted of Melbourne, Kooyong in the

Figure 2. Waverley Park and its car parking, 1999 (left); Docklands and its mixed land uses with pedestrian bridge to Southern Cross Station in background, 2000 (right). Source: Fairfaxphotos.

middle eastern suburbs was replaced by the National Tennis Centre (2km from the CBD) and Waverley (20km from the CBD) with Docklands (only 1km).[25] The new Melbourne Rectangular Stadium, designed to seat 31,000 fans, is being co-located with the Tennis Centre and MCG. In parallel, in Brisbane the QEII stadium at Nathan (10km from the CBD) was abandoned by the Brisbane Broncos rugby league team for a refurbished and expanded Lang Park (2km from the CBD). Peripheral locations for stadia are out of favour. The second process is that stadium developments are being sited where high quality public transport services can service a significant catchment of the city's population. Even the Olympic Stadium at Sydney Olympic Park, Homebush, which sits in the middle suburbs, is serviced by a rail station that handled 90,000 departures perfunctorily following the opening ceremony of the 2000 Games, and over 500 services per day during the games, though it is mostly used only for events now.[26]

Travel demand management (TDM) and modern stadia

Following the trajectory of urban planning and management generally, there has clearly been an about-face in the transport context of major sports stadium developments. Planning movements such as the New Urbanism (which ironically looks to 'old urbanism' as its source) and Smart Growth, promote a restructuring of the city towards public transport, walking and cycling, in conjunction with changes in urban design.[27] Linking public transport to activity centres is thus of the highest priority. Stadium developments have shifted towards 'transit-oriented development' (TOD) – a term variously defined, but that involves clustering development and integrating it with public transport services.[28]

The shift is due partly to the problems of managing private vehicle traffic and car parking at stadium sites. Few sites are available, even in low-density Australian cities, that can accommodate the land take needed for car parking surrounding large stadia (i.e. >20,000 seats) where authorities will require provision of parking if public transport is not available. The only sites available are beyond the urban fringe in locations far from the bulk of the population and unsupported by public transport. Market pressures are pushing stadium investments into closer proximity to public transport and the inner-city.

Modern sports stadia are also integrating with surrounding land uses in new ways. As noted by van Dam[29] stadia have moved to be inwardly mono-functional (serving only one sport – i.e. by removing running tracks from football stadia) but outwardly multi-functional. Hotels, bars, ancillary facilities, even commercial offices and other urban uses are now often co-located with a stadium development. Function rooms within stadia are seen as critical generators of revenue on non-match days.[30] When placed in proximity to a public transport node, such a stadium precinct inevitably meshes with TOD planning principles for location efficiency and mixed use.[31] Pedestrian accessibility becomes a key success factor.[32] Pedestrian access maximizes the benefits accruing from increased consumption by event patrons at facilities proximate to the stadium, such as hospitality venues, accommodation and commercial precincts reachable on foot, which acts in contradiction to the use of large open-air parking lots.

The mass convergence of thousands of spectators on stadium precincts, and their dispersal after the game, generates heavy traffic flows, parking and congestion problems in surrounding streets, if prohibitions on parking and other travel demand management (TDM) measures are not applied.[33] TDM is essentially 'any action or set of actions aimed at influencing people's travel behavior in such a way that alternative mobility options are presented and/or congestion is reduced'.[34] TDM may be used to manage congestion, but also to meet other policy goals, such as limiting greenhouse gas emissions from the transport sector or reducing vulnerabilities to Peak Oil.[35] As noted by Meyer, key elements of TDM generally include:

- Actions to ensure efficient use of road space, through:
  - Traffic management
  - Preferential treatment for public transport and/or high occupancy vehicles
  - Provision for cyclists and pedestrians
  - Parking controls
- Actions to reduce vehicle use in congested areas
- Actions to improve public transport.[36]

Travel demand management may be applied at specific sites (e.g. at a particular workplace or residential development) or at an area-wide level (e.g. TravelSmart community programmes). TDM may also be applied across different travel markets serving diverse trip purposes (e.g. trips to work, to school, to shopping or to recreation). Furthermore, TDM can be used to mitigate existing mobility/congestion problems in the short term, or it can provide a long-term approach to transport problems.

Cars provide patrons with great flexibility as to their route and their time schedule, notwithstanding the time necessary to park and walk to the stadium entrance. No timetable needs to be consulted. This is not the case with public transport. The challenge that sports events transport planners have set for themselves is to make the public transport on offer as seamless and convenient as possible. This includes TDM measures such as special-events services, public transport fare discounts, promotion and advertising. It also includes bringing the public transport as close to the stadium as possible. At its best, such as at Lang Park in Brisbane, this means integrating bus stations underneath the stadium itself, and investment in high-volume rail station infrastructure, including priority pedestrian links to and from the stadium.

TDM in contemporary Australian stadia

Major sporting stadia in Australia now almost universally apply TDM measures under a Transport Management Plan (TMP) to manage traffic flows and parking, primarily by discouraging private motor vehicle travel and encouraging public transport usage. The 'Gabba, Lang Park and Robina Stadium (Skilled Park), the three largest stadia in

Table 1. Travel Demand Management Measures applied at Robina Stadium.

Vehicle Management	Public Transport
• Road closures before, during and after events, except for local access and stadium transport services in the immediate vicinity of the stadium and around the bus marshalling zone; • Residents permits required for access in residential streets; • Private vehicles are prevented from stopping at any time or during event zones along major access roads around the stadium; and, • Limited number of 2-hour parking spaces.	• Bus marshalling zones; • A purpose built pedestrian route between the Robina train station and bus interchange and the stadium; • Special bus and train services, in addition to scheduled services; • Separate locations for limousine service, taxi rank, and disability set down/pick up and general set down/pick up zones; and • Free public transport fares for pre-purchased ticket-holders.

Source: Major Sports Facilities Authority 2004.

South-East Queensland, are all examples of stadia using TMPs. A variety of initiatives for managing traffic around events at these venues have been developed in consultation with key stadium and event stakeholders to ensure that any impacts on local traffic, businesses and residents are minimized and the efficiency and effectiveness of public transport for patrons is maximized. The TDM measures applied by the management authority Stadiums Queensland for Robina Stadium are shown in Table 1.[37]

At Robina Stadium, the public transport services on offer are less impressive than in Brisbane and there have been longer wait times and growing resistance to the lack of parking – especially as the stadium is a greenfields development. The local member has gone so far as to call for a parking structure to be built adjacent to the stadium, within the boundaries of the TOD.[38]

The TDM measures at Lang Park are so onerous that a 'Traffic Area' surrounding the stadium – effectively anything within a 15-minute walk – is affected by strict and rigidly enforced on-street parking restrictions for as many as four hours before and after the game. Yet it is not all 'sticks' that are used to condition fans away from car use. The Queensland Government has introduced 'carrots' such as package pricing such that a public transport fare is 'built in' to any pre-purchased ticket price. This approach has been used for major events around the world and the first time many Australians used it was at the Olympic Games in Sydney. Stadium ticket holders obtain 'free' public transport to and from the stadium, simply showing their ticket or membership card to a bus driver or ticket inspector. In addition, special events buses run from major bus interchanges and the central business district for two hours before kick off and after the game. A high quality public transport incentive is therefore dangled before the sports patron.

Such a scheme was first introduced in Queensland by state and local government as part of the Lang Park redevelopment, partly in response to the advocacy of local community groups concerned about the development of a mega-stadium in an existing residential area, and the possible impacts on residential amenity from car parking. The motives and initial success of the TDM scheme were made explicit by the then Minister for Transport, Stephen Bredhauer in Queensland Parliament, who commented after the opening game:

> The transport strategy for the stadium is one that is public transport focused and seeks to actively discourage reliance on private vehicle travel ... These arrangements were highly successful. They exceeded all expectations, with more than 85 per cent of all attendees travelling by public transport on the day.[39]

Due to the positive results at Lang Park, the scheme was soon expanded to the 'Gabba and to recently opened Robina Stadium. All have been generally regarded as successes by transport authorities, although there is some criticism of the arrangements at Robina. Similar schemes have been applied at stadia as diverse as Subiaco and the smaller Perth Oval (Members Equity Stadium) in Perth, and, most ironically, from 2008 at auto-dominated Westlakes in Adelaide.[40] That Perth and Brisbane are the Australian cities to have most embraced TDM for sports events is no great surprise as both TransPerth and TransLink, respectively, are regarded as providing these cities with superior public transport planning arrangements to all other metropolitan regions in the country.[41]

There are some equity concerns about the TDM approach used in Queensland, including the use of 'free' public transport. The free fare offer overcomes the unwillingness of some spectators to use public transport because of their increased travel costs.[42] It also allows for 'park'n'ride' public transport operations – where spectators may drive to on- or off-street parking adjacent to a busway or rail station and travel only the last part of their journey to the game. But the fare is not actually 'free' at all. A state (i.e. taxpayer) subsidised fare is hypothecated into the price of the pre-purchased ticket. In this way, all taxpayers are subsidizing sports patrons, who, due to ticket price rises, are increasingly of a higher-income demographic.[43] Further, patrons cannot pay less for their ticket by not using public transport, say by walking or cycling to the stadium. However, this is not necessarily different to the circumstances Manville and Shoup discuss where 'free' on-street or off-street parking, or heavily subsidised parking is made available in places such as car-dominated sports stadia.[44]

Impacts of TDM and TOD on the patron experience

The actions of stadium developers, governments and transport operators in changing both the location of stadia within the city, and the transport offer available to patrons, has led to significant shifts in the patron travel and sport-event experience. Some of these shifts, it can be argued, have impacted on the psycho-social experience of the sport spectator. As noted by Marcus, the travel experience, whether driving and parking or via public transport, is a patron's first and last impression of both a stadium and a sport event. And the experience is often not a good one.[45] The motivations for patrons to travel to sports stadia include both the desire to experience excitement and express identification with a team.[46] The concept of pilgrim is perhaps a little over-worked in reference to the stadium-goer, but clearly the reverential attitudes and 'worship' of fans for their teams and players makes clear the spectator experience 'can be said to possess some of the characteristics of a religion in Durkheim's sense'.[47] The journey is also the transition between the calm of home and the tension and turmoil of the match, allowing for the slow reduction of stress levels, particularly on the way home. We suggest that new or, more correctly, renewed productions of identity and identification are apparent in the spectator's journey by public transport.

At car-dominated stadia, the mass-produced, mass-consumed car was manifestly visible. Home may be far from the stadium, but to the arriving driver, personal time and space was often reconfigured via high speed travel on a freeway or arterial road, until arrival at the inevitable queue close to the stadium, where the 'freedom' and autonomy of the road would end, as increased control of the road environment was used to direct the driver in and to a parking space.

Back to Waverley

To return to our case of Waverley Park, the car park there, with its informally marked bays and parking attendants, was primarily used as storage place for vehicles during the game, but it had many other functions as well. It allowed for display of both car customization and of fan ornamentation of their vehicles which, although not unique to Australia, certainly took on a local flavour. One could see cars decked out with team car seat covers, number plate surrounds, flags, see-through windscreen decals and bumper stickers, with children's scarves streaming from where there were jammed in the passenger windows. Self-presentation theory suggests that the drivers of such vehicles are presenting themselves in a manner congruent with their self-image, obtaining 'a sense of personal identity from driving their car'.[48] The rather barren Waverley car park provided space for meeting and for other social activities, such as a pre-game meal or cup of coffee from the 'boot' of the car ('tailgating' as it is known in the US[49]). Concession stands and newspaper sellers, media caravans, St John's ambulances, and a litany of other uses would cluster near the entry points to the stadium itself. Should any space be empty of cars it would often be consumed by children and youth playing football. Mild forms of 'hooning' were not uncommon, with young men displaying their prowess and testing both the limits of the law, and the patience of other patrons.[50] And a 'sonic envelope' of pre- or post-match commentary from car-radio speakers playing stations broadcasting inside the ground (or at other games) would mesh with the sounds of arriving or departing car engines and celebratory horn honking.[51] Yet, it was not always a happy experience. The car is most commonly theorised as a source of freedom, autonomy and independence.[52] However, in the Waverley car park (or at Westlakes for that matter) the car could on occasion be more of a prison, trapping a departing driver and passengers in a seemingly immobile queue for the limited egress points that connect to the road network.

The new experience

The modern TDM stadia, by contrast, offer different experiences. Public transport, with its constraints of schedules and routes, is generally not perceived as giving people a sense of control, freedom or independence.[53] But that does not mean it must be unpleasant, especially where the public transport on offer matches or exceeds the performance of car travel for the trip. The public transport to Lang Park, for example, is one of the highest quality offers in Australia, particularly in terms of travel time, which expands the spatial catchment of the stadium as well as offering reduced travel times to those living close by. Generally clean and comfortable express buses run to underneath the stadium on the exclusive busways. Additional train services run. 'Free' public transport and branded services reduce complexity for the traveller, with short walking distances required at the stadium end.

The public transport journey often starts on foot, with a walk to a bus stop or train station near a stadium-goer's place of work or residence. A public transport vehicle will then be boarded, which though simple in concept to the user, is actually part of a complex and highly organized system that conditions patrons into a particular mode of existence. Public transport managers are faced with significant tasks in planning, designing and delivering events services. But they are not the only people who must be disciplined. The public nature of public transport means an attitude of reciprocity and self-discipline is required, transforming each individual into a 'responsible' social actor, as opposed to the malignantly deviant (i.e. fare dodgers, vandals or deliberately unruly passengers) or the 'ignorant members of the public' who are just unaware of the unwritten rules by highly developed protocols of public transport usage in a city.[54] The queue, particularly that at public transport services after a game, is an example of mutual fatedness where the rules of 'polite' behaviour are generally observed.

Research supports the existence of 'communitas' at events,[55] such as sport events at mega-stadia. There is a growing research base on how the social and cultural aspects of sport contribute to both social capital and community development.[56] Indeed, Fairley and Gammon identify sport fan communities as being particularly important.[57] Though such communities may be constituted in many ways, including via digital communications and live 'big screen' viewing sites, the private sphere and limited meeting opportunities of car-based transport to stadia may stymie the capacity of sports fans from the same neighbourhoods to identify and meet each other. That situation is now reversed with patrons 'forced' to their nearest train and bus stops.

Where additional public transport services are run just for the sport-event, these tend to be populated solely by stadium-goers. This represents an 'intense moment of travel and co-presence' and, given the colour of the modern merchandised fan, a return to spectacle and procession.[58] Crowded into waiting areas, public transport vehicles and concourses, these travel spaces provide an experience-based sociality, where accidental encounter and spontaneity are likely, across social classes.[59] At major Lang Park fixtures, one may see MPs, prominent football identities and businessmen with less well-heeled patrons on the bus, given there are few other options for travel to the game. Often these services are full of banter and good-humour. It is a small return towards Sennett's vision of the city as 'a human settlement in which strangers are likely to meet'.[60]

Such encounters may also occur in the large commodified 'entertainment precincts' that have developed in close vicinity to contemporary stadia. These allow for 'networked sociality' based around places to meet before or after the game: public and semi-public spaces such as bars, cafés, restaurants and pubs.[61] As an example, the lively Caxton Street, near Lang Park, is pedestrianised on game days and lies on a pedestrian route from the stadium to Brisbane's largest rail station (Roma Street). Such spaces were mostly absent at Waverley and other car-dominated stadia, which were part of the segregated zoning of the mid- to late-twentieth Century.

Beyond questions of sociality, the path-dependent pattern of auto-mobility in contemporary society, laid down throughout most of the twentieth century, has at least been broken by stadia using TOD and TDM. Sports stadia are one of the first major land uses to make the transition. It may prove to be a small but significant shift in breaking society's attachment to, and reliance on, the car. Decisions to choose particular modes of travel (car or public transport) are seen as a product of a reasoning process.[62] As Anable notes, however, 'the combination of instrumental, situational and psychological factors affecting travel choice' will differ in distinct ways for various population groups.[63] The sports patron is faced with a different set of factors to the general commuter in the city. Though they may try to resist, sports patrons are effectively 'forced' to use the public transport system in Brisbane to get to a game. As such, there are undoubtedly many game attendees who have used public transport for the first time in years, if not decades. Familiarity and experience is a key element of voluntary behaviour change, particularly under trans-theoretical theory, which describes the different stages of behaviour as being: 1) pre-contemplation, 2) contemplation, 3) preparation, 4) action, and 5) maintenance.[64] A positive public transport journey may lead to attitudinal change and the formation of intentions and modified behaviour patterns, leading to the choice of public transport for future journeys.

A sports patron's experience of violence and vandalism is also altered, though this is not a common feature of the contemporary sports scene in Australia.[65] At Westlakes in Adelaide visiting fans were routinely advised not to drive and park at the stadium should they have 'interstate plates' due to problems with vandalism. The car parks of the auto-dominated mega-stadia are too vast for CCTV and police control; an unregulated space, where, at least in the early days, 'hooning' in its less aggressive forms took place. Car park 'rage' is managed as best it can by traffic wardens and the police, but crowds are reasonably dilute out in the expanses of a parking lot. In the denser environs of a concourse and public transport station, there is actually greater potential for friction. Guilianotti has noted how prolific the instruments of regulation and control have become in the stadium landscape to control this problem.[66] Policing, marshalling and surveillance of public transport infrastructure and the stadium environs creates less opportunity for even minor anti-social behaviour. The walkways, concourses and platforms of public transport infrastructure are well suited to surveillance technology and stadia are deliberately designed to avoid 'blind spots'. This is allied with other changes. Stadium managers use pre- and post-game entertainment to diminish the peak of travel demand that can occur at the start or end of a game, and other techniques are used to encourage stadium-goers into their numbers seats to become, in Foucault's terms, 'docile bodies'.[67]

Sports patrons may be shifting to public transport, but there have also been other changes in both the types of patron attracted to sports such as AFL, start times and days of the week, and the activities of patrons in an era of flexible work practices, and Friday and Monday night football. More women are attending sports events, particularly AFL matches in cities such as Sydney.[68] Travel habits between the home, work and recreation are changing as time and money constraints affect the way in which people conduct their activities and therefore seek out opportunities to minimize the amount of travel they require. Changes to television programming have meant sporting matches no longer start at 2.00 p.m. kick-off on Saturday afternoon (as the majority were up to the mid-1980s) and twilight and evening games have become more frequent, with weekday as well as weekend matches scheduled. The origin from which sports patrons leave to reach a stadium destination is less likely to be their place of residence. Leaving straight from work, university or some other location to the stadium and heading for drinks after the match is more common. The effects of these changes on travel behaviour are mostly unexplored.

Appraising public transport catchments to stadia

What does this mean for the appraisal of stadium developments? Metz suggests the human mobilities strand of social geography seems 'limited by a reluctance to engage with economic aspects of travel behaviour'.[69] Our thinking about the nature of stadia in an era of TOD and TDM fostered ideas about new tools for examining stadium proposals.

The stadium travel market and accessibility

Baim notes that since travel costs are borne by patrons once a stadium is built, there is a clear market-orientation for professional sports, influencing location decisions.[70] Stadium developments designed around TDM and TOD therefore have implications for market assessment. Conventional approaches to transport planning, such as micro-simulation models and 4-step traffic models,[71] are inadequate for appraising the likely transport performance or catchment of a stadium under TDM. We need to consider such land uses through the lens of accessibility: public transport accessibility.

Accessibility essentially describes an individual's ability to reach goods, services, activities and destinations, collectively.[72] The ease with which destinations can be reached depends not just on the transport network but also the patterns of land use. Halden states that: '[a]ccessibility measures seek to define the level of opportunity and choice taking account of both the existence of opportunities, and the transport network options available to reach them'.[73]

The recent development of geographic information systems (GIS) has allowed the development of workable accessibility planning tools. In Northern Ireland a detailed study compared in-town and out-of-town locations for a proposed stadium site for Belfast. The study used GIS to appraise destination accessibility to a range of urban features.[74] Their approach was to 'differentiate specific locations within Belfast City Centre and highlight the key issues relating to each potential site'. Yet while they identified proximity of stadium locations to local public transport stops, they ignored the actual access of residents via that public transport system from the stops to their places of residence. As such, Berry, Carson and Smyth's analysis of the transport potential of the proposed sites, and the public transport catchment each would easily service, was limited.

An alternative approach

We demonstrate an approach using GIS to develop catchment analyses for stadium locations that seeks to determine public transport catchments, in terms of both spatial reach and the number of residents who can access a proposed stadium site easily by public transport. This method focuses on such aspects as the walk access from home to a public transport stop; wait times and travel time on the vehicles; interchange with other public transport services; and, the walk access from the final public transport stop to the proposed stadium site. Ease of access may be defined in terms of travel time considering all the legs of the journey.

A new AFL stadium for the Gold Coast

Queensland's Gold Coast is Australia's sixth largest city with over 550,000 residents. The AFL Commission has committed to establishing a team in the city from 2011, and at the time of writing, the GC-17 bid team has just submitted a formal application to the AFL Commission for the 17th AFL license.[75] A major consideration for the team is where it will play. A number of locations for an oval stadium servicing AFL, cricket and potentially athletics have been mooted on the Gold Coast, which may play a role in a future bid to host the Commonwealth Games. A series of investigations were undertaken in 2007 and 2008, and the state and local governments and the AFL focused their interest on several new sites including at Nerang, Helensvale and Coomera where a new venue close to the Gold Coast rail line could be constructed. However, the Gold Coast City Council and the AFL now seem determined to redevelop the existing Carrara stadium site, where an inadequate facility with temporary stands is in place.[76] Cararra is neither on the rail line, nor within walking distance of any priority public transport infrastructure. Figure 3 provides the set of proposed and existing stadium locations, as well as the location of the stadium's competitor in the sports market – the rectangular Robina Stadium, which services rugby league and soccer.

It is beyond the scope of this essay to provide full detail on the method used to undertake the accessibility analysis, or the strengths and weaknesses of the proposed and existing sites. For further information see the report by Burke, Evans and Hatfield.[77] In summary, several spatially-based datasets were used, including the Gold Coast road network, public transport network information, and 2006 Australian Bureau of Statistics population data. Since people generally conceive travel length in terms of time, particularly when walking or using public transport, we used time-based measures instead of distance measures and included wait and transfer times for public transport. A total travel time of 45minutes or less from the place of origin to the stadium was considered 'high accessibility'. This roughly equates to a 30-minute public transport journey plus walking and wait/transfer time – what most fans would readily consider. Total travel times of 75minutes or less from the place of origin to the stadium was considered 'reasonable accessibility'. This roughly equates to a 60-minute public transport journey plus walking and wait/transfer time. Total travel times in excess of 75minutes were considered beyond what all but the 'heroic' team supporter would be willing to countenance. Although

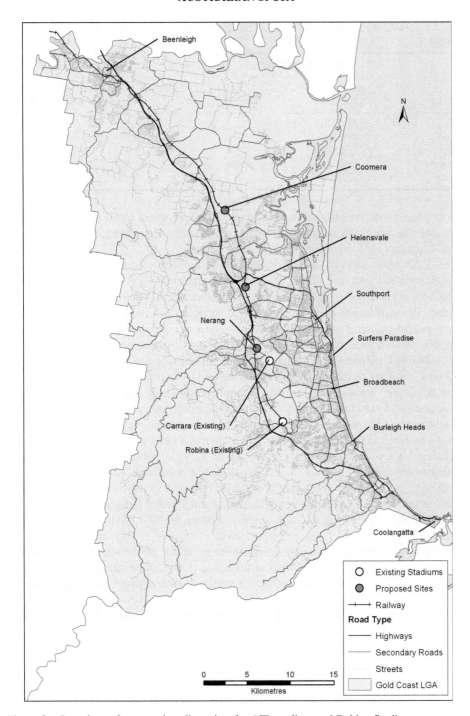

Figure 3.   Locations of proposed stadium sites for AFL stadium and Robina Stadium.

Table 2. Public transport accessibility of the Gold Coast residential population to proposed stadium locations.

Location	High Accessibility		Reasonable Accessibility	
	Population within 45 minutes	% Total population	Population within 75 minutes	% Total population
Carrara	229,840	48.7	388,797	82.5
Nerang	251,216	53.3	434,793	92.2
Helensvale	138,510	29.4	413,933	87.8
Coomera	169,986	36.0	424,660	90.0
Robina	172,006	36.5	388,620	82.4

arbitrary and not derived from direct observation of sports event travel on the Gold Coast, these measures are likely to provide a meaningful comparison of the accessibility offered for AFL patrons by each of the proposed sites.

Like all such models, our approach has a number of limitations, beyond the simplification of travel time preferences. The method used does not take into account any differences in residents' social, economic, physical and travel preferences. It assumes that any person, regardless of their ability or social standing, will have equal opportunities to access public transport services. It assumes equal preferences for the use of public transport, regardless of the mode available (rail or bus). And all residents are assumed to be possible AFL patrons. The population area modelled is limited to the 2006 boundaries of Gold Coast City to make use of 2006 census data. Results may differ if one were to consider future populations, tourist accommodation (for visiting fans), different population areas (i.e. including populations to the north and south of Gold Coast City) and new public transport networks. Future testing and refining may resolve some of these limitations, but it is useful to demonstrate the approach here.

Table 2 shows the proportion of the Gold Coast's population that were within 45minutes and within 75minutes access of each stadium location via public transport. At the existing stadium site at Carrara, the public transport system can currently service 48.7% of the Gold Coast population within 45minutes, and a comparatively low 82.5% within 75minutes. Were the stadium moved to Nerang it could service 10% more of the population (and more of those in growth areas of the city). This could prove highly advantageous in helping the stadium compete for the sports patron with Robina Stadium, which would find itself with a dramatic difference in catchment areas. Our assessment suggests that the short term decision by the AFL and Gold Coast City Council to save money and redevelop at Carrara will limit the catchment of the new stadium, affecting the viability of the future AFL club and the Australian Rules code in the city, including in its battle with rugby league.

Conclusion

The new 'location, location, location' mantra of stadium developers heralds a return to the city centre and to sites supported by high-capacity public transport infrastructure. Two processes are apparent. Firstly, with the nationalization of sporting codes and the rationalization of teams and grounds in Australia, large mega-stadia have emerged. Most are in the form of new or redeveloped grounds in the core of cities, or at the least where major public transport routes can service city populations. Secondly, TOD and TDM are redefining the patron transport experience, in the stadium surrounds and on the journey to and from the ground. The 'carrot' and 'stick' approach of TDM is conditioning sports fans to accept public transport as the preferred mode of access. The success of TDM measures in Queensland suggests further roll-out is likely in both Australia and abroad. With public transport the priority, proactive transport planning will be a pressing concern when considering stadium development.

The research has added to understanding of travel to and from the stadium within the more holistic sport's patron experience, which has been given lesser attention in the academic literature. The return of sports fans to public transport in Australian cities is creating new opportunities for experience-based sociality in public spaces, which may have positive aspects.[78] The docile behaviour of Australian stadium goers is reinforced by public transport, which by its nature requires attitudes of reciprocity and self-discipline to adhere to the formal or unwritten protocols that allow the system to operate efficiently, and to get everyone to and from the game.[79] In addition, the research has demonstrated a promising approach to appraise market catchments for stadium proposals where public transport is the only real means to get there.

The tasks for future research are many. We need better understandings of traveller's behaviour to and from stadia, not the least to help manage sports events and transport systems. Further examination is needed of public transport generally within the 'human mobilities' stream of social science, which (understandably) has focused mostly on the car.[80] We need to identify groups who may be included and excluded by these new stadium locations – particularly as for some time the 'rich' have been reclaiming the centres of Australian cities where stadia are being located or redeveloped.[81] In part, this may be accomplished by testing and revising improved accessibility models like that demonstrated, in order to better understand stadium-transport relationships. It may also prove worthwhile determining if events-related public transport may play a role in influencing modal change for other trip purposes.

Acknowledgements

The authors wish to thank Translink and Queensland Transport for the provision of public transport data and for funding research on Transit-Oriented Development. The research on accessibility modelling has also has been generously supported by the Queensland Development Research Institute (QDRI) and the Australasian Centre for the Governance and Management of Urban Transport (GAMUT). The authors also wish to thank two anonymous reviewers whose input improved the final essay.

Notes

[1] Post to Bigfooty.com, 10 September 2008 on the topic 'It's The Football Stupid' – Possible explanation for falling AFL attendances in Adelaide'. www.bigfooty.com/forum/showthread.php?t=492248.

[2] See Bale and Moen, *The Stadium and the City*; Redhead, 'Those Absent From the Stadium are Always Right'; and Fredline, 'Host and Guest Relations'; Gibson, 'Sport Tourism'.

[3] Lipsitz, 'Sports Stadiums and Urban Development'; Thornley, 'Urban Regeneration and Sports Stadia'.

[4] See Lertwachara and Cochran, 'An Event Study'; Nelson, 'Prosperity or Blight?'; Wassmer, 'Metropolitan Prosperity from Major League Sports in the CBD'.

[5] Bale, *Sport, Space and the City*.

[6] Siegfried and Zimbalist, 'The Economics of Sports Facilities', 100.

[7] Macdonald, 'Most Valuable Player'.

[8] See Leonard, *A Sociological Perspective of Sport*, 331–2.; Buraimo, Forrest and Simmons, 'Freedom of Entry'.

[9] Horak, 'Moving to Suburbia'; Spirou and Bennett, *It's Hardly Sportin'*, 59–82.

[10] Berry, Carson and Smyth, *A Multi-purpose Sports Stadium.*
[11] Bale, 'In the Shadow of the Stadium'; Humphreys, Mason and Pinch, 'The Externality Fields of Football Grounds'.
[12] Mott MacDonald, 'Predicting People Movement'.
[13] Bale, *Sport, Space and the City*, 40–2.
[14] Eight AFL games are played each week (the majority of which are played at the MCG, Docklands, Subiaco, Westlakes, the 'Gabba and SCG) over a 22-round home and away regular season contested by 16 AFL clubs and were attended by an average of 38,286 persons per game in 2008 (see www.footywire.com/afl/footy/); Eight NRL games are also played per week over a 25-round home and away regular season contested by 16 NRL clubs and were attended by an average of 15,917 persons per game in 2008.
[15] Urry, 'The "System" of Automobility', 27.
[16] Blainey, *A Game of Our Own*, 98.
[17] Huggins and Tolson, 'The Railways and Sport in Victorian Britain', 110.
[18] Blainey, *A Game of Our Own*, 157.
[19] Fløysand and Jakobsen, 'Commodification of Rural Places', 208.
[20] Hay, Haig-Muir and Mewett, '"A Stadium as Fine as any on Earth" or "Arctic Park"?', 158.
[21] Hay *et al.*, 'Waverley Park', 10–11.
[22] Dovey et al., *Fluid City*, 160–1.
[23] See www.waverleypark.com.au/.
[24] See R. Hodder, 'Stadium Village'. *Herald Sun*, 2000.
[25] Moriarty, 'Inequality in Australian cities', 214.
[26] Hensher and Brewer, 'Going for Gold at the Sydney Olympics', 383.
[27] For more on these Planning Movements see Smart Growth Network, *About Smart Growth*, 5–7; and Leccese *et al.*, *Charter of the New Urbanism*.
[28] Cervero, *Transit-Oriented Development in the United States*, 5–7.
[29] van Dam, 'Refurbishment, Redevelopment or Relocation?', 138.
[30] Leask and Digance, 'Exploiting Unused Capacity'.
[31] Daisa, 'Traffic, Parking, and Transit-Oriented Development', 115–16.
[32] Berry, Carson and Smyth, *A Multi-purpose Sports Stadium*, 24.
[33] Bale, *Sport, Space and the City*, 101–6.; Humphreys, Mason and Pinch, 'The Externality Fields of Football Grounds', 403.
[34] Meyer, 'Demand Management as an Element of Transportation Policy', 576.
[35] Chapman, 'Transport and Climate Change'.
[36] Meyer, 'Demand Management as an Element of Transportation Policy', 583–4.
[37] Stadiums Queensland (formerly the Major Sports Facilities Authority) is the State Government body charged with the management of major sports facilities that are declared under the Queensland Government's Major Sports Facilities Act 2001.
[38] ABC News, 'MP Wants Football Stadium Car Park'.
[39] Bredhauer, 'Ministerial Statement', 2,453.
[40] South Australian National Football League, 'A New Era for Footy Express'.
[41] Mees, O'Connell and Stone, 'Travel to Work in Australian Capital Cities'.
[42] Humphreys, Mason and Pinch, 'The Externality Fields of Football Grounds', 408.
[43] See Australian Bureau of Statistics, *Sports Attendance, Australia*; or Guilianotti, *Football*, 79.
[44] Manville and Shoup, 'Parking, People, and Cities'.
[45] Marcus, 'A Parking Home Run', 19.
[46] Dunning, *Sport Matters*, 119.
[47] Ibid., 6–7.
[48] Steg, 'Car Use', 150.
[49] Hinch and Higham, *Sport Tourism Development*.
[50] For 'hooning' see Butler-Bowdon, 'Roads Hogs to Road Rage'.
[51] A concept provided by Featherstone, 'Automobilities', 9.
[52] Butler-Bowdon, *Roads Hogs to Road Rage*, 82.
[53] Anable and Gatersleben, 'All Work and No Play?', 165.
[54] Nahuis, 'The Politics of Innovation', 232.
[55] Getz, 'Event Tourism', 414.
[56] Nicholson and Hoye, *Sport and Social Capital.*; Perks, 'Does Sport Foster Social Capital?'.
[57] Fairley and Gammon, 'Something Lived, Something Learned'.

[58] Urry, 'Small Worlds', 119.
[59] Wittel, 'Towards a Network Sociality', 68.
[60] Sennett, *The Fall of Public Man*, 39.
[61] Urry, 'Small Worlds', 120.
[62] See Yago, 'The Sociology of Transportation'. And for a non-public transport argument, Fishbein and Ajzen, *Belief, Attitude, Intention, and Behavior*, 177.
[63] Anable, '"Complacent Car Addicts"', 65.
[64] Seethaler and Rose, 'Application of Psychological Principles', 73.
[65] Lynch, 'Disorder on the Sidelines of Australian Sport', 50.
[66] Guilianotti, *Football*, 82.
[67] Bale, *Sport, Space and the City*, 30.
[68] The AFL's marketing department cites figures from Morgan Research claiming that 50% of AFL supporters are female; this compares to 39% of the National Rugby League's supporters. Of the attendances at AFL games every weekend, about 45% are female.
[69] Metz, *The Limits to Travel*, 129.
[70] Baim, *The Sports Stadium*, 219.
[71] For the main form of city-level transport models such as the Brisbane Strategic Transport Model, see Bureau of Transport Economics, *Urban Transport Models*; Pas, 'The Urban Transportation Planning Process'.
[72] Litman, 'Non-Motorized Transportation Demand Management'.
[73] Halden, 'Using Accessibility Measures', 214.
[74] Berry, Carson and Smyth, *A Multi-purpose Sports Stadium*, 52.
[75] N. Smart, 'GC17 Team Puts Coast Case Forward'. *Gold Coast Bulletin*, October 14, 2008.
[76] 'City Commits $20 m to AFL Stadium'. *Gold Coast Bulletin*, October 10, 2008.
[77] Burke, Evans and Hatfield, *A Sporting Chance*.
[78] Wittel, 'Towards a Network Sociality'.
[79] Nahuis, 'The Politics of Innovation'.
[80] Featherstone, 'Automobilities'; Sheller, 'Bodies, Cybercars'; and Urry, 'The "System" of Automobility'.
[81] Badcock, 'Recently Observed Polarising Tendencies'.

References

ABC News. 'MP Wants Football Stadium Car Park', April 22, 2008. http://www.abc.net.au/news/stories/2008/04/22/2223712htm?site=news.

Anable, J. 'Complacent Car Addicts" or "Aspiring Environmentalists"? Identifying Travel Behaviour Segments using Attitude Theory'. *Transport Policy* 12, no. 1 (2005): 65–78.

Anable, J., and B. Gatersleben. 'All Work and No Play? The Role of Instrumental and Affective Factors in Work and Leisure Journeys by Different Travel Modes'. *Transportation Research – A* 39, nos. 2/3 (2005): 163–81.

Australian Bureau of Statistics. *Sports Attendance, Australia – 2005–06*. Canberra: ABS, 2007.

Badcock, B. 'Recently Observed Polarising Tendencies and Australian Cities'. *Australian Geographical Studies* 35, no. 3 (1997): 243–59.

Baim, D.V. *The Sports Stadium as a Municipal Investment*. Contributions in economics and economic history: no. 151. Westport, CT: Greenwood Press, 1994.

Bale, J. 'In the Shadow of the Stadium: Football Grounds as Urban Nuisances'. *Geography* 75, no. 4 (1990): 325–34.

Bale, J. *Sport, Space and the City*. Caldwell, NJ: Blackburn Press, 2001.

Bale, J., and O. Moen. *The Stadium and the City*. Keele: Keele University Press, 1995.

Berry, J., D. Carson, and M. Smyth. *A Multi-purpose Sports Stadium: In-town Versus Out of Town Location*. Belfast: University of Ulster Press, 2007.

Blainey, G. *A Game of Our Own: The Origins of Australian Football*. Revised edn. Melbourne: Black Inc., 2003.

Bredhauer, S. 'Ministerial Statement: Suncorp Stadium, Public Transport'. Hansard: Queensland Parliament, 2003.

Buraimo, B., D. Forrest, and R. Simmons. 'Freedom of Entry, Market Size, and Competitive Outcome: Evidence from English Soccer'. *Southern Economic Journal* 74, no. 1 (2007): 204–13.

Bureau of Transport Economics. *Urban Transport Models: A Review*. Canberra: Bureau of Transport Economics, 1998.

Burke, M., R. Evans, and E. Hatfield. *A Sporting Chance: Accessibility of Proposed AFL Stadium Locations on the Gold Coast.* Brisbane: Urban Research Program, Griffith University, 2008.

Butler-Bowdon, E. 'Roads Hogs to Road Rage'. In *Cars and Culture: Our Driving Passions*, edited by C. Pickett, 66–83. Sydney: Harper Collins, 1998.

Cervero, R. *Transit-Oriented Development in the United States: Experiences, Challenges, and Prospects.* Washington, DC: Transportation Research Board, 2004.

Chapman, L. 'Transport and Climate Change: A Review'. *Journal of Transport Geography* 15, no. 5 (2007): 354–67.

Daisa, J. 'Traffic, Parking, and Transit-Oriented Development'. In *The New Transit Town: Best Practices in Transit-oriented Development*, edited by H. Dittmar and G. Ohland, 114–29. Washington, DC: Island Press, 2004.

Dovey, K., L. Sandercock, Q. Stevens, I. Woodcock, and S. Wood. *Fluid City: Transforming Melbourne's Urban Waterfront.* Sydney and Oxfordshire, UK: University of New South Wales Press; Routledge, 2005.

Dunning, E. *Sport Matters: Sociological Studies of Sport, Violence and Civilization.* London and New York: Routledge, 1999.

Fairley, S., and S. Gammon. 'Something Lived, Something Learned: Nostalgia's Expanding Role in Sport Tourism'. In *Sport Tourism: Concepts and Theories*, edited by H. Gibson, 50–65. London: Routledge, 2006.

Featherstone, M. 'Automobilities: An Introduction'. *Theory, Culture & Society* 21, nos. 4/5 (2004): 1–24.

Fishbein, M., and I. Ajzen. *Belief, Attitude, Intention, and Behavior: An Introduction to Theory and Research.* Reading, MA; London; Sydney: Addison-Wesley, 1975.

Fløysand, A., and S.E. Jakobsen. 'Commodification of Rural Places: A Narrative of Social Fields, Rural Development, and Football'. *Journal of Rural Studies* 23, no. 2 (2007): 206–21.

Fredline, E. 'Host and Guest Relations and Sport Tourism'. *Sport in Society* 8, no. 2 (2005): 263–79.

Getz, D. 'Event Tourism: Definition, Evolution, and Research'. *Tourism Management* 29, no. 3 (2008): 403–28.

Gibson, H.J. 'Sport Tourism: A Critical Analysis of Research'. *Sport Management Review* 1, no. 1 (1998): 45–76.

Guilianotti, R. *Football: A Sociology of the Global Game.* Cambridge: Polity Press, 1999.

Halden, D. 'Using Accessibility Measures to Integrate Land Use and Transport Policy in Edinburgh and the Lothians'. *Transport Policy* 9, no. 4 (2002): 313–26.

Hay, R., M. Haig-Muir, and P. Mewett. '"A Stadium as Fine as any on Earth" or "Arctic Park"? – The Tortured Past and Uncertain Future of a Cultural Icon'. *Journal of Australian Studies* 66 (2000): 158–68.

Hay, R., M. Haig-Muir, P. Mewett, C. Lazenby, and N. Lewis. 'Waverley Park: Whose Social History?' *Sporting Traditions: Journal of the Australian Society for Sports History* 18, no. 1 (2001): 1–17.

Hensher, D., and A. Brewer. 'Going for Gold at the Sydney Olympics: How did Transport Perform?' *Transport Reviews* 22, no. 4 (2002): 381–99.

Hinch, T., and J.E.S. Higham. *Sport Tourism Development, Aspects of Tourism.* Clevedon, UK: Channel View Publications, 2004.

Horak, R. 'Moving to Suburbia: Stadium Relocation and Modernization in Vienna'. In *The Stadium and the City*, edited by J. Bale and O. Moen, 81–93. Staffordshire, UK: Keele University Press, 1995.

Huggins, M., and J. Tolson. 'The Railways and Sport in Victorian Britain: A Critical Reassessment'. *The Journal of Transport History* 22, no. 2 (2001): 99–115.

Humphreys, D.C., C.M. Mason, and S.P. Pinch. 'The Externality Fields of Football Grounds: A Case Study of the Dell, Southampton'. *Geoforum* 14, no. 4 (1983): 401–11.

Leask, A., and J. Digance. 'Exploiting Unused Capacity: Sports Stadia and the MICE Industry'. *Journal of Convention & Exhibition Management* 3, no. 4 (2002): 17–35.

Leccese, M., K. McCormick, and Congress for the New Urbanism. *Charter of the New Urbanism.* New York: McGraw-Hill, 2000.

Leonard, W.M. *A Sociological Perspective of Sport.* 4th edn. New York: Macmillan, 1993.

Lertwachara, K., and J.J. Cochran. 'An Event Study of the Economic Impact of Professional Sport Franchises on Local U.S. Economies'. *Journal of Sports Economics* 8, no. 3 (2007): 244–54.

Lipsitz, G. 'Sports Stadiums and Urban Development'. *Journal of Sports and Social Issues* 8 (1984): 1–17.

Litman, T. 'Non-Motorized Transportation Demand Management'. In *Sustainable Transport: Planning for Walking and Cycling in Urban Environments*, edited by R. Tolley, 573–87. Cambridge, UK: Woodhead Publishing Ltd, 2003.

Lynch, R. 'Disorder on the Sidelines of Australian Sport'. *Sporting Traditions: Journal of the Australian Society for Sports History* 8, no. 1 (1991): 50–75.

Manville, M., and D. Shoup. 'Parking, People, and Cities'. *Journal of Urban Planning and Development* 131, no. 4 (2005): 233–45.

Marcus, J. 'A Parking Home Run'. *Parking* 45, no. 1 (2006): 19–25.

Mees, P., G. O'Connell, and J. Stone. 'Travel to Work in Australian Capital Cities, 1976–2006'. *Urban Policy and Research* 26, no. 3 (2008): 363–78.

Metz, D. *The Limits to Travel: How Far Will You Go?* London: Earthscan/James & James, 2008.

Meyer, M.D. 'Demand Management as an Element of Transportation Policy: Using Carrots and Sticks to Influence Travel Behavior'. *Transportation Research Part A: Policy and Practice* 33, nos. 7/8 (1999): 575–99.

Moriarty, P. 'Inequality in Australian Cities'. *Urban Policy and Research* 16, no. 3 (1998): 211–18.

Mott MacDonald. 'Predicting People Movement'. In *Panstadia International Quarterly Report*, no. 1 (2001): 44–7.

Nahuis, R. 'The Politics of Innovation: Self-service on the Amsterdam Trams'. *Technology in Society* 27, no. 2 (2005): 229–41.

Nelson, A.C. 'Prosperity or Blight? A Question of Major League Stadia Locations'. *Economic Development Quarterly* 15, no. 3 (2001): 55–65.

Nicholson, M., and R. Hoye. *Sport and Social Capital*. Oxford: Butterworth-Heinemann, 2008.

Pas, E.I. 'The Urban Transportation Planning Process'. In *The Geography of Urban Transportation*, edited by S. Hanson, 53–77. New York: Guilford Press, 1995.

Perks, T. 'Does Sport Foster Social Capital? The Contribution of Sport to Lifestyle of Community Participation'. *Sociology of Sport Journal* 24, no. 4 (2007): 378–401.

Redhead, S. 'Those Absent From the Stadium are Always Right: Accelerated Culture, Sport Media, and Theory at the Speed of Light'. *Journal of Sport & Social Issues* 31, no. 3 (2007): 226–41.

Seethaler, R., and G. Rose. 'Application of Psychological Principles to Promote Travel Behaviour Change'. *Transport Engineering in Australia* 9, no. 2 (2004): 67–84.

Sennett, R. *The Fall of Public Man*. Cambridge: Cambridge University Press, 1977.

Sheller, M. 'Bodies, Cybercars and the Mundane Incorporation of Automated Mobilities'. *Social & Cultural Geography* 8, no. 2 (2007): 175–97.

Siegfried, J., and A. Zimbalist. 'The Economics of Sports Facilities and Their Communities'. *The Journal of Economic Perspectives* 14, no. 3 (2000): 95–114.

Smart Growth Network. *About Smart Growth*. Washington, DC: Sustainable Communities Network, 2007.

South Australian National Football League. 'A New Era for Footy Express'. In *AAMI Stadium News*. Adelaide: SANFL, 2007.

Spirou, C., and L. Bennett. *It's Hardly Sportin': Stadiums, Neighborhoods, and the New Chicago*. DeKalb, IL: Northern Illinois University Press, 2003.

Steg, L. 'Car Use: Lust and Must; Instrumental, Symbolic and Affective Motives for Car Use'. *Transportation Research Part A: Policy and Practice* 39, nos. 2/3 (2005): 147–62.

Thornley, A. 'Urban Regeneration and Sports Stadia'. *European Planning Studies* 10, no. 7 (2002): 813–18.

Urry, J. 'Small Worlds and the New "Social Physics"'. *Global Networks* 4, no. 2 (2004): 109–30.

Urry, J. 'The "System" of Automobility'. *Theory, Culture & Society* 21, nos. 4/5 (2004): 25–39.

van Dam, F. 'Refurbishment, Redevelopment or Relocation? The Changing Form and Location of Football Stadiums in the Netherlands'. *Area* 32, no. 2 (2000): 133–43.

Wassmer, R.W. 'Metropolitan Prosperity from Major League Sports in the CBD: Stadia Locations or Just Strength of the Central City? A Reply to Arthur C. Nelson'. *Economic Development Quarterly* 15, no. 3 (2001): 266–71.

Wittel, A. 'Towards a Network Sociality'. *Theory, Culture and Society* 18, no. 6 (2001): 31–50.

Yago, G. 'The Sociology of Transportation'. *Annual Review of Sociology* 9, no. 1 (1983): 171–90.

'Brave new world' or 'sticky wicket'? Women, management and organizational power in Cricket Australia[1]

Megan Stronach and Daryl Adair

School of Leisure, Sport and Tourism, University of Technology, Sydney, Australia

In 2003 the men's Australian Cricket Board (ACB) and Women's Cricket Australia (WCA) amalgamated to form a gender integrated national body, Cricket Australia. This essay shows that this new organization has served the interests of women well in a number of key areas, including junior development, coaching of talented youth, financial support and scholarships. There have also been modest improvements to the publicity and profile of the women's game. Yet these benefits are, arguably, compromised by an arm's length managerial strategy in which women have little decision-making voice in the state organizations, and are absent from the board of CA itself. The men who run the game of cricket have recourse to substantial amounts of revenue and sponsorship income, which are deployed as they see fit. We argue that if women's cricket is to emerge out of the shadow of the men's game, it is vital to have female representation on the CA board and more generally among state cricket organizations.

Introduction

Hoye and Stewart have rightly observed that 'Australian sporting structures are notoriously difficult to change'. They conclude that such trenchant conservatism is a problem in the Australian context because many of 'our traditional systems of sport management are infected with duplication and inefficiency'.[2] The goal of change is therefore important, even if processes of bringing about reform are typically complex and difficult. Indeed, Hoye and Stewart conclude that 're-structuring and amalgamation issues are some of the most difficult facing sport organisations'.[3] Taking these leads, the following essay analyses change in one of the exemplars of conservatism in Australian sport – the management of cricket. In 2003 the Australian Cricket Board (ACB) and Women's Cricket Australia (WCA) amalgamated to form a new body – Cricket Australia (CA).[4] In one sense, we reveal cricket administrators seeking to overcome what Hoye and Stewart describe as 'management ... infected with duplication'.[5] However, in another sense we demonstrate that there was a range of pressures leading towards merger, and these impacted very differently on WCA and the ACB. Indeed, the subsequent creation of CA, with a board composed entirely of males, remains a stark reflection of fundamental disparities in the participation, profile and power of men and women in cricket. Ongoing dominance of male decision making within the management of the game in Australia was, therefore, not unexpected. But in the context of an integration process – which brought male and female cricket organizations under the same banner – the complete absence of women from executive positions in CA seems, as liberal observers might well put it, 'just not cricket'. Rather than empowering women as decision makers in this 'brave new cricketing world', CA has not allowed females any runs on the managerial board – the equivalent, one might say, of a 'sticky wicket' in cricket parlance.

This deprivation of female influence in the board room of Australian cricket is inconsistent with government-led campaigns to empower women by providing them with opportunities to be decision makers in various managerial contexts. Indeed, the Honourable Julie Bishop, Minister Assisting the Prime Minister for Women's Issues, is emphatic about the need for change: 'The Australian Government is committed to increasing the number of women in leadership roles. This commitment includes increasing the number of women appointed to Australian Government boards and other decision-making bodies.'[6] However, according to a recent report by a government agency, much still needs to be done. The *2006 Australian Census of Women in Leadership* found there were only six (3%) female CEOs in the ASX200;[7] that women held only 12% of executive management positions within this group of companies; and although there were 1,487 available seats at boardroom tables in the ASX200, just 129 were occupied by women (8.7%).[8]

Sport organizations by comparison

In comparing management of sport institutions by gender, there are precedents for pessimism. Historical research shows that Australian sport has long discriminated against females, depriving them of full opportunities.[9] Most pointedly, sociological studies during the early and mid 1990s showed that women had comparatively little managerial voice or authority in supposedly gender-neutral National Sporting Organizations (NSOs) and the Australian Sports Commission (ASC).[10] But, as Adriaanse has recently reported, there have been some changes in the board room.[11] The ASC board jumped from 25% women to 42% women between 1990 and 1996; the Confederation of Australian Sport (CAS) board rose from 13% in 1990 to 30% in 1996; while female general managers or executive directors of NSOs increased from 16% to 25% in the same period.[12] In 2002, the last year in which the ASC published gender statistics for boards under its remit, some of these figures had declined – but nothing quite like the paucity of female representation on boards reported by the ASX200. From that perspective, women in senior sport management have thus made significant strides. Yet this very conclusion makes the omission of females from the CA board all the more startling.[13]

This essay is concerned with gender representation and power in the management of Australian cricket, though it has a particular interest in the place of women in that context. The study will show that the amalgamation of two autonomous, albeit interrelated sport organizations did not come about simply, nor was it a marriage of equals. The ACB was the flagship body for Australian cricket and also represented the interests of men's

Table 1. Female representation in key decision-making positions.

Sport organization	1996	2002	Difference
NSO – Exec Director or General Manager	25%	17%	− 8
NSO – President	13%	19%	+6
AOC – Executive Board	13%	17%	+4
ACGA – Executive Board	0%	25%	+25
CAS – Board	30%	20%	− 10
ASC – Board	42%	41%	− 1

cricket – which dominated the sport. This symbiotic, gendered relationship had been forged over many years and would not easily succumb to change. The co-existence of WCA, which had long represented the interests of women's cricket, accentuated the gender-specific and largely separate management of the game of cricket in Australia. By comparison with the ACB, WCA was an administrative minnow – with a skeleton staff, few resources and little in the way of external financial support. Indeed, as this essay will show, WCA continually relied on the ACB for assistance in a range of key areas, from funding through to the staging of junior development programmes. Hence, although these two organizations existed for the common promotion of the game of cricket, they were fundamentally unequal in size, scope, resources and power. WCA was, in fact, largely dependent on the ACB for its survival. Aside from this benevolent paternalism the two organizations were separate, which reflected the gendered structure and status of cricket. The game had long been dominated by men – in terms of player numbers, administrative strength, media coverage, broadcasting of games and superior resources. At the elite level the contrast was particularly stark: both the Australian men's and women's teams were outstanding performers on the international stage, but only one of these groups was able to make cricket into a career. This was also true of the game's senior administrators: the ACB employed salaried staff while WCA relied on part-time volunteers.[14]

Gender, power, representation

This essay is sociological in its emphasis on gendered power relationships negotiated during change. The study is located within a feminist paradigm, and therefore contributes to a larger body of literature that has highlighted gender disparities and the persistence of male dominance in sport management. Researchers in Australasia, North America and Europe have shown that although governments and their agencies have introduced gender equity policies in sport administration, there has typically been either trenchant resistance to gender inclusive structural change, or resentment towards women who have been 'elevated' after the implementation of affirmative action or gender mainstreaming strategies.[15] Shaw and Penney, for example, found hostility on the part of many existing sports managers towards gender inclusive policies 'imposed upon them' from governments and their agencies. This was particularly so, the authors argued, when state funding was tied to expectations of compliance with such policies – for that typically meant a need for change in the gender balance of management within sports organizations, which threatened the dominant position of men.[16]

Coupled with the issue of gender equity and sport management, this essay is concerned with a particular aspect of governance – organizational change through merger or acquisition.[17] There is a strong body of literature on the phenomenon of amalgamation or takeover of sport leagues, clubs and teams (sometimes involving relocation of one or more party),[18] the integration or acquisition of sports telecasters and their media products,[19] as well as the merger or takeover of manufacturers of sporting goods and apparel.[20] However, there is presently much less research dedicated to the gender dimensions of organizational amalgamations or acquisitions in sport. Yet it is fertile ground for assessments of both long- and short-term change in sports administration. For example, nearly 20 years ago Sport Canada, the federal body responsible for governance of amateur sport, decreed that single-sex national sporting organizations (NSOs) should integrate. This had varying consequences in Canadian college sports. In the relatively gender neutral sport of field hockey, 'provisions were made in the structure of the new sex-integrated NSO to ensure women's continued representation'.[21] By contrast, in traditionally male-dominated ice hockey, women have generally had little voice and even less decision-making power.[22] This helps to explain why at one university 'the budget for the women's ice hockey team was $41,000 (CDN) compared to the budget for the men's team which was over three times that amount at nearly $145,000 (CDN)'.[23]

The sport of soccer, too, has been the subject of single-sex amalgamations and acquisitions in recent years. In the UK the Football Association took 'control' of the women's game from 1992,[24] while in the Antipodes the male-run football body New Zealand Soccer assumed 'entirely ... the control and operation of women's soccer' by the end of 2001.[25] In both cases the female organizations were made redundant. In Australia, female observers generally consider that during the amalgamation of men's and women's sport organizations, women believe they typically have more to lose in the process.[26] Netball Australia's Joyce Brown contends: 'In my experience, in some sports that merge, it is the women's section that is actually taken over and you don't get women in the decision-making area.'[27] Margot Foster offers similar sentiments: 'the impact of amalgamation is that it is more likely than not that the women will back off or acquiesce in a combined organisation leaving the whole organisation in the control of men who may or may not have an interest in the women's side of the sport'.[28] According to Van Sterkenburg and Knoppers, the global media helps to legitimize gender inequities during merger, with female sports managers typically represented 'as strong, but simultaneously as mentally unsure of themselves and as dependent on men'.[29]

Yet it may be the case that gender integration in sport management is preferable to a situation where one or more of the parties risks financial or operational extinction. In the United States, the Association for Intercollegiate Athletes for Women (AIAW) governed women's collegiate athletics between 1960 and 1980, but was defunct by 1982 after the male-run National Collegiate Athletic Association usurped the AIAW role by signing up women's sports to complement its traditional portfolio of commercially lucrative, televised, 'NCAA' products. Rather than inviting the AIAW to function under the NCAA banner, thereby empowering women sports administrators, the NCAA opportunistically embraced women's sports in the early 1980s, in the process eroding the operational capacity of the AIAW. With the implementation of Title IX legislation, the NCAA felt threatened by what it took to be an imminent feminization of the college sporting landscape; the organization also envisaged a wider broadcast audience if it could capture women's sports in its programming.[30] It is ironic, then, that many women's sports and AIAW member colleges acquiesced in, or were persuaded to accept, the demise of their representative body. They soon competed in national championship events run exclusively by the NCAA, which had long boasted major television coverage of many sports. By 1982, NBC cancelled its contract to broadcast sports under the banner of AIAW, and although the latter then sued the NCAA for damages the case was not won. The NCAA has since retained its governance of men's and women's collegiate athletics, but according to feminist critics this assimilationist takeover of female sport by a traditionally male-run organization has had negative consequences in key areas of women's representation – namely coaching, public relations, administration and board membership.[31]

Much of the literature on organizational change emphasizes the underlying importance of interests and values. Reform may be driven by external or internal factors, or a combination of both, but there are always stakeholder interests under negotiation during such a process. While the stated objective of organizational change can, for example, be fiscal savings via economies of scale (i.e. upsizing a company), the costs and benefits of such new arrangements may well impact unevenly on sectors within an organization and among constituent stakeholders. There can be consensus about outcomes, negotiation to modify outcomes, or opposition to outcomes. Organizational reform in sport – whether in a company, volunteer group, or NSO – is therefore inherently political and an exercise of power.[32] Although logic and rationality are often assumed to be central to such decision making, structural factors like position and hierarchy, as well as discursive factors like voice and influence, may be just as critical.[33] As Hoye and Cuskelly conclude: 'power is present in all sport organisations and is used ... to influence decisions, manipulate organisational outcomes, and pursue individual and group self-interests'.[34] The authors then refer to the work of other scholars. Robbins and Barnwell state that power can be conceived egoistically as 'an individual's capacity to influence decisions'.[35] Moreover, according to Slack, power can be construed coercively as 'the ability to get someone to do something they would otherwise have not done'.[36] In the context of the present study, a concluding quote by Hoye and Cuskelly seems particularly apt: 'The nature of the power that an individual [or group] is able to accumulate is only relative to the amount of power held by another actor [or group], and may also vary according to the nature of the decision being taken'.[37] This takes us back to the exercise of power during organizational change; and, in the case of the ACB and WCA, various rationales and pressures to form a single cricket body representing both men and women.

There is extensive literature on mergers and acquisitions in various types of organizations and fields. Much of the research focuses on factors leading to amalgamation or takeover. Here the interest is with the pre-merger status of two (or more) organizations to be put together. There are often substantial differences in power and resources, which typically lead to varying expectations about the role and authority of particular stakeholders in an 'integrated' enterprise.[38] The management of mergers or acquisitions is therefore replete with strategic, economic and political complexities, not the least of which is who will lead a refashioned enterprise and who is expected to follow.[39] If it is a merger of 'equal' partners, then the new entity is likely to reflect this parity of status in its management; the reverse is likely of 'unequal' partnerships. There is also the question of identity: how does a renovated organization represent itself? This is not simply a question of culture and form; it is as much about politics and dominance. The signs and symbols, aims and ideals of a new entity not only position the organization in a broader market or industry, they also circumscribe the place of merged or acquired stakeholder groups within the revamped polity.[40] Finally, researchers point to the importance of post-merger or post-acquisition management. This is an acknowledgment that in practice amalgamations and takeovers are rarely instantaneous; indeed, the change is often a process of trial and adjustment over time.[41] A common thread in the merger scholarship is the goal of synergy and its value to organizational relevance and efficiency. In these respects the recommendations of Terry and O'Brien are instructive:

> In order to reduce intergroup rivalry ... newly merged organizations should engage in efforts to encourage the development of a common ingroup identity. Facilitating intergroup contact that emphasizes cooperative interdependence is one way in which this could be achieved ... as is increasing the salience of a relevant outgroup or competitor, such that 'us' reflects the superordinate identity of the new organization rather than the self-inclusive pre-merger organization ... [where] 'them' resides outside rather than within the new organization.[42]

What type of merger, therefore, was apparent in the formation of CA, and how were males and females both represented and empowered in the management of the organization? Do we see the emergence of Terry and O'Brien's recommended superordinate identity and authority, or the persistence of a self-inclusive, pre-merger decision-making paradigm?

Researching the position of women administrators in Australian cricket

To better understand the changes that came about in the women's side of cricket, it is prudent to examine the administration of the sport from an historical perspective, and to identify key pressures impacting on WCA in the years leading up to creation of CA as a single organization representing both women and men. This approach allows an overview of the distinctive place of women's cricket in the Australian sporting landscape, and ways in which the management and identity of the women's game has evolved today.

To produce an informed analysis, primary data for this study was drawn from both publicly available and privately held documents pertaining to the management of women's cricket in Australia. These included annual reports, policy statements, media releases, committee meeting minutes, letters and emails. The researchers were also able to draw upon commentaries about women's cricket by historians, magazine authors and various Australian newspapers. In order to supplement and substantiate these documents, semi-structured interviews were conducted with key individuals involved in the administration of women's cricket both in the lead up to, and following, amalgamation. Comments were also elicited from a sample of elite women cricketers, both past and present.[43] This documentary and oral archive has enabled the authors to analyse the demise of WCA and its replacement with CA from the perspective of female stakeholders. We begin this analysis with an overview of key historical developments in women's cricket in Australia. This is followed by discussion of specific operational pressures faced by WCA which, when combined, made the looming prospect of merger with the ACB all the more likely – even necessary.

Critical historical milestones

- 1920s – Interstate competition for women's cricket in Australia conceived.
- 1931 – Formation of Women's Cricket Council (AWCC) with founding members Victoria, NSW and Queensland. South Australia, Western Australia, ACT and Tasmania affiliate in subsequent years. Aims of the organization: to promote women's cricket in Australia and to arrange interstate and international matches.
- 1930s – Women's cricket develops soundly during this decade, but the hiatus to sport afflicted by the Second World War reverses growth with the result that women's cricket seems to almost disappear in the two decades after.
- 1970s – Feminist ideology in Australian society brings incremental improvements to gender equity in the workplace, and the notion of 'women's rights' slowly begins to influence sport opportunities for females in a positive manner.[44]
- 1980s and 1990s – The low profile of Australian women in cricket is apparent in the sporting press, when the outstanding performances of the nation's elite level female players appear as virtual footnotes alongside those of the men's game.
- 1994 – 'Annetts affair' shocks the sporting world, and women's cricket becomes the subject of unprecedented media attention, gossip and innuendo. Denise Annetts, an international cricketer with world records in the game, makes a stunning public allegation. As Cashman puts it:

  [Annetts] vented her frustration over her omission from the Australian team by claiming she was dropped because she was heterosexual and married. The whiff of a lesbian scandal in sport attracted a voracious media eager to confirm speculation about the presence of lesbianism in cricket and to cast doubt on the organisational and administrative fairness of the sport's governing body.[45]

Later that year, for the first time since 1937, journalists are assigned to the Australian women's New Zealand tour.[46]

- 1994 – Women's cricket reports growth of interest from players new to the game, many of whom were previously unaware that serious competition for women cricketers even existed.[47] The surge is thought to be helped by a stellar cricketing performance from Australian female all-rounder Zoe Goss, who competes in a high profile celebrity match broadcast on national television. Playing in the otherwise male 'Bradman XI' against a male 'World XI' at the SCG, Goss scores 29 runs and 2-60, and becomes an instant media star after cheaply dismissing world number one batsman Brian Lara.
- 1995 – Favourable media reporting of women's cricket, together with support from the ACB, leads to a number of new developmental initiatives including coaching courses and development programmes. This results in increased numbers of girls and boys participating in school cricket.
- 1997 – Australia wins Women's World Cup. A media conference upon the team's return and a parade for the team at the SCG is organized by the ACB. The AWCC Annual Report describes 'unprecedented media attention', which also highlights 'the importance of ACB support to women's cricket in Australia'.[48]
- The Australian Sports Commission (ASC) facilitates a management improvement workshop for WCA directors and state presidents.
- Zoe Goss is appointed part-time women's cricket promotional officer for the AWCC.
- 1998 – AWCC restructures and changes name to Women's Cricket Australia (WCA).[49] A series of strategic planning workshops result in updating of constitution and by-laws and a full review of the National Development Plan. Market research is undertaken to establish demographic and psychographic profiles of female cricketers, and coaches surveyed for feedback about future planning. For the first time WCA engages a media and public relations company to enhance the profile of the sport.
- April 1998 – WCA conducts a workshop to discuss the pros and cons of WCA-ACB amalgamation.
- 2000 – Susan Crow resigns as Executive Officer of WCA, a position she had held for five years, and Australian cricket team captain Belinda Clark is the new appointee.
- 19 September 2001 – ACB Chairman, Denis Rogers, and WCA President, Quentin Bryce AO, announce that the two organizations will integrate their operations.

Pressures leading to amalgamation

WCA Annual Reports between 1996 and 2000 indicate that there were major stresses on the administration of women's cricket. These included funding and sponsorship problems, coaching and development issues, and, most telling of all, pressure from external bodies to consider amalgamation with men's cricket. Cumulatively, they influenced a decision by WCA to approach the ACB and consider amalgamation of the two organizations. However, the weak pre-merger status of WCA made it vulnerable during negotiations. From a decision-making point of view, the ACB could choose to exploit this situation to safeguard its own power base, or view integration as an opportunity to empower women into areas of policy, influence and authority within a revamped body.

Financial pressure

As Figure 1 illustrates, in the years leading up to amalgamation, WCA received considerable financial support from the ASC and the ACB. During 1996/97 WCA sought a corporate sponsor of its own, planning to use any such revenue to systematically advance the development of women's cricket. However, while a marketing firm had been employed by WCA, these consultants were unable to secure corporate sponsorship for women's cricket. Subsequently, ACB funding was vital to the participation of the Australian team at the 1997 Women's World Cup; the team's involvement without a commercial sponsor was already prohibitive. Indeed, a sense of frustration was apparent in women's cricket ranks, epitomized by an otherwise sympathetic report in the Adelaide *Advertiser*: 'Australia's women cricketers might soon be known as the Southern Scabs, not Southern Stars, because a lack of finances is preventing them playing host to touring sides'.[50] With Australia struggling in a fiscal sense to host international women teams on home soil, it was noted that the resources and funding of England and New Zealand's women's cricket bodies had been strengthened since 1995 by amalgamating with their men's organizations.[51] A seemingly successful precedent had thus been set in other cricket playing nations.

Due to ongoing financial constraints, WCA had only two staff members remaining in 1998. These were Executive Director Susan Crow and Coaching and Development Manager Christina Matthews, both based in ACB offices. This amenable location fostered close working relationships between WCA, the ACB and state men's cricket associations. Indeed, it seems no coincidence that discussions about reform and restructure of the women's game were 'on the table' at this time. Concurrently, though, there had been a significant addition to revenue for women's cricket: corporate sponsorship from the Commonwealth bank of $105,000 per annum for the next three years. WCA's initiative to work with a financial consultant to secure private funding had thus paid off. However, the money was always earmarked for a specific purpose: costs associated with travel and

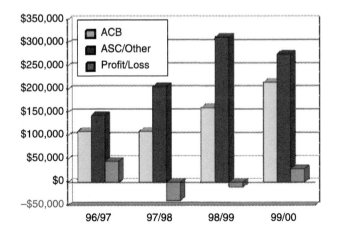

Figure 1. WCA financial situation, 1996–2000

related expenses for the national women's team and the national youth (under 23 years) team.[52] So WCA still relied heavily on the ACB and the ASC for finance to enable it to operate in other areas.

Despite the operating shortfalls of 1998 and 1999, WCA's trading position improved in 2000, and the organization traded slightly in the black.[53] On the face of it, then, the planning and marketing strategies implemented by WCA had been successful. However, the bigger picture was still tenuous. Although sponsorship had been secured to address the expenses of the two elite teams, there was little money available to promote women's cricket at grassroots level. There was, in other words, a continued reliance on the ACB to facilitate local interest in the women's game, and WCA's overall financial situation remained precarious. Could WCA continue to operate by relying on subsidies from the ACB and the ASC? We return to this question momentarily.

Coaching and development

The second major pressure on WCA during the late 1990s was in coaching and development. These areas, vital to the growth of women's cricket, were both driven by the ACB, which provided coaching courses and development programmes open to all young cricketers, boys and girls. By the end of 1997 each state, with the exception of Western Australia, had a women's cricket development officer employed by the state men's cricket association under cooperative arrangements with the women's associations. That intervention provided much needed stability and greater networking opportunities for the regional development officers. Through sponsorship provided by Nestle, the ACB hosted the MILO cup – the Under-16 Girls Cricket Championships, which was the first venture involving WCA and the Australian School Sport Council. Meanwhile, at the elite level, high performance training for women was funded and run through AIS scholarship programmes. In 1998, Coaching and Development Manager Christina Matthews reported candidly: 'There is no doubt that the development of the game for women and girls would be greatly hindered if not for the cooperation of the ACB particularly at the development and coaching level'.[54]

The WCA/ACB alliance in coaching and development activities had worked well for several years. Yet for women's cricket, the overwhelming reliance on ACB funds and management of the coaching and development operation underscored the perennial problem that WCA was not able to function independently as an NSO. If anything, the collaboration provided substance to the argument that a permanent alliance between WCA and the ACB was needed. As Susan Crow conceded, an amalgamation arrangement would 'allow the women's game, now run by a handful of people across Australia, to tap into the ACB's resources and expertise'.[55] Yet there was no prospect of an 'amalgamation of equals', something that Crow freely admitted: women's cricket is 'going to be a cost for the ACB ... until we are in a position to attract the crowds and television audiences they do'.[56]

Pressure from external bodies

The third pressure on WCA was imposed by external funding and accreditation bodies. During the late 1990s the ASC made it clear to single gender organizations operating dual gender sports, that it expected them to merge their operations or risk losing Commonwealth funding. In its report *Amalgamation Guidelines for Recreation and Sporting Organisations* (1997), the ASC argued for managerial efficiencies associated with NSO amalgamations.[57] This view was given particular encouragement by the federal government which, via the ASC, posited neo-liberal economic advantages for dual sex sports moving to a single, combined bureaucracy.[58] Indeed, several dual gender sports in Australia have now amalgamated their men's and women's associations: field hockey, soccer, lawn bowls and most recently golf. These developments have varied considerably according to sport, and warrant full treatment in their own right by way of further research.[59] For example, in 2002 the integration of lawn bowls came after what *The Daily Telegraph* describes as 'five years of wrangling, haggling, backbiting and mistrust'.[60] In amateur golf, *The Age* reported in 2005 that amalgamation between men and women 'was forced by the Government's funding arm, the ASC, which told the two bodies it would withdraw its funding of more than $1 million a year by June 30 unless the union could be conceived'.[61] In the context of the present study, a key point is that women's sport organizations with similar player numbers to their respective men's association, such as hockey and lawn bowls, were in a better bargaining position in terms of amalgamation than situations where female numbers were comparatively small.[62] The latter case applied in cricket – a traditionally male-dominated sport. Fully cognizant of this state of affairs, independent WCA Board member Phillip Endersbee commented:

> The Federal government is putting pressure through the Sports Commission on sports bodies. They want to provide funding through one national organisation … but it's a huge challenge to merge a women's sport with one of the last male bastions and make sure that it retains its own personality.[63]

So WCA approached the ACB in an unenviable position, interpreting the amalgamation process as necessary simply for the survival of women's cricket. In a paper entitled 'A Partnership in Cricket', WCA President Quentin Bryce outlined her belief that, on balance, an integrated approach to the management of cricket could be beneficial to both organizations.[64] But by that time WCA was so financially dependent on the ACB that it is difficult to imagine that it would have much clout to achieve this vision of a male-female 'partnership' in cricket. By the year 2000, amalgamation of WCA and the ACB had been on the agenda of each sport organization for several years, so it was no surprise to insiders when Bryce and the ACB Chairman, Denis Rogers, announced a trial merger between the two. The WCA Board had been developing a proposal for amalgamation as part of a *Draft Heads of Agreement* for some time.[65] And it was noted in the *WCA Board Meeting Minutes* of 30 June 2000 that a number of 'sticking points' with the ACB had been identified, and further work would be needed by WCA to develop a document acceptable to the ACB.[66]

This comment could be seen as a sign of WCA's precarious position – it seemed an admission that the organization needed to 'toe the line' with the ACB. Outwardly WCA looked forward with optimism to a 'partnership in cricket', but inwardly these female administrators feared a male takeover of their association. Yet the writing was on the wall: WCA was about to enter the reform process from an unfavourable bargaining position.

Trial integration

In September 2001, a trial integration of the two organizations was announced. The WCA executive announced to its female constituents anticipated benefits, such as opportunities to streamline the administration of cricket, further development of the game at all levels, more efficient and effective use of resources, reduction of financial pressures on touring teams, and improved access to, and use of, facilities. Henceforth WCA would be known simply as Women's Cricket, a programme of the ACB, and the Women's Cricket logo would no longer be used. Overseeing the transition would be the newly created Women's Cricket Advisory Committee (WCAC), to be chaired by the WCA President. Its role would be to make recommendations to the ACB's Board of Directors on matters affecting the fulfilment by the ACB of its obligations as agreed in the Heads of Agreement and be responsible for ensuring that the two bodies were able to merge successfully. This committee included three representatives from the ACB as well as representatives from the states and the ACT.[67]

Although WCA had entered the amalgamation process somewhat 'cap-in-hand', the WCAC provided a forum to advocate for the needs of women within the new structure. But even at this early point there was a peculiar lack of WCA representation – other than the chair. However, Ms Rina Hore, who was both a Vice President of WCA and a Cricket NSW Board member, was soon appointed to the committee, and meetings were also attended by Dr Julie Savage (Vic. delegate), Christine Garwood (SA delegate) and Belinda Clark (who by then was re-employed by the ACB in the position of Women's Cricket Operations Manager).

The role of the WCAC on amalgamation

Curiously, according to minutes of meetings of this group (for example, *Meeting Minutes of 20 September 2002*),[68] it appears that the WCAC focused principally on operational matters, rather than issues pertaining to the amalgamation. The latter, it seems, were handled by a self-appointed body of stakeholders. This sub-group comprised Ms Bryce, Ms Hore and Mr Brian Freedman, each of whom was a WCA Board member, as well as ACB management executives Mr Ross Turner, Ms Belinda Clark and later Mr James Sutherland. While that collective was not formally appointed, the arrangement did ensure active involvement of key WCA board members in the amalgamation discussions.[69]

Given WCA's vulnerability at the time of the trial integration process, it is difficult to understand why it had put itself in an even weaker position by not ensuring equal representation on the committee formed to oversee integration of the game's management (the WCAC). Inexplicably, during the two-year trial period the WCAC met only five times, well short of the scheduled eight meetings. This was puzzling. This body was, after all, formed to 'provide direction of specific women's cricket issues as they [arise]',[70] and an early topic for debate was that of pregnancy among players – certainly a specific concern of females. It was also unclear about the degree to which women would have a managerial voice within a merged WCA-ACB structure. With this issue in mind, a Women's Cricket Reference Group (WCRG) was formed to review the ongoing strategic direction of women's cricket nationally in the new structure. This body was chaired by ACB Director Tony Harrison and comprised Mr Tony Steele, Dr Harry Harinath, Ms Rina Hore, Dr Julie Savage and Ms Jo Broadbent – all high-profile individuals with long-standing interest and expertise in women's cricket.[71]

Brave new world? Cricket Australia

On 2 April 2003 the ACB reported to its directors that the trial integration had, in its view, been successful, and recommended that 'women's cricket (be) permanently integrated into the Australian Cricket Board effective as of 1 July 2003'.[72] Referring back to WCA's expectations of amalgamation, the ACB was able to list benefits that had resulted from the trial. Women's cricket had been embraced in the overall strategic direction of Australian cricket – as evidenced in the 2002/04 strategic plan *From*

Backyard to Baggy Green. This initiative was consistent with the ACB's mission statement which sought to advance cricket as Australia's national sport. Specifically, strategic initiative 3.5 'Nurture and Grow Women's Cricket' aimed to extend cricket to women and girls with the view to increasing overall national participation in the game. Moreover, bringing more females into cricket was expected to raise the volume of cricket consumers, such as by purchasing CA merchandise. Women's cricket operations had been successfully integrated into ACB operations through the Game Development area, while human and material resources had been effectively utilized through high performance cricket programmes, namely the ACB Centre of Excellence and sports science and sports medicine programs.[73]

WCA was formally dissolved at a special meeting on 20 June 2003. Assets (some $219,000) were distributed to the ACB. The AWCC Jubilee Fund, with a balance of $3,037, was distributed to the ACB, this time specifically for the purpose of providing disadvantaged females with an opportunity to access cricket. The ACB Annual Report of 2002/03 stated that WCA had now officially integrated with the ACB after its two-year trial period and Chairman Bob Merriman noted that, 'cricket will only prosper as a national sport if it appeals to and is supported by all Australian regardless of gender or background'.[74] From 1 July 2003 the ACB changed its name to Cricket Australia (CA) and adopted a new logo and slogan, 'Long Live Cricket!' The organization's vision at the time was 'Cricket – Australia's favourite sport'. As a project within the Cricket Operations Department, discussion of women's cricket is now included in the CA annual report, and the front cover of that document now includes action photographs of female cricketers alongside their male counterparts.

As Table 2 indicates, the ACB was able to report significant financial and administrative benefits stemming from the initial merger phase. However, numbers can be read in various ways. The increase in female numbers of 18% between 2002/03 and 2003/04 is impressive. Yet the most startling increase in women cricketers came well before merger. Between 1997/98 and 1998/99 female participation in cricket rose 41%. This was, no doubt, due in no small part to ACB support of junior programmes and so on. But WCA still had to run competitions for girls and women, and sustain the rising interest in cricket among females. In short, although WCA was run by a skeleton staff, they were certainly competent – but resource poor.

Table 2. Benefits of amalgamation.[75]

Sponsorship increased by:	$93,000
Administrative savings:	$160,000
Investments to teams increased by:	$211,000
Participation numbers increased by:	18%
Merged state/territory bodies:	4 (Qld, Tasmania, ACT, NT)

Perspectives of female stakeholders

In the WCA Annual Report of 2002–03, President Bryce admitted 'feeling cautious' about pending merger arrangements.[76] She was especially concerned with a need to preserve traditions: 'One of the very big challenges for cricket is to maintain the lovely traditions and history but being able to change, being thoroughly contemporary, being relevant, being inclusive.'[77] Private communication between past WCA board members reveals personal feelings of sadness at the demise of a women's organization for cricket. One admitted candidly: 'From my very personal perspective, I grieved some years ago for the

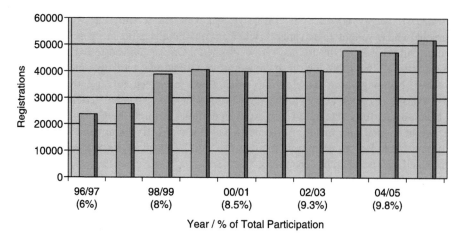

Figure 2.   Females participating in cricket in Australia 1996–2006.
Sources: WCA, *Annual Reports 1996/97, 1997/98, 1998/99, 1999/2000*; ACB, *Annual Report 2001/02*; Cricket Australia, *National Cricket Census 2002/03, 2003/04, 2004/05*.

AWCC/WCA I knew. But I accept the inevitability [of change] and now look forward to a bright future.'[78]

Interviews with current and former elite level players revealed a 'realist' rather than an 'idealist' position about the future of top level women's cricket. In terms of changes to the game's administration, most women were generally accepting and confident about handing over the reins of management to male control. The interviewees did not automatically expect their game to have a profile like men's cricket, nor did they demand gender-blind distribution of available resources or payment of salaries. Respondents were typically pragmatic and optimistic. One commented:

> The amalgamation of Women's Cricket and Cricket Australia has certainly assisted in the growth of the game. Financial assistance and the commitment from State Associations are positive and Cricket Australia is continuing to educate those States. Some do it better than others but with our National body's support it will continue to be positive.

Another interviewee saw growth stemming from the new arrangements:

> That fact that women's cricket is now integrated with the ACB would probably be the main reason [for the current growth]. Instead of things being run by amateurs, there is a professional group managing the game throughout the country.

A minority of interviewees sounded words of caution:

> When you are struggling each week for players this [idea of rapid growth] seems far from the truth. However I do believe the profile in schools has improved. Integration with the men's cricket is not all positive but I think at a grass roots level has helped to raise the profile and awareness of cricket as sport that can be enjoyed by women and girls.

Most typical was the 'time will tell' philosophy:

> It [the administration] is a bit in the air at the moment. I think we need some time for integration to kick in. To see if working with the men can bring advantages of which it already has. The new form of administration needs the time to work out the problems and where the needs will be.[79]

Many respondents seemed content with the support they were receiving from CA, even though it was at a much lower level than that of their male colleagues. Comments included 'we are supported well by Cricket Australia', 'recent integration ... has aided players financially', and 'you don't have to pay anything and you can actually win money'. However, several interviewees called for better promotion of their sport and their national team: 'we don't get the same recognition', 'the sport may grow if they publicise it more than they do now', and 'we need our national team to be recognised, celebrated and promoted more through Cricket Australia and the media in order to attract more interest and more players for the future'. A senior player commented: 'If we want women's cricket to improve we need more tours and financial support, and more training in order for us to get better, play longer and start attracting spectators'.[80]

A seat at the table?

The attitude of the men's cricket organizations towards the proposed WCA-ACB amalgamation is most significant. In light of external pressure being brought to bear on both organizations to amalgamate, it would not have been surprising to find that the men accepted amalgamation on their terms as a 'fait accompli', or that they really had nothing to lose. Yet according to interviews with David Johnston, Chief Executive of the Tasmanian Cricket Association, this was not the case. Johnston believes that while there was some initial reluctance from a few members of the 'old guard', the more forward-thinking administrators within the organization viewed the amalgamation as a major opportunity to further the development of cricket, and the best way forward for the game. The ACB planned to promote cricket as Australia's favourite sport, and in order to do this, their plans needed to include the women's game. Therefore, they foresaw major benefits to cricket from the proposed new structure. Some of the men experienced reservations about the costs involved in setting up new structures for amalgamation, but most felt that in the long term this would be a strategic investment for the future of cricket.[81] Clearly this new arrangement handed the men's organization an unprecedented opportunity to market the game even more broadly, with a view to increasing not only participation numbers but also consumers of the sport across both genders.

What about women involved in the merger process? Key female officials do not believe that they merely 'acquiesced' to the ACB's requirements. However, David Johnston admits that 'a little massaging of egos was needed to avoid conflicts' throughout the integration process.[82] Belinda Clark recalls that difficult discussions were 'resolved with underlying goodwill as both sides wanted the integration to be effective'.[83] Yet women now have little clout in all decision-making areas. This is undoubtedly due to the lack of women at CA and state board levels, which is symptomatic of a more general problem for female representation in dual gender sporting organizations. 'But', says Johnston, 'including women members on the national and state Game Development and Women's Cricket sub-committees is helping women's point of view to be put forward'.[84] Clark agrees, believing that 'in an ideal world WCA would [be represented at board level. This was the major thing that was compromised during the [integration] processes.'[85] She also commented on the increased number of women contributing to the sport as a whole, not just to women's cricket: 'Females are more involved now than previously and this can only serve to assist to "un-marginalise" the game. Changing attitudes on both men's and women's side of the game takes time and a concerted effort from people in key roles.'[86]

All that said, the recent Parliament of Australia Senate Report, *About Time! Women in Sport and Recreation in Australia*, reveals the following figures, which underscore management inequities by gender in key Australian sports. We use the dual gender sports of hockey and cricket to make statistical comparisons.

Comparative figures: women at board level

- NSOs: National average 1 female to 7 males.
- Hockey Australia: Neither gender to constitute less than 35% on board.
- Cricket Australia: Women have a 1 in 98 female representation at board level.[87]

Comparative figures: women in senior management

- NSOs: 13% women in senior management in top 40 funded NSOs.
- Hockey Australia: 10.2% females in senior management.
- Cricket Australia: 2 out of 44 CEOs or senior management staff are female (7%).[88]

In cricket, therefore, women are clearly underrepresented in managerial roles. This appears to suggest that there are plenty of men deemed capable of holding a board or committee seat in cricket, but few women are considered to have similar ability. Current exceptions to this trend are Rina Hore, a Director of Cricket NSW, Belinda Clark, Manager of the Cricket Centre of Excellence in Queensland, and Christina Matthews, Marketing Manager for Cricket NSW. However, as we have seen from interviews in this study, few female stakeholders seem particularly concerned about a lack of 'female' voices in CA. They have, of course, long been in the shadow of men in cricket culture and administration. It may be difficult, in that context, for them to view women as 'natural' managers of Australia's major summer sport. Indeed, the absence of women from contemporary cricket management seems an international phenomenon. The England Cricket Board became a dual gender body in 1998, but there are no females on the board. The best that can be said is that of four 'regional development officers', two are women.[89] Even the International Cricket Council, which like the ASC is pushing for all its national organizations to become gender amalgamated,[90] does not have a female representative on its board![91] It seems that New Zealand leads the way: gender integrated management of cricket began in 1998 and the New Zealand Cricket Board has one female member out of a total of eight.[92]

In Australia, change appears to be in the wind. CA's 2007 'Females in Cricket' strategy notes an intention to 'appoint at least one female on all Australian Cricket Boards by June 2009 based on merit'.[93] It remains to be seen whether this intention turns out to be more than just lip service, as there is no mention of constitutional changes to mandate that goal. It may indeed be up to the Australian federal government to mandate gender reform in sport management, as has already been done in Norway, where since 1987 a minimum proportion of women board members has been expected in dual gender sports with a single administration.[94] The Commonwealth has, indeed, recently put money into the development of females in sport via the programme Sports Leadership Grants for Women (2007/08), totalling $400,000 with 176 successful applicants in fields such as coaching, management and governance.[95] The IOC, too, has recognized that its male-dominated management structure needs gender reform. In 1996, 'as part of its Women and Sport Policy, the IOC set targets for women's membership of National Olympic Committees and International Sporting Federations ... at least 10% female representation by Dec 2000 increasing to 20% by Dec 2005'.[96] Adriaanse notes that these figures have not been met: in 2007 there were only 16 women (13.9%) among a total of 115 IOC members, and there is presently only one woman on the IOC board of 15 persons.[97] But at least there are aspirational targets.

The ASC is critical to improvements in the role and status of women in leadership positions within sport. It has announced several policy initiatives and programmes to improve governance in sport and the effectiveness of boards in NSOs, and women have been included in this dialogue.[98] Most notably, in 2003 the ASC organized *Sport Needs More Women: A National Forum for the Sports Industry*. This two-day symposium brought together some 250 participants, at which ASC CEO Mark Peters emphasized that, 'Australia would be best served by a sporting culture that enabled and valued the full involvement of women in every aspect of sport'.[99] Two key initiatives emerged from the conference:

1. The National Leadership Program – a senior leadership training programme for women designed to prepare them for board and senior leadership positions in sport.
2. The National Industry Framework on Women and Sport – will provide sporting organizations with benchmarks to track their progress in boosting the involvement of women in all aspects of sport.[100]

Four years after the creation of CA, some positive signs have emerged. The women's cricket website has been updated – for the first time in six years. A new logo for women's cricket has appeared. Some states are making match payments to their elite female teams and women are finally assured of a voice on their own reference committee, now known as the 'Females in Cricket' reference committee. The structure of this committee emanated from the 2007 strategic review of women's cricket by CA, but the committee will, for the foreseeable future, continue to comprise a majority of male decision-makers.[101] At least the women's cricket selection panel, which is responsible for choosing representatives for the Southern Stars and the Shooting Stars (under-23 national youth team), now includes long-time female stalwarts of the game, Marg Jennings (chair), Wendy Weir and Christina Matthews. So women's representation has improved in this operational area. The Women's World Cup to be played in Australia in 2009 will provide an excellent opportunity to promote the women's game. Hopefully, women will be actively involved in top-level planning, marketing and management of this global cricket event.

Conclusion

The amalgamation of WCA and ACB was virtually inevitable owing to the pressures and policies outlined in this essay. But the manner in which amalgamation took place was open to negotiation, as were the consequences of amalgamation. From an outsider's perspective the amalgamation of men's and women's cricket therefore appears to be little more than a capitulation by the women's organization. The women wanted to develop a 'partnership in cricket' but instead appear to have bent over backwards to comply with the requirements of the men's organization. The men wanted cricket to become the country's most popular sport, and the amalgamation provided them with an enormous opportunity to increase both participation and consumer numbers. From an insider's perspective, many women recognized the dependence of women's cricket on the men's organization and most therefore believe their sport has improved as a result of the amalgamation.

Certainly the amalgamation strategy had good intentions, but we maintain that in managerial terms the outcome has been more of a takeover. Women's cricket scarcely has a voice within CA – certainly at the upper levels of management. Meanwhile, the Australian women's cricket team continues remarkable ongoing success with win/loss ratios over the past 10 years of 80% in test matches, 88% in ODIs and 100% in Twenty20 matches. However, in CA's current opinion, the women's game 'continues to drift along with low public awareness and limited commercial appeal'.[102] So 'more of the same', despite CA's superior managerial, marketing and promotional resources.

Notes

[1] In this essay we use the terms merger, amalgamation and integration interchangeably. This is a stylistic device: the common meaning we attribute to these words are 'any combination of two or more enterprises into a single enterprise'. *Random House Unabridged Dictionary*. The underlying nature and complexity of combining enterprises are discussed later in the essay.

[2] Hoye and Stewart, 'Power and Organisational Change', 63.

[3] Ibid.

[4] Prior to 1998, Women's Cricket Australia (WCA) was known as the Australian Women's Cricket Council (AWCC). For the convenience of readers, we have referred singularly to WCA except where specific reference to AWCC helps inform the essay.

[5] Hoye and Stewart, 'Power and Organisational Change', 63.

[6] *Appoint Women: An Australian Government Initiative*. http://www.appoint women.gov.au/about/minister.htm.

[7] The ASX 200 refers to the top 200 companies listed on the Australian Stock Exchange in a particular year.

[8] Equal Opportunity for Women in the Workplace Agency (EOWA), *The 2006 Australian Census of Women in Leadership*.

[9] King, 'The Sexual Politics of Sport'; Thompson, '"Thank the Ladies for the Plates"'; Stell, *Half the Race*, 250–70; Randall, 'Women and Sport in Australia'; Lenskyj, 'Sport and the Threat to Gender Boundaries'; Burroughs and Nauright, 'Women's Sports and Embodiment in Australia and New Zealand'; Cashman, *Paradise of Sport*, 72–91; Phillips, *Australian Women at the Olympic Games*; Adair and Vamplew, *Sport in Australian History*, 48–62.

[10] Australia, Parliament, House of Representatives, Standing Committee on Legal and Constitutional Affairs. Equity for women in sport: a joint seminar – held by the House of representatives Standing Committee on Legal and Constitutional Affairs and the Australian Sports Commission, Parliament House, Canberra, ACT Wednesday 27 February and Thursday 28 February 1991 (official Hansard Report); McKay, *Why so Few?*; McKay, 'Masculine Hegemony'; McKay, *Managing Gender*.

[11] Adriaanse, '"A Seat at the Table"'.

[12] Adriaanse's figures are drawn from the Australian Sports Commission (ASC) report *Benchmark Data Summary*.

[13] Adriaanse, '"A Seat at the Table"'.

[14] Cashman and Weaver, *Wicket Women*; Burroughs, Seebohm and Ashburn, 'Add Sex and Stir'; Burroughs, Seebohm and Ashburn, 'A "Leso Story"'.

[15] McKay, *Managing Gender*; Rintala and Bischoff, 'Persistent Resistance', Welch, *Towards Gender Equity in Sports Management*; Aitchison, Jordan and Brackenridge, 'Women in Leisure Management'; Shaw and Slack, '"It's Been Like That for Donkey's Years"'; Whisenant, Pedersen and Obenour, 'Success and Gender'; Rees, 'A New Strategy'; Aitchison, 'Feminist and Gender Research'; Shaw, 'Gender Suppression'; Shaw and Frisby, 'Can Gender Equity be More Equitable?'; Hoeber, '"It's Somewhere on the List"'; Password, 'Exploring the Gaps'.

[16] Shaw and Penney, 'Gender Equity Policies'.

[17] In this essay we use the terms acquisition or takeover interchangeably. This is a stylistic device: the common meaning we attribute to these words are 'the act or action of acquiring; *specifically*: the obtaining of controlling interest in a company' (emphasis in the original). *Merriam-Webster's Dictionary of Law*. These phenomena range considerably: from 'friendly' acquisitions involving agreement from two or more parties, through to 'hostile' takeovers where there is disagreement by one or more party.

[18] For examples on three continents, see Phillips and Nauright, 'Sports Fan Movements to Save Suburban-based Football Teams'; Duke and Renson, 'From Factions to Fusions?'; Stevens, 'The Canadian Hockey Association Merger'.

[19] Andrews, 'Sport and the Transnationalizing Media Corporation'; Grainger and Andrews, 'Resisting Rupert Through Sporting Rituals?'; Warf, 'Oligopolization of Global Media and Telecommunications'.

[20] M. Tran, 'Adidas to Take Over Rival Reebok'. *Guardian Unlimited*, August 3, 2005. http://www.guardian.co.uk/business/2005/aug/03/money1; Reuters, 'Germany's Puma Leaps on French Bid'. *Spiegel Online International*, April 10, 2007. http://www.spiegel.de/international/business/0,1518,476389,00.html.

[21] Lenskyj, 'Whose Sport?', 147.

[22] Adams and Stevens, 'Change and Grassroots Movement'.

[23] Hoeber and Frisby, 'Gender Equity for Athletes', 192.

[24] Williams, 'The Fastest Growing Sport?', 121.

[25] Cox and Thompson, 'From Heydays to Struggles', 222.

[26] Phillips, 'How Hockey Avoided Merger Meltdown'.

[27] Brown, J. quoted in M. O'Regan (ed.), 'Football Culture, Netball Culture'. *The Sports Factor*, ABC Radio National, 15 March 2002. http://www.abc.net.au/rn/sportsfactor/stories/2002/505198.htm.

[28] Foster, 'Women in a Sporting Administration Environment', 8.

[29] Van Sterkenburg and Knoppers, 'Dominant Discourses', 303.

[30] Title IX legislation is a United States law enacted on 23 June 1972, that states: 'No person in the United States shall, on the basis of sex, be excluded from participation in, be denied the benefits of, or be subjected to discrimination under any education program or activity receiving federal financial assistance'.

[31] Jensen, 'Women's Collegiate Athletics'; Lopiano, 'A Political Analysis'; Hult, 'Women's Struggle for Governance in US Amateur Athletics'; Lovett and Lowry, 'Women and the NCAA'; Whisenant, Pedersen and Obenour, 'Success and Gender'.

[32] Kikulis, Slack and Hinings, 'Toward an Understanding of the Role of Agency and Choice'; Kikulis, Slack and Hinings, 'Does Decision Making Make a Difference?'; Auld, 'Professionalisation of Australian Sport'; Skinner, Stewart and Edwards, 'Amateurism to Professionalism'; Hill and Kikulis, 'Contemplating Restructuring'; Kikulis, 'Continuity and Change'; Amis, Slack and Hinings, 'Values and Organizational Change'.

[33] Edwards, Gilbert and Skinner, *Extending the Boundaries*, 57–67.

[34] Hoye and Cuskelly, 'Board Power and Performance', 103.

[35] Robbins and Barnwell, *Organisation Theory*, 223.

[36] Slack, *Understanding Sport Organizations*, 179.

[37] Hoye and Cuskelly, 'Board Power and Performance', 103.

[38] Pfeffer, 'Merger as a Response to Organizational Interdependence'; Giessner *et al.*, 'The Challenge of Merging'.

[39] Seo and Hill, 'Understanding the Human Side of Merger and Acquisition'.

[40] Olie, 'Shades of Culture'; Terry and O'Brien, 'Status, Legitimacy, and Ingroup Bias'.

[41] Cusella, '"Managing after the Merger"'; Boen, Vanbeselaere and Cool, 'Group Status'.

[42] Terry and O'Brien, 'Status, Legitimacy, and Ingroup Bias', 287.

[43] Full transcripts of these interviews are held by the lead author.

[44] Cashman, *Paradise of Sport*, 72–91.

[45] Cashman *et al.* (eds), *The Oxford Companion to Australian Cricket*, 596. For detailed analysis of women's cricket, media and sexuality, see Burroughs, Seebohm and Ashburn, 'Add Sex and Stir'; Burroughs, Seebohm and Ashburn, 'A "Leso Story"'.

[46] Burroughs, Seebohm and Ashburn, 'A "Leso Story"', 33.

[47] Ibid., 41.

[48] WCA, *Annual Report, 1997/98*, 7.

[49] Cashman and Weaver, *Wicket Women*, 82–3, 149; WCA, *Annual Report, 1997/98*; Official Home Page of Women's Cricket in Australia: http://www.southernstars.org.au/wca.htm.

[50] N. Tugwell, 'Host of Problems for [Southern] Stars'. *Advertiser*, December 29, 2000.

[51] Ibid.; Thompson, 'Girls Don't Just Want to Have Fun'.

[52] WCA, *Annual Report, 1998/1999*.

[53] WCA, *Annual Report, 1999/2000*.

[54] WCA, *Annual Report, 1997/1998*.

[55] C. Saltau, 'Women's Cricket to Join with ACB'. *The Age*, November 9, 1999.

[56] Ibid.

[57] ASC, *Amalgamation Guidelines*.
[58] Environment, Communications, Information Technology and the Arts Reference Committee, *Women in Sport and Recreation in Australia*.
[59] A brief synopsis can be found in Cooke, 'All Together Now'.
[60] R. Kershler, 'Bias Put to Rest in New Bowls Amalgamation'. *The Daily Telegraph*, July 16, 2002.
[61] M. Blake, 'Golf's Peak Amateur Bodies to Amalgamate – Golf'. *The Age*, February 16, 2005. See also M. Blake, 'Cash Threat Over Amalgamation Deadlock – Golf'. *The Age*, January 22, 2005; M. Blake, 'Amalgamation Forces Phillips to Quit – Golf'. *The Age*, June 1, 2005.
[62] Bartlett, 'Amalgamation of Men's and Women's Sports'; Phillips, 'How Hockey Avoided Merger Meltdown'.
[63] Endersbee, quoted in Trethewey, 'Putting the Runs on the Board', 28.
[64] WCA, *Annual Report 1999/2000*, 5.
[65] 'Boards Talk of Amalgamation'. *Australian*, December 26, 2000.
[66] WCA, *Board Meeting Minutes*, 30 July 2000.
[67] ACB/WCA, 'Draft Heads of Agreement', 1 July 2001, 2–3.
[68] ACB, *Minutes Women's Cricket Advisory Committee*, 20 September 2002, 2.
[69] ACB, *Report to Directors*, 23 May 2003, 1.
[70] WCA, *Report to WCA Members: Women's Cricket Reference Group*, 28 May 2003, 2.
[71] ACB, *Annual Report 2002/2003*, 15.
[72] ACB, *Report to Directors*, 3 April 2003, 3.
[73] Ibid., 4.
[74] ACB, *Annual Report 2002/2003*, 5.
[75] ACB, *Report to Directors*, 3 April 2003, 3.
[76] 'Boards Talk of Amalgamation'.
[77] http://www.southernstars.org.au/wca.htm.
[78] Written correspondence between WCA members, 17 June 2003, held by the lead author.
[79] Full transcripts of these interviews are held by the lead author.
[80] Ibid.
[81] Johnston, personal communication with lead author, 15 May 2006.
[82] Ibid.
[83] Clark, personal communication with lead author, 22 May 2006.
[84] Johnston, personal communication with lead author, 15 May 2006.
[85] Clark, personal communication lead author, 22 May 2006.
[86] Ibid.
[87] Parliament of Australia Senate Report, *About Time!*, 77.
[88] Ibid., 95.
[89] 'ECB Structure'. http://www.ecb.co.uk/ecb/about/ecb-structure,28,BP.html.
[90] Patwardhan, 'Women Seek BCCI's Expertise'.
[91] 'ICC Structure and Contacts'. 30 October 2007. http://icc-cricket.yahoo.com/about-icc/executive.html.
[92] 'NZ Cricket Organisation Chart'. http://www.blackcaps.co.nz/content/corporate/publications/ORGCHARTAugust2007.pdf.
[93] CA, 'Females in Cricket', 111.
[94] Hovden, 'From Rights-based to Utility-based Equalization'.
[95] 'More Australian Women Take up the Challenge of Sports Leadership'. ASC media release, September 7, 2007. http://www.ausport.gov.au/fulltext/2007/ascmedia/07.09.07.asp.
[96] Adriaanse, '"A Seat at the Table"', 6.
[97] Ibid.
[98] ASC, *Sport Innovation and Best Practice*; ASC, *Governing Sport*; ASC, *Submission to the Senate*; Office for Women, Australian Government, 'Advancing Women in Leadership'. http://ofw.facs.gov.au/downloads/pdfs/decade_of_achievements_women_leadership.pdf.
[99] 'Australian Sports Commission Events: Sport Needs More Women 2003'. http://www.ausport.gov.au/events/womensforum2003/index.asp.
[100] Ibid.
[101] CA, 'Females in Cricket', 100, 108.
[102] Ibid., 84.

References

Adair, D., and W. Vamplew. *Sport in Australian History*. Melbourne: Oxford University Press, 1997.

Adams, C., and J. Stevens. 'Change and Grassroots Movement: Reconceptualising Women's Hockey Governance in Canada'. *International Journal of Sport Management and Marketing* 2, no. 4 (2007): 344–61.

Adriaanse, J. '"A Seat at the Table": Experiences and Contributions of Women on Sport Boards'. Doctoral Assessment Seminar Paper, Faculty of Business, University of Technology Sydney, 9 November 2007.

Aitchison, C.C. 'Feminist and Gender Research in Sport and Leisure Management: Understanding the Social-cultural Nexus of Gender-power Relations'. *Journal of Sport Management* 19, no. 4 (2005): 422–41.

Aitchison, C.C., F. Jordan, and C. Brackenridge. 'Women in Leisure Management: A Survey of Gender Equity'. *Women in Management Review* 14, no. 4 (1999): 121–7.

Amis, J., T. Slack, and C.R. Hinings. 'Values and Organizational Change'. *Journal of Applied Behavioral Science* 38, no. 4 (2002): 436–65.

Andrews, D.L. 'Sport and the Transnationalizing Media Corporation'. *Journal of Media Economics* 16, no. 4 (2003): 235–51.

ASC. *Amalgamation Guidelines for Recreation and Sporting Organisations*. Canberra: ASC, 1997.

ASC. *Benchmark Data Summary – Female Representation in Sport*. Canberra: ASC, 2003.

ASC. *Sport Innovation and Best Practice – Governance*. Canberra: ASC, 2004.

ASC. *Governing Sport: The Role of the Board*. Canberra: ASC, 2005.

ASC. *Submission to the Senate Inquiry into Women in Sport and Recreation in Australia*. Canberra: ASC, 2006.

Auld, C. 'Professionalisation of Australian Sport: The Effects on Organisational Decision Making'. *European Journal for Sport Management* 4, no. 2 (1997): 17–39.

Bartlett, J. 'Amalgamation of Men's and Women's Sports: Case Study, Queensland and Hockey Three Years on'. In *Competing Interests in Sport: Proceedings of the 8th Annual ANZSLA Conference, Queenstown NZ, August 1998*, 60. Essendon, VIC: ANZSLA, 1999.

Boen, F., N. Vanbeselaere, and M. Cool. 'Group Status as a Determinant of Organizational Identification After a Takeover: A Social Identity Perspective'. *Group Processes and Intergroup Relations* 9, no. 4 (2006): 547–60.

Burroughs, A., and J. Nauright. 'Women's Sports and Embodiment in Australia and New Zealand'. *International Journal of the History of Sport* 17, nos. 2–3 (2000): 188–205.

Burroughs, A., L. Seebohm, and L. Ashburn. 'Add Sex and Stir: Homophobic Coverage of Women's Cricket in Australia'. *Journal of Sport and Social Issues* 8, no. 19 (1995): 266–84.

Burroughs, A., L. Seebohm, and L. Ashburn. 'A "Leso Story": A Case Study of Australian Women's Cricket and its Media Experience'. *Sporting Traditions* 12, no. 1 (1995): 27–46.

CA. 'Females in Cricket: Background Strategy Document'. Jolimont, VIC: CA, 2007.

Cashman, R., and A. Weaver. *Wicket Women: Cricket and Women in Australia*. Sydney: NSW University Press, 1991.

Cashman, R. *Paradise of Sport: The Rise of Organised Sport in Australia*. Melbourne: Oxford University Press, 1995.

Cashman, R., *et al.*, eds. *The Oxford Companion to Australian Cricket*. Melbourne: Oxford University Press, 1996.

Cooke, G. 'All Together Now: Unity is Strength'. *Sports Connect* 2, no. 1 (June 2004). http://www.ausport.gov.au/journals/connect/vol2no1/21unity.asp.

Cox, B., and S. Thompson. 'From Heydays to Struggles: Women's Soccer in New Zealand'. *Soccer and Society* 4, no. 2 (2003): 205–24.

Cusella, L.P. '"Managing after the Merger": Case Analysis'. *Management Communication Quarterly* 13, no. 4 (2000): 668–78.

Duke, V., and R. Renson. 'From Factions to Fusions? The Rise and Fall of Two-club Rivalries in Belgian Football'. *International Review for the Sociology of Sport* 38, no. 1 (2003): 61–77.

Edwards, A., K. Gilbert, and J. Skinner. *Extending the Boundaries: Theoretical Frameworks for Research in Sport Management*. Altona, VIC: Common Ground Publishing, 2002.

Environment, Communications, Information Technology and the Arts Reference Committee. *Women in Sport and Recreation in Australia.* Official Committee Hansard, Senate, Australian Commonwealth Government, 3 August 2006.

Equal Opportunity for Women in the Workplace Agency (EOWA). *The 2006 Australian Census of Women in Leadership: A Study of Women Board Directors and Executive Managers in the Top 200 Companies on the Australian Stock Exchange.* http://www.eowa.gov.au/ Australian_Women_In_Leadership_Census/2006_Australian_Women_In_Leadership_Census/ 2006.asp.

Foster, M. 'Women in a Sporting Administration Environment'. Paper delivered to the *World Trotting Conference*, Sydney, November 20–22, 1999, 8.

Giessner, S., T. Viki, S. Otten, D. Terry, and S. Tauber. 'The Challenge of Merging: Merger Patterns, Premerger Status, and Merger Support'. *Personality and Social Psychology Bulletin* 32, no. 3 (2006): 339–52.

Grainger, A., and D.L. Andrews. 'Resisting Rupert Through Sporting Rituals? The Transnational Media Corporation and Global-local Sport Cultures'. *International Journal of Sport Management and Marketing* 1, nos. 1–2 (2005): 3–16.

Hill, L., and L.M. Kikulis. 'Contemplating Restructuring: A Case Study of Strategic Decision Making in Interuniversity Athletic Conferences'. *Journal of Sport Management* 13, no. 1 (1999): 18–44.

Hoeber, L. '"It's Somewhere on the List but Maybe it's one of the Bottom Ones": Examining Gender Equity as an Organisational Value in a Sport Organisation'. *International Journal of Sport Management and Marketing* 2, no. 4 (2007): 362–78.

Hoeber, L., and W. Frisby. 'Gender Equity for Athletes: Rewriting the Narrative for this Organizational Value'. *European Sport Management Quarterly* 1, no. 3 (2001): 179–209.

Hovden, J. 'From Rights-based to Utility-based Equalization: Gender Political Discourses in Norwegian Sport'. *Idrottsforum/org* 20 April 2004. http://www.idrottsforum.org/articles/ hovden/hovden.html.

Hoye, R., and G. Cuskelly. 'Board Power and Performance within Voluntary Sport Organisations'. *European Sport Management Quarterly* 3, no. 2 (2003): 103–19.

Hoye, R., and B. Stewart. 'Power and Organisational Change: The Case of the Melbourne Women's Hockey Association, 1995–1998'. *Sporting Traditions* 18, no. 2 (May 2002): 47–66.

Hult, J.S. 'Women's Struggle for Governance in US Amateur Athletics'. *International Review for the Sociology of Sport* 24, no. 3 (1989): 249–61.

Jensen, J. 'Women's Collegiate Athletics: Incidents in the Struggle for Influence and Control'. In *Fractured Focus: Sport as a Reflection of Society*, edited by R. Lapschick, 151–61. Lexington MA: Lexington Books, 1986.

Kikulis, L.M. 'Continuity and Change in Governance and Decision Making in National Sport Organizations: Institutional Explanations'. *Journal of Sport Management* 14, no. 4 (2000): 293–320.

Kikulis, L.M., T. Slack, and C.R. Hinings. 'Does Decision Making Make a Difference? Patterns of Change Within Canadian National Sport Organizations'. *Journal of Sport Management* 9, no. 3 (1995): 273–99.

Kikulis, L.M., T. Slack, and C.R. Hinings. 'Toward an Understanding of the Role of Agency and Choice in the Changing Structure of Canada's National Sport Organizations'. *Journal of Sport Management* 9, no. 2 (1995): 135–52.

King, H. 'The Sexual Politics of Sport: An Australian Perspective'. In *Sport in History*, edited by R. Cashman and M. McKernan, 68–85. St Lucia: University of Queensland Press, 1979.

Lenskyj, H. 'Whose Sport? Whose Traditions? Canadian Women and Sport in the Twentieth Century'. *International Journal of the History of Sport* 9, no. 1 (1992): 141–50.

Lenskyj, H. 'Sport and the Threat to Gender Boundaries'. *Sporting Traditions* 12, no. 1 (1995): 47–60.

Lopiano, D.A. 'A Political Analysis of the Possibility of Impact Alternatives for the Accomplishment of Feminist Objectives within American Intercollegiate Sport'. In *Fractured Focus: Sport as a Reflection of Society*, edited by R. Lapschick, 163–76. Lexington, MA: Lexington Books, 1986.

Lovett, D.J., and C.D. Lowry. 'Women and the NCAA: Not Separate – Not Equal'. *Journal of Sport Management* 9 (1995): 244–8.

McKay, J. 'Masculine Hegemony, the State and the Incorporation of Gender Equity Discourse: The Case of Australian Sport'. *Australian Journal of Political Science* 29, no. 1 (1994): 82–95.

McKay, J. *Why so Few? Women Executives in Australian Sport*. Canberra: ASC, 1992.

McKay, J. *Managing Gender: Affirmative Action and Organizational Power in Australian, Canadian and New Zealand Sport*. New York: State University of New York Press, 1997.

Olie, R. 'Shades of Culture and Institutions in International mergers'. *Organization Studies* 15, no. 3 (1994): 381–405.

Parliament of Australia Senate Report. *About Time! Women in Sport and Recreation in Australia*. Canberra: Australian Government Printing Service, 2006.

Password, F. 'Exploring the Gaps Between Meanings and Practices of Gender Equity in a Sport Organization'. *Gender, Work and Organization* 14, no. 3 (2007): 259–80.

Patwardhan, D. 'Women Seek BCCI's Expertise'. 30 May 2005. http://www.rediff.com/cricket/2005/may/30deep1.htm.

Pfeffer, J. 'Merger as a Response to Organizational Interdependence'. *Administrative Science Quarterly* 17, no. 3 (1972): 382–94.

Phillips, D.H. *Australian Women at the Olympic Games*. 3rd ed. Sydney: Walla Walla Press, 2002.

Phillips, M.G., and J. Nauright. 'Sports Fan Movements to Save Surburban-based Football Teams Threatened with Amalgamation in Different Football Codes in Australia'. *International Sport Studies* 21, no. 1 (1999): 23–38.

Phillips, S. 'How Hockey Avoided Merger Meltdown'. *Sports Connect* 1, no. 1 (October 2003). http://www.ausport.gov.au/journals/connect/vol1no1/11hockey.asp.

Randall, L.M. 'Women and Sport in Australia'. *Current Affairs Bulletin* 70, no. 3 (August 1993): 19–26.

Rees, T. 'A New Strategy: Gender Mainstreaming'. Paper presented to the 5th European Women and Sport Conference, Berlin, Germany, April 18–21, 2002.

Rintala, J., and J. Bischoff. 'Persistent Resistance: Leadership Positions for Women in Olympic Sport Governing Bodies'. *Olympika* 6 (1997): 1–24.

Robbins, S.P., and N. Barnwell. *Organisation Theory: Concepts and Cases*. 3rd ed. Sydney: Prentice Hall, 1998.

Seo, M.G., and S. Hill. 'Understanding the Human Side of Merger and Acquisition: An Integrative Framework'. *Journal of Applied Behavioral Science* 41, no. 4 (2005): 422–43.

Shaw, S. 'Gender Suppression in New Zealand Regional Sports Trusts'. *Women in Management Review* 21, no. 7 (2006): 554–66.

Shaw, S., and W. Frisby. 'Can Gender Equity be More Equitable? Promoting an Alternative Frame for Sport Management Research, Education, and Practice'. *Journal of Sport Management* 20, no. 4 (2006): 483–510.

Shaw, S., and D. Penney. 'Gender Equity Policies in National Governing Bodies: An Oxymoron or Vehicle for Change?' *European Sport Management Quarterly* 3, no. 2 (2003): 78–102.

Shaw, S., and T. Slack. '"It's Been Like that for Donkey's Years": The Construction of Gender Relations and the Cultures of Sport Organizations'. *Sport in Society* 5, no. 1 (Jan 2002): 86–106.

Skinner, J., B. Stewart, and A. Edwards. 'Amateurism to Professionalism: Modelling Organisational Change in Sporting Organisations'. *Sport Management Review* 2, no. 2 (1999): 173–92.

Slack, T. *Understanding Sport Organizations: The Application of Organization Theory*. Champaign, IL: Human Kinetics, 1997.

Stell, M.K. *Half the Race: A History of Australian Women in Sport*. Sydney: Angus and Robertson, 1991.

Stevens, J. 'The Canadian Hockey Association Merger and the Emergence of the Amateur Sport Enterprise'. *Journal of Sport Management* 20, no. 1 (2006): 74–100.

Terry, D., and A. O'Brien. 'Status, Legitimacy, and Ingroup Bias in the Context of an Organizational Merger'. *Group Processes and Intergroup Relations* 4, no. 3 (2001): 271–89.

Thompson, J. 'Girls Don't Just Want to Have Fun'. *Wisden Cricket Monthly*, March 2005. http://content-www.cricinfo.com/wcm/content/story/144732.html.

Thompson, S.M. '"Thank the Ladies for the Plates": The Incorporation of Women into Sport'. *Leisure Studies* 9, no. 2 (1990): 135–43.

Trethewey, J. 'Putting the Runs on the Board'. *Skills Bank* (2001): 28.

Van Sterkenburg, J., and A. Knoppers. 'Dominant Discourses About Race/ethnicity and Gender in Sport Practice and Performance'. *International Review for the Sociology of Sport* 39 (2004): 301–21.

Warf, B. 'Oligopolization of Global Media and Telecommunications and its Implications for Democracy'. *Ethics, Place and Environment* 10, no. 1 (2007): 89–105.

Welch, M. *Towards Gender Equity in Sports Management: Report of the European Symposium on Gender Equity in the Management and Governance of Voluntary Sports Organisations*. Leeds: Federation Of Yorkshire Sport and the School of Leisure and Sports Studies At Leeds Metropolitan University, 1999.

Whisenant, W.A., P.M. Pedersen, and B.L. Obenour. 'Success and Gender: Determining the Rate of Advancement for Intercollegiate Athletic Directors'. *Sex Roles* 47, no. 9 (2002): 485–91.

Williams, J. 'The Fastest Growing Sport? Women's Football in England'. *Soccer and Society* 4, no. 2 (2003): 112–27.

Asia's place in the imaging of Australian sport

Richard Cashman

School of Leisure, Sport and Tourism, University of Technology, Sydney, Australia

Since the 1970s, the Australian-Asian sport relationship has intensified and has developed greater depth. There have been an increasing number of tours to and from Asia, Australian involvement in Asian competitions, player exchanges, Australian investment in Asia and vice versa, as well as coach and information exchange. Australian players and spectators have become more familiar with Asian sport and what it means to play in Asia and against Asian players. Australian sport, as a result of globalization, has become more closely tied to Asian sport and this interconnectedness is likely to increase in the future. The greater involvement of Australian sport in Asia has had subtle changes in the imaging of Australian sport as a result of an increasing prominence of 'multiculturality' and 'polyethnicity'. It remains to be seen whether this increasing awareness of 'each other' will necessarily result in greater cultural understanding or lesser stereotyping on both sides.

Introduction

Joseph Maguire suggested that there has been an 'intensification of global interconnectness' since the late 1960s that has 'unleashed new sets of independency chains' linking people around the globe. A global economy and a transnational cosmopolitan culture have been advance through new and improved communication networks.[1]

However, the future realization of a 'single global market', which is the view of hyperglobalisers such as Kenichi Ohmae, is unlikely.[2] Rather, a transformationist model is more appealing in that while there is greater interdependence between the global and the local, the 'the distinctions between international and domestic, and external and internal affairs has become blurred, and the future direction of this process remains uncertain at this point in time'.[3] There continues to be an ongoing intensifying, a deepening and stretching of links between the global, regional and local.

Globalization has also enhanced the organization and status of sub-global regional competitions, which have become important stepping-stones in global competition. It has contributed to the emergence of second tier mega sports events, such as the Asian and Commonwealth Games and a host of other games. Regional competitions, such as the Asian Champions League and the Asian Cup, have been modelled in part on successful European competitions, such as the European Champions League and the UEFA Cup.

Before 1945, there were far fewer sporting organizations that spanned a continent. Global interconnectness has resulted in tighter and more defined regional organizations in sport. The 207 current member nations of the Fédération Internationale de Football Association (FIFA) belong to six separate football federations representing Africa, Asia, Europe, Oceania, North and South America. The Asian Football Federation (AFC) that was formed in 1954 currently has 46 member nations. These are divided between four football federations: ASEAN (including Indonesia, Malaysia and Australia), East Asia (including China and Japan), West Asia (including Iran, Iraq and Qatar) and Central and South Asia (including India, Afghanistan and Uzbekistan).

From the 1970s Australian soccer officials would have preferred to be part of the AFC rather than Oceania because the Asian competition was stronger and more lucrative. However, Australia's first serious move to join the AFC in the 1970s was rebuffed because Asian countries feared the impact of Australian playing strength on Asian football. Adding Australia to the AFC would probably reduce Asian World Cup opportunities.[4] Australian had to settle instead for membership of the weaker Oceania Football Confederation. However, a second request to join the AFC in 2005 proved successful and Australia then left the weaker Oceania Football Federation for the stronger one.

The global sports system also continues to evolve as 'global marketing strategies also celebrate difference' in that 'cultural industries constantly seek out new varieties of ethnic wares'. Maguire added that contemporary globalization:

> involves the creolization of sports cultures. When both national identity itself – and the sport forms of the culture as a whole – are undergoing a pluralization process, it is increasingly difficult to sustain the notion that a *single* sport represents *the nation*. The global movement of sport labour reinforces the problems of multiculturality and polyethnicity.[5]

Asia provides Australia with a rich storehouse of 'otherness' and 'difference'.

Another important result of globalization has been the altered balance of global power with the emergence of China and India as significant powers in recent times. In the past decade China has grown to be the world's fourth largest economy and the third largest trading nation with a spectacular annual growth rate of around 10% per year. India is following closely behind. One consequence is that China and India are becoming more prominent in the organization of major sports events and are seen as potential lucrative sports media and markets. These two powers are building on and extending the global sporting role of Japan and South Korea in earlier decades. The Australian-Asian sports nexus has also advanced because the Australian economy is riding high on the coattails of a booming Chinese economy and, to a lesser extent, the South Asian economy – another fast rising economy. China is the principal buyer for Australia's extensive mineral resources and became Australia's largest trading partner in 2007. Educational, cultural and political links have multiplied as a result in recent decades. Sport along with culture has followed and enhanced closer economic ties and has added depth to the burgeoning relationships between Australia and various Asian nations. Involvement in Asian sport above all has become lucrative for many Australian clubs and sports organizations and businesses.

Maguire has noted in what he regards as the fifth 'global sportization phase' from the late 1960s, that African, Asian and South American nations became more prominent and the control of global sport by British, European and North American interests waned. Western sports leadership and power has been contested in various ways in the past few decades.[6]

Since the late 1960s, there has been greater interconnectness between Australian and Asian sport. Cricket, soccer and the Olympic Games are the best examples (see case studies below) of the intensification of the Australian-Asian nexus. However, there are few Australian sports that have not been affected by the potential new relationships.

Issues and approaches

There are many questions that can be posed about the closer nexus between Australia and Asian sport, which manifests itself more intensely in some sports than others. Australia has developed deep relationships in cricket with India (and the subcontinent more generally), Japan and South Korea in soccer and China in the Olympics.

To what extent is this new focus transforming the traditional Australian sports orientation? Has an increasing contact with Asia led to a greater awareness of 'multiculturality' and 'polyethnicity' both in sport and society more generally? Has a sporting confrontation with Asia and its sporting culture forced Australian sports leaders to reimagine and even rebrand sporting culture?

There has also been a long and ongoing debate about whether Australia is a European country, that happens to be located in the Asia-Pacific region, or whether it has become or is becoming an Asian or an Asian-Pacific country. The increasing presence of Asians in Australia (as immigrants and tourists) has made such issues more prominent. Former Prime Minister Paul Keating believed that Australia should make 'an intense effort' to integrate itself more fully into the Asian region and that this would be the starting point for the assertion of an 'unambiguous' post-colonial identity.[7] However, while this 'perceived rush to become an Asian nation' proved attractive to sections of the educated middle class, many other Australians were wary of such a development.[8] Some Asian leaders, such as the former Malaysian Prime Minister Mahathir Mohamad, also questioned whether Australia was entitled to regard itself as Asian.

Finally it is worth reflecting on whether sport enhances (or detracts from) Asian economic, political or cultural relationships more generally. To what extent is sporting engagement with Asia separate or linked to other initiatives? And does sport merely follow the flag or does it contribute something of its own, adding depth to the burgeoning Australian relationship with Asia?

To explore the above, the essay will introduce three case studies of sports where the Asian relationship has become more significant since the 1970s: cricket, soccer and the Olympic Games. There will also be brief references to some other sports, such as horseracing, field hockey, rugby, swimming and tennis, which have developed an Asian profile.

Australian-Asian contacts before the 1970s

Contact and exchanges between Australian and Asian sport were relatively rare before 1945 and, to a lesser extent, before the 1970s. The occasional exchanges that did take place were usually at a low level and did not loom large in the Australian sports calendar or the country's imagination.

Two Chinese soccer tours in the 1920s did attract sizeable crowds, partly because of the novelty factor. The first Chinese soccer tour of 1923 was not undertaken by a national side; rather it was 'touted as a Chinese university side, however it was made up of students, young merchants, accountants and bank clerks, amateurs from the South China Athletic Association in Hong Kong'.[9] Australian-born K.L. Kwong, a professor at the National College of Commerce in Shanghai, organized a second tour in 1927 with the team made up of university students. While the White Australia Policy, which aimed to exclude non-Anglocentric immigration to Australia, may have discouraged contacts with Asia, Andrew Honey has noted that this did not stop contacts because visiting non-white sports teams were treated as 'exceptions to the policy of non-"white" exclusion' partly because they were temporary and occasional visitors. The two Chinese tours were followed by teams from the Dutch East Indies (1928), Java (1931), India (1938) and Chinese Republic, Hong Kong (1941).[10]

There was less to attract Australian sporting interest in Asia before 1945 because of the relatively limited organization of many Asian sports and the rudimentary character of most Asian economies in this period. Japan was an exception to the rule: it developed strength in swimming, which was realized in the 1932 and 1936 Olympic Games, where Japan became a dominant force in the pool. Two Japanese swimmers, one being Kiywa Takaishi, competed in the NSW Championships in 1927.[11] Legendary Australian soldier Weary Dunlop, while still a medical student, was a member of a Combined Universities rugby team that made a nine-match tour of Japan and Hong Kong in 1934.

There were few common sports in which Asians and Australians excelled. The Indian men's hockey team dominated Olympic competition – winning six times in a row from 1924 to 1956 and again in 1964 and 1980. Pakistan won the men's gold medal in 1960, 1968 and 1984. The Australian men's hockey team only achieved its first Olympic medal (a silver) in 1976 and finally won the gold medal in 2004, at a time when India and Pakistan were less dominant in world hockey. The Australian women's hockey team has been prominent and successful in this sport and over a longer period than the men. A women's team undertook an ambitious tour in the 1930s to various European countries and Africa – but it did not travel to Asia where few women played this sport.[12] The Australian women won the Olympic gold medal in 1988, 1996 and 2000. While field hockey was defined initially in Australia more as a game for women and girls, the reverse was true in India and Pakistan, where field hockey was almost exclusively a male sport. Women's field hockey has been prominent in South Korea but much less so in India and Pakistan.

It is also clear that Asian sport did not rate with Australian sports officials and fans before 1945 and the primary success that mattered was largely against British, European and North American opposition. These were the critical members of the Australian imaginary grandstand and opinions expressed in these countries carried a lot of weight in Australia well into the twentieth century.[13]

Australian cricket administrators adopted a patronising stance and did little to encourage Indian cricket in the 1930s. Australia did not play its first Test against India until 1947, even though India acquired Test status in 1932 and played three series against England in the 1930s. When the Maharaja of Patiala proposed a private Australian tour to India in 1935 – with the Maharaja footing all the bills – the Australian Board of Control for International Cricket (the Australian Cricket Board) refused permission for a handful of stars (Bill Woodfull, Alan Kippax and Bill Ponsford) to tour. The Board dictated that the team could not play in the Australian colours or be known as the Maharaja of Patiala's Touring Australian team. The Maharaja had to settle instead for a motley crew of veterans (many aged 49 or above) and a handful of younger cricketers yet to make their mark.[14]

Martial arts were probably the Asian sports that were first taken up seriously in Australia from the 1970s. Damien McCoy has noted that before the 1970s the interest in martial arts outside Asia was confined to a 'few enthusiasts'.[15] This all changed with greater commercial contact between Australia and Asia, the earlier end of colonialism, increased contact through the Korean and Vietnamese wars, a rising interest in eastern philosophies and the emergence of cult figures, such as Bruce Lee, in film and television. McCoy has tracked the impressive growth of participant numbers in karate, judo, taekwondo and various other forms of martial arts in Australia and the participation of Australian teams in international competitions. By the 1980s Australia hosted three international karate competitions: the Asian Pacific Karate Championships in 1981 and 1989 and the World Karate Championships in 1986. The Taekwondo Asian Games were held in Darwin in 1986.[16]

Cricket

While the status of martial arts remains relatively low in Australia, cricket has long been one of the flagship sports of Australia. The game is played in every state, has a wide player and supporter base and is the sport that comes closest to being the national sport. The rise of subcontinental cricket in the Australian consciousness has been relatively recent but has been impressive in its dimensions. Cricket was the first major sport in which a significant relationship developed between Australia and Asia from the 1970s.

From 1945 until the 1970s administrators continued to regard Indian and subcontinental cricket as inferior. The Australian Cricket Board did relatively little to encourage the development of cricket on the subcontinent. India toured Australia and played five Tests in 1947/48 but did not return until two decades later, in 1967/68, to play another four Tests. Australia toured India a little more frequently but two of the first three tours (1956/57 and 1964/65) were tacked on the end of Ashes campaigns – the main game – and only three Tests were played against India on each occasion. Australia played a stand-alone five-Test series in 1959/60 and another five-Test series in 1969/70 prior to a tour of South Africa.

Pakistan did not fare much better, touring Australia first in 1964/65 (for one Test) and playing two three-Test series in 1972/73 and 1976/77. Tours to Pakistan were also an extension of the Ashes or Indian series. Just one Test was played in Pakistan in 1956 when Australia lost on the mat at Lahore. Three Tests were played in 1959/60 and another one in 1964/65.

The relationship between Australia and the subcontinent changed significantly in the 1970s for a number of reasons. Firstly, there was a dramatic improvement in the performance of subcontinental teams. India won a series against a strong England team, led by Ray Illingworth by 1–0 (in a three-Test series) in 1971. This was essentially the same English team that had beaten Australia 2–0 in 1970/71. India maintained a competitive team during the 1970s and surprised the West Indies to win the third Cricket World Cup in 1983 after the West Indies had won the initial two in 1975 and 1979.

There was also improvement in the Pakistan side. Pakistan had a convincing win over Australia by eight wickets in the Third Test of the 1976/77 series to square the three-Test series 1–1. Imran Khan had the outstanding figures of 12/165 in this Test. The spectacular rise of the West Indies, since the celebrated series of 1960/61, demonstrated that contests against countries other than England could rival, and at times, overshadow the Ashes series.[17]

The support of India for establishment cricket, during the World Series Cricket (WSC) crisis of 1977 to 1979, also elevated the worth of Indian cricket in the mind of Australian cricket officials. Because no Indian cricketer signed up for WSC, the Australian Cricket Board was able to promote a five-Test series against a full-strength Indian side as a counter attraction to the WSC Supertests. The establishment 1977/78 Test series was closely fought with Australia prevailing in the final Test to win the series 3–2.

Closer ties in the 1980s

Despite an increasing respect for the cricketers of the subcontinent, Australian players did not rate playing on the subcontinent highly and developed a negative mindset to touring there. Many Australian cricketers of the 1950s and 1960s regarded travel to India an ordeal and developed what Mike Coward referred to as a 'rat and riot' mentality.[18] Another popular view which persisted for decades was that the Pakistanis were (and still are in the opinion of many) cheats and that Pakistani umpires gave many home town decisions.

The Australian loss on the mat in 1956 at Karachi was discounted because it was believed that the matting was stretched (or loosened) to benefit the home side.

There was a significant shift in attitudes towards playing on the subcontinent in the 1980s. Prominent players, such as Allan Border, recognized that negative attitudes towards the subcontinent promoted a defeatist mentality that became a self-fulfilling prophecy. Border realized that to achieve international success Australian players had to come to terms with playing on the subcontinent and accept the different conditions there: the pitches, the weather, the crowd. He encouraged Australians players to take a more positive attitude towards playing and touring on the subcontinent.[19]

Border's views were shared by players, officials and some members of the media. Prominent Australian cricket officials such as Alan Crompton, Fred Bennett and Malcolm Gray recognized that that the subcontinent was a rich market for cricket growth. Bennett also lobbied vigorously for the admission of Sri Lanka to Test status.[20] Steve Waugh was another Australian captain who not only appreciated the rich tapestry of Indian cricket but its society and culture as well. Waugh set up his own charity in India. Prominent Australian cricket journalist Mike Coward reminded his readers that the subcontinent was the site of an ancient civilization that had developed a vibrant and interesting cricket culture, adding to the strength and variety of world cricket. Coward's book, *Cricket Beyond the Bazaar*, catalogued the changing Australian attitude towards cricket on the subcontinent.

The new stance of Australian cricketers yielded some immediate results. The performance of the Australian team on the subcontinent improved in the 1980s and Australia won its first World Cup victory at Calcutta in 1987. Border and Waugh, who relished playing in India, became much-loved cricketers on the subcontinent. Pakistan proved to be the 'last frontier' but Australia finally won a series 1−0 (with two draws) there in 1998/99 − Australia's first success in almost 40 years.

Despite a changing relationship in the 1980s, the second tied Test at Madras in 1989, did not rate (and still does not rate) as highly as the first tied Test between Australia versus the West Indies in Brisbane in 1960. The Madras Test was equally dramatic and exciting until the final wicket fell on the fifth day and perhaps was more heroic given the enervating climate. But it did not occur on Australian soil, nor was it televised (though there was virtually no television of the 1960 Test).

The changing balance of world cricket

Since the 1970s when the West Indies won the initial two World Cups (in 1973 and 1977) and dominated Test match cricket from the late 1970s and during the 1980s, the balance of power has shifted to the subcontinent and Australia. India won the World Cup in 1983, Pakistan in 1991 and Sri Lanka in 1996. The other four World Cups were won by Australia (1987, 1999, 2003, 2007). Australia has also dominated Test cricket in the last decade.

While Australia has had the best cricket team in the world during the past decade and an unrivalled cricket system, the real power in the game (in terms on media, audiences, revenue and sponsorship) has shifted to the subcontinent, which generated 60 per cent of the revenue generated in world cricket in 2003/04 − through television rights and sponsorship.[21] It is not surprising then that there was a significant shift in the governance of global cricket in the 1990s when the former dominant countries (England, Australia, South Africa, New Zealand and the West Indies) − the older and largely 'white'-dominated empire − were outvoted by the newer cricket nations, headed by the four countries of the subcontinent in the International Cricket Council (ICC). The powerful Indian official, Jagmohan Dalmiya, was elected President of the ICC in 1997.

The subcontinent has dominated world cricket agendas since then. A bid to stage the 2011 World Cup on the subcontinent was successful even though World Cups had been held there in 1987 and 1996 and Australia and New Zealand, which also bid (unsuccessfully), could argue that it was their turn to host the World Cup on the basis of an informal rotation system. The World Cup had been staged only once in Australia and New Zealand, in 1991.

The Indian Cricket League, a rebel Twenty20 competition promoted by Zee Telefilms, threatens to challenge and possibly undermine future official Twenty20 competitions. The activities of Subhash Chandra, Chairman of Zee Entertainment Enterprises Limited, mirror that of Australian media mogul, Kerry Packer, who had the money and the clout to hijack global cricket in the 1970s.

The subcontinent looms larger in Australian cricket because of the size of the audience there. With the emergence of an Indian middle-class audience (estimated as high as 300 million and growing) augmented by an expatriate audience of an estimated 20 million, there is already a huge market for cricket in a country that is besotted with the game. The growth of this market has been accelerated by the deregulation of the Indian economy and the media in 1991. Since then, the Indian cricket audience had been previously well served by ESPN-Star, broadcast from Hong Kong, and more recently by Zee Telefilms that broadcast a wide range of subcontinental and international cricket. The Indian cricket market is growing at a rapid rate and twice as fast as the British market.[22]

India is the new commercial power in international cricket and 70% of the advertising revenue for 2003 World Cup emanated from India.[23] The television rights for coverage of international cricket were sold by the Board of Control for Cricket in India (BCCI) to Zee Telefilms (Zee TV) for US$308 million which was approximately seven times the value when the rights were last sold in 1999.[24] Dabkowski noted in 2004 that 'few people know that India – or companies based in India – account for about 60 per cent of the total revenue being poured into world cricket'.[25]

Cricket Australia (CA) has profited from this market by selling the rights for Australian cricket off-shore. CA, which secured 64% of its revenue from media rights in 2003/04, signed two contracts, a four-year deal with ESPN-Star for Australian cricket coverage on the subcontinent, and another six-year contract with the British BSkyB for British coverage of Australian games.[26] Dabkowski stated that 'the exact size of the [ESPN-Star] deal is confidential but insiders believe that it is probably the biggest TV rights deal ever done by [the] Australian cricket's governing body'.[27]

Another unusual feature of globalization is that the Indian company, Hero Honda motorcycles, which is a sponsor of Indian cricket, appeared on billboards on Australian cricket grounds during the series between Australia and Zimbabwe in 2003/04. The advertising was not aimed at the Australian domestic audience since this company does not operate in Australia but the much larger Indian audience following these Tests.[28]

In the past two decades a significant number of Australians have played various roles on the subcontinent as coaches and advisors. While Greg Chappell resigned as coach of the Indian cricket side in 2007, Geoff Lawson was appointed coach of Pakistan in the same year. Jamie Siddons is the current coach of Bangladesh having succeeded Australian Dav Whatmore. Coaches of Sri Lanka have included Dav Whatmore, Bruce Yardley, John Dyson, Tom Moody and current coach Trevor Bayliss. Dennis Lillee was recruited to establish a fast bowling clinic in Madras (now Chennai) in the 1990s. Fast bowler Brett Lee produced a hit song with Indian actress, Asha Bhosle, which topped the charts in India.

Some Australian universities have also recognized that cricket could be used to promote educational goals on the subcontinent. The University of New South Wales (UNSW) used a cricket tour to promote its brand in India and to advance its educational goals there. The University's first grade side, managed by former Test cricket player Geoff Lawson, toured India from 10–23 April 2005. In addition to playing cricket the team visited schools to inform students of educational and sporting opportunities at UNSW.[29] Griffith University sponsors the scoreboard at the Gabba ground Brisbane. The sponsorship in part is aimed at those watching the cricket games at this venue.[30]

Changes in the imaging of Australian cricket

The regular visit of cricket teams from India, Pakistan, Sri Lanka and Bangladesh has reshaped Australian cricket. Firstly, there is the interesting phenomenon that significant numbers of Asian-born (or first generation Australian-born of Asian immigrants) cricket fans have flocked to matches in Australia to support the visiting teams thereby demonstrating multiculturalism in a tangible way. Michael Roberts has noted that the visits of Sri Lankan sides had brought an 'added dimension' to Australian cricket in that their supporters 'enliven proceedings with their shouts, and own brand of music, sway and sound, *baila* as it is called'.[31]

Increasing contact with Asian cricketing nations has also added new narratives to Australian cricket. The Australian 1996 World Cup team opted to forfeit its points in its match against Sri Lanka in Colombo, which had been the scene of recent bomb blasts. Despite the loss of these points, Australia met Sri Lanka in the final in Pakistan but lost.

Cultural misunderstanding and the issue of race have become more prominent in recent cricket narratives. The Second Test between Australia and India at Sydney (2–6 January 2008) proved so volatile and controversial that the media referred to the Test and the post-match crisis as Bollyline – combining Bollywood (the popular name for the Bombay-based Hindi film industry) and Bodyline, (the most controversial series in Australian cricket history in 1932/33). The drama was exacerbated by some poor umpiring decisions, a perceived Australian win-at-all-cost attitude and the referee's three-match suspension of Harbhajan Singh on the grounds of an alleged racist comment.

There were two significant outcomes of the Bollyline affair. In his post-match conference the Indian cricket captain Anil Kumble complained that 'only one team was playing with[in] the spirit of cricket, that's all I can say'.[32] Kumble, in a sense, held up a mirror in which the Australian cricket public could reflect on its team's behaviour. Judging by the storm of public protest that followed, it is clear that a significant number of Australians agreed with Kumble, though others defended the Australian team.

The second outcome related to racial vilification and hinged on the use of the words 'monkey' and 'bastard'. The Indian hierarchy was sufficiently outraged by the charge that Singh had used the word 'monkey' with racist intent to lay a counter-charge against Brad Hogg that he was similarly guilty because of his reference to Indian players as 'bastards'. The Australian public must have been surprised to discover that a commonplace word in Australian speech – which can even be used in a friendly sense – is deeply offensive to Indians. The extended media debate thus focused on matters of race and issues of inter-cultural sensitivities.

Soccer

Australia first reached the FIFA World Cup in 1974 but then struggled for another 32 years before it was able to repeat this achievement in 2006. A primary reason for many frustrating campaigns was that Australia was disadvantaged by being classified in the Oceania region, one of the weaker regions in world soccer. As a result, Australia was denied tough competition with teams in its immediate neighbourhood. New Zealand was the only country of Oceania to provide serious opposition. Another hurdle was that the best team in Oceania usually had to qualify for the World Cup playing the fourth-ranked South American team – which was always a difficult assignment.

While Australia struggled internationally for the three decades after 1974, soccer advanced significantly in Asia. South Korea appeared in the World Cup in 1954 and has played in every World Cup since 1986, advancing to the semi-final in 2002. Japan has gained entrance to the last three World Cups and co-hosted the 2002 World Cup with South Korea. North Korea attended the World Cup in 1966 when it reached the quarter-finals and China appeared for the first time in 2002. Soccer in Asia was strengthened by the inclusion of teams from West Asia, such as Iran, Iraq, Saudi Arabia and the United Arab Emirates, which provided at least one additional Asian representative to the World Cup from 1978.

A significant reorientation took place on 1 January 2006 when the Football Federation of Australia moved from the Oceania Football Confederation (OFC) to the Asian Football Confederation (AFC). This development had been endorsed by the AFC on 23 March 2005 and approved by FIFA on 29 June 2005.

Frank Lowy, the prime instigator of the move to Asia, believed that it would improve the standard of Australian football, give the national team a fairer change of qualifying for future world cups and provide A-League teams with access to the Asian Champions League. Players' union chief Craig Foster stated that the involvement of A-League teams in the Asian Champions League will 'bring new foreign and domestic investors to Australian clubs', lead to an increase in 'A-League salaries' which will help keep the best players in Australia and make the country 'an attractive destination for quality foreign players both from Asia and Europe'. John O'Neill, the then chief executive of the FFA, stated that 'forging such close links with soccer's biggest developing marketplace offers unimagined sporting and commercial opportunities for Australian clubs' that will in turn 'attract companies and broadcasters keen to tap into billions of people that straddle a region incorporating such rapidly emerging economies' of China and India. O'Neill added that soccer is the one sport 'capable of engaging fully with Asia' and that such an engagement 'will transform the game from top to bottom'.[33]

Anthony Bubalo, a researcher for the Lowy Institute, stated that the 'basic numbers' of the Australian involvement Asia are 'startling':

> Beginning next January [2006] each year Australian national and club teams will play dozens of home and away games against counterparts in a sporting confederation that incorporates more than half the world's population ... and contains three of the world's top five economies: Japan, China and India (measured on purchasing power).
>
> The commercial potential of this new sporting relationship is obvious. Sponsors of Australian teams will gain exposure to a massive new audience: some 250 million Chinese were, for example, estimated to have watched the 2004 Asian Cup final between China and Japan. And there will undoubtedly be spin-offs in the tourism and travel sectors.[34]

Foster predicted that the move to Asia will not only secure higher-quality players and raise the overall standard of the game, but also generate money 'through higher sponsorship and TV revenues'.[35] This prediction was realized when it was reported in April 2006 that FoxSports had paid $120 million for the rights to broadcast soccer for the next seven years. The deal will enable FoxSports to broadcast 90 A-League games per season plus six Socceroo games plus the rights to Australian games in Asian tournament.[36]

This represented a major breakthrough for the code that had struggled to gain media exposure on an ongoing basis.

The move to Asia has already had some impact on the A-League. A small number of Asian players play in the A-league while some Australian players appear in Asian leagues. Additional Asian players in the A-League have the potential to create greater regional interest in the A-League which will attract new sponsors and provide existing sponsors with a larger audience. There is also the likelihood of greater Asian investment in the A-League. The Singapore-based World Sport Group, which was a key player in the FoxSports deal, came close to purchasing Perth Glory in 2007 before the club opted for a Perth-based syndicate.[37]

Since it threw in its lot with Asian soccer, Australia also had the opportunity to develop significant rivalries against prominent Asian teams. In its 2006 World Cup campaign Australia had a dramatic encounter with Japan that it won when it scored three goals in the last ten minutes. This added interest to the next contest between the two sides at the 2007 Asian Cup – when Australia and Japan were two of the pre-Cup favourites. This time Japan reversed the result when it won through a penalty shootout. When the wealthy Japanese team Urawa Red Diamonds played Sydney FC in Sydney on 21 March 2007, a contingent of 2000 fans travelled to Sydney to support the team. The Urawa Red Diamonds have a large fan base and regularly play in front of crowds of over 40,000.[38]

It is clear that the move to Asia by FFA occurred primarily for pragmatic rather than ideological reasons: the lure of additional revenue, media exposure, a greater profile and a stronger status in world soccer. The alignment with Asia also puts Australian soccer in a stronger position in its battle with the country's three other football codes: Australian football, rugby and rugby league. The engagement with Asia may lead to subtle changes in the way that the sport in played and organized. After Australia's first Asian Cup experience, when it reached the quarter-finals, there were many calls to promote those players who could adapt to the heat and humidity (as well as the environment more generally) of Asia.

Anthony Bubalo has speculated on the meaning of Australian soccer's move to Asia given that 'Australia remains, anachronistically, a member of the West Europe and Others Group (WEOG) in the United Nations'. Bubalo added that:

> Football may also provide a way to by-pass the tortuous debate over whether Australia is an Asian nation. Identity reflects different elements, from geography and culture to ethnicity. By some of these measures Australia is 'Asian' and by others it clearly isn't. Football will add another meaningful strand – at both popular and institutional levels – to a web of ties placing Australia in the region. Where some Asian leaders have used the notion of 'Asian values' as a cipher for divergent political interests and outlooks, 'football values' could well become a bridge. In this respect it is worth noting that Australia is not just joining the Asian football club. Should Australia qualify for future World Cups, it will become an Asian representative in international sport's biggest event, at a time when Asia is trying to assert itself as a footballing power.
>
> At the same time, it should be recognised that membership of the AFC will not make Australia any more Asian than the Persian Gulf countries that are also members of the Confederation. Nor will football help Australia overcome all of the prejudices, misconceptions and historical legacies – both Australian and Asian – that still complicate its ties with the region. Indeed football may reinforce stereotypes, given the role sporting rivalries often play as manifestations of national animosities ...
>
> One can also question whether the deepening and broadening of Australia's engagement with Asia actually matters. The Howard government has argued on a number of occasions that what really counts is less the building of deeper cultural and popular ties than the creation of practical relations between Australia and individual Asian states based on shared interests.[39]

The Australian Olympic caravan: taking Australian sports business to Asia

Sydney and Beijing were rivals to stage the 2000 Olympic Games when Sydney prevailed by the narrowest of margins, 45 votes to 43. While Beijing was favoured in many quarters, human rights was the city's bid weakness since the memory of the events of Tiananmen Square in 1989 was still fresh in 1993, when the bid was decided. While the Sydney bid team was careful not to be seen to capitalize on this issue, some of its supporters in other countries (notably in the United States) were less reticent.

Beijing, when it next bid for the Olympic Games in 2001, was prepared to learn from the defeat of 1993 and to tap into Sydney's Olympic expertise. A close Sydney-Beijing relationship became a reality because prominent Sydney Games officials, such as Sandy Hollway, and companies such as Telstra, recognized benefits that might accrue from nurturing the Beijing bid. Hollway visited Beijing a number of times before the successful bid offering much pro bono advice for the Beijing bid team, as did the Telstra team. Hollway and others recognized that the increasing cultural, political and economic links with China. Sydney and Beijing belong to the same Asia-Pacific region and there is only a two-hour time difference between the two cities.[40]

It was due to the influence of people such as Sandy Hollway, David Churches, Bob Adby and David Richmond that the Sydney-Beijing Olympic Secretariat (SBOS) was set up by February 2002, initially in the Premier's Department but later in the Department of State and Regional Development in the New South Wales Government. This was an imaginative and even inspired idea to publicize and facilitate the export of Australian expertise in the Olympic Games as well as event management more generally. SBOS assisted Australian firms by providing informal strategic advice and assistance; by offering independent and realistic assessment of opportunities; by delivering a specialized information resource and by linking firms with Australian promotional activities in China.[41]

Communication between Sydney and Beijing was enhanced by the close links between many Australian and Chinese officials. Sandy Hollway for instance worked closely with Wang Wei, secretary-general and vice-president of the Beijing Organising Committee for the Olympic Games (BOCOG). A reference from Hollway supporting an Australian firm to Wang Wei carried weight because SBOS and its Chinese partners effectively screened such applications beforehand.[42]

The acclaimed success of the Sydney 2000 Olympic and Paralympic Games is the prime reason why Australian Olympic expertise continues to be so highly valued internationally in Beijing and elsewhere. Although there have been a number of summer and winter Olympic Games since 2000, Australian expertise continues to be more valued than that of other countries, particularly in Asia.

Australia is the first country to develop an international Olympic caravan of international experts who travel from one Games city to another. Australian members of the caravan share a sense of belonging to a common enterprise, to advance the reputation of Australia as a clever, innovative and professional dispenser of Olympic knowledge. Many people who worked with the Sydney Olympic Organising Committee (SOCOG) or some other Sydney Olympic body before 2000, have continued to work for the Australian Olympic export cause – sometimes on a paid basis and at other times on a pro bono basis – as if the Games have never ended.

As the transfer of Olympic knowledge is a relatively recent phenomenon, Sydney was fortunate that Beijing won the bid to stage the 2008 Games just one year after the completion of the Sydney Games. Sydney and Beijing have developed many economic, cultural and political ties over the past few decades. London's success in winning the bid to stage the 2012 Games is also beneficial for Australia because of long-standing cultural, political and economic ties.

As a result the Australian Olympic presence in Beijing is probably more prominent than that of any other country. The Sydney firm of PTW Architects designed the Aquatic Centre, known as the Watercube, which is one of the two iconic buildings of the Beijing Olympic Games, the other being the main stadium (known as the bird's nest) which was designed by a Swiss company. Australian companies also assisted with the design of the shooting centre, the sailing facility at Qingdao and the equestrian centre in Hong Kong as well as the temporary venues for archery, hockey and tennis.

The Watercube is a symbol both of Australian prominence and of Australian excellence. Surveys have shown that it is the venue most loved by the host community. The Chinese Government is also pleased that this venue has been funded by overseas Chinese compatriots – Chinese people from Taiwan, Singapore and many other countries. The Watercube symbolizes the leadership role of mainland China for the Chinese diaspora.

It is important to note that many of the above contracts, won by Australians, involved working with Chinese companies at the design, building and management stage. Australian companies have had to understand how to do business in China and have adapted well to local culture and its protocols.

Doing business with Asia through sport has become big business in recent decades. While profitable in its own right, sport enhances and adds depth to other political, cultural and even educational activities. The potential for future sports business in Asia appears unlimited particularly as some of the leading Asian nations become more prominent globally.

Other sports

The above case studies could be replicated in a number of others sports, such as rugby, horseracing, tennis, swimming and field hockey, each adding further dimensions to the story of an increasing Australian involvement in Asia. While Japan is still regarded as one of the minnows of world rugby, a Japanese team toured Australia in 1975 playing two Tests and another nine matches. Numerous Australian clubs have toured Japan and there are strong links between Japanese rugby and Australian universities.[43] Australian rugby administrators supported Japan's unsuccessful bid to stage the 2011 Rugby World Cup – a bid which was won by New Zealand. Swimmer Ian Thorpe has become a cult figure in Japan and his visits there have been immensely popular.

There has been a long history of the export of Australian thoroughbreds and walers to Asia. Although horseracing is far less developed in Asia than Australia, a number of Australian jockeys have raced in Hong Kong and Singapore. Asian horses are the latest to make an impact on the Melbourne Cup and two Japanese horses (ridden by Japanese jockeys) secured a quinella in the 2006 Melbourne Cup – Delta Blues won and Pop Rock came second.

Asian players have also become more prominent in the Australian tennis grand slam that advertises itself as the Grand Slam of the Asia-Pacific. Chinese players secured their first grand slam title at the Australian Open in 2006 when Yan Zi and Zheng Jie won the women's doubles.

Conclusions

Since the 1970s, the Australian-Asian relationship has intensified and has developed greater depth. There have been an increasing number of tours to and from Asia, Australian involvement in Asian competitions, player exchanges, Australian investment in Asia and vice versa, as well as coach and information exchange. Australian players and spectators have become more familiar with Asian sport and what it means to play in Asia and against Asian players. Australian sport, as a result of globalization, has become more closely tied to Asian sport and this interconnectedness is likely to increase in the future.

The greater involvement of Australian sport in Asia has had subtle changes in the imaging of Australian sport as a result of an increasing prominence of 'multiculturality' and 'polyethnicity'. It remains to be seen whether this increasing awareness of 'each other' will necessarily result in greater cultural understanding or lesser stereotyping on both sides, as Anthony Bubalo has suggested. At the very least Australian players and spectators will become more aware of how they look to people of other cultures because of a growing Asian commentary on Australian sport, teams and athletes. The comments of respected Asian sports leaders, such as Anil Kumble, may cause many Australians to pause and reflect on the nature of Australian sports culture. Australian sporting officials, clubs, businesses and spectators have also had to observe new protocols and be sensitive to cultural differences.

The greater orientation of Australian soccer to Asia is likely to have some subtle changes in the way that Australians define their place in sport. The primary field for Australian soccer is now the Asian region and Australia will go to future World Cups as a representative of Asia. It remains to be seen whether this will lead to any change in Australian identity, such as a greater recognition that Australians are not Europeans who happen to live in the Asia-Pacific but are part of a multicultural society – Indigenous, European, Asian and Pacific – that fits comfortably in the Asian-Pacific region.

Australian athletes, officials and business personnel have a compelling incentive to come to terms with Asia and to adapt to Asian protocols and sensitivities. The Asian sports market is both powerful and lucrative and is likely to become more so in future. Pragmatism will determine that Asia will loom ever larger in the imaging of Australian sport.

Notes

[1] Maguire, 'Global Sport', 1.
[2] Ohmae, *The End of the Nation State*.
[3] Lamb, 'Globalisation, Governance and International Cricket', 44.
[4] Mosely, '"Playing Ball with Asia"', 59.
[5] Maguire, 'Global Sport', 11.
[6] Ibid.
[7] Watson, *Recollections of a Bleeding Heart*, 170.
[8] Bubalo, 'Football Diplomacy', 7.
[9] Honey, 'Sport, Immigration Restriction and Race', 44.
[10] Honey, 'Sport, Immigration Restriction and Race', 44–5; Mosely, '"Playing Ball with Asia"', 53–74.
[11] Honey, 'Sport, Immigration Restriction and Race', 45.
[12] Stell, *Half the Race*, 52.
[13] Cashman, *Sport in the National Imagination*, 145–51.
[14] Coward, *Cricket Beyond the Bazaar*, 89–113.
[15] McCoy, 'Martial Arts', 239.
[16] Ibid., 238–50.
[17] Coward, *Cricket Beyond the Bazaar*, 80–9.
[18] Ibid., 4.
[19] Ibid., 1, 10–12.
[20] Cashman *et al.*, *Oxford Companion to Australian Cricket*, 9, 261–5.
[21] Lamb, 'Globalisation, Governance and International Cricket', 187.
[22] Ibid., 183.

[23] Ibid., 180.
[24] Gupta, 'Zee vs ESPN-Star: It's Match of the Season', quoted in ibid, 182.
[25] S. Dabkowski, 'Indian Cricket Fever Spins Plenty of Dollars for Australia', *The Age*, January 3, 2004.
[26] Lamb, 'Globalisation, Governance and International Cricket', 183–4.
[27] S. Dabkowski, 'Indian Cricket Fever Spins Plenty of Dollars for Australia', *The Age*, January 3, 2004.
[28] Lamb, 'Globalisation, Governance and International Cricket', 189–90.
[29] Cashman, Hughes and Zavos, *The Pavilion on the University Green*, 221.
[30] Communication from Kristine Toohey.
[31] Roberts and James, *Sri Lanka and Australia at Cricket*, 122
[32] www.cricinfo.com, January 6, 2008.
[33] Michael Lynch, 'Why Asia is our Road to Riches', *The Age,* March 25, 2005.
[34] Anthony Bubalo, 'Comrades On and Off the Pitch', *The Australian*, September 30, 2005.
[35] Michael Lynch, 'Why Asia is our Road to Riches', *The Age,* March 25, 2005.
[36] ABC website, www.abc.net.au, April 21, 2006.
[37] Fox Sports News, www.foxsports.com.au, June 15, 2006.
[38] Urawa Red Diamonds website: www.urawa-reds.co.jp.
[39] Bubalo, 'Football Diplomacy', 3, 7.
[40] Communication from Sandy Hollway and John Hunter, Telstra.
[41] Cashman, *The Bitter-Sweet Awakening*, 119–23.
[42] Communication from Eric Winton of SBOS.
[43] Pollard, *Australian Rugby Union*, 353.

References

Bubalo, Anthony. 'Football Diplomacy'. Sydney: Policy Brief, Lowy Institute for International Policy, November 2005. http://www.lowyinstitute.org.

Cashman, Richard. *Sport in the National Imagination: Australian Sport in the Federation Decades.* Sydney: Walla Walla Press, 2002.

Cashman, Richard. *The Bitter-Sweet Awakening: The Legacy of the Sydney 2000 Olympic Games.* Sydney: Walla Walla Press, 2006.

Cashman, Richard, Anthony Hughes and Zolton Zavos. *The Pavilion on the University Green.* Sydney: Walla Walla Press, 2005.

Cashman, Richard, Warwick Franks, Jim Maxwell, Brian Stoddart, Amanda Weaver, and Ray Webster, eds. *The Oxford Companion to Australian Cricket.* Melbourne: Oxford University Press, 1996.

Coward, Mike. *Cricket Beyond the Bazaar.* Sydney: Allen & Unwin, 1990.

Honey, Andrew. 'Sport, Immigration Restriction and Race: the Operation of the White Australia Policy'. In *Sport, Federation, Nation*, edited by Richard Cashman, John O'Hara, and Andrew Honey, Chap. 3, 26–46. Sydney: Walla Walla Press, 2001.

Lamb, Peter. 'Globalisation, Governance and International Cricket'. PhD diss., University of Sydney, 2005.

Maguire, Joseph. 'Global sport: Identities, Societies and Civilizations'. Paper presented at the International Olympic Academy, Greece, 28 May–3 June, 1999.

McCoy, Damien. 'Martial Arts'. In *Sporting Immigrants: Sport and Ethnicity in Australia*, edited by Philip A. Mosely, Richard Cashman, John O'Hara, and Hilary Weatherburn, 238–50. Sydney: Walla Walla Press, 1997.

Mosely, Philip A. '"Playing Ball with Asia": Asian-Australian Links through Soccer'. In *The World Game Downunder*, edited by Bill Murray and Roy Hay, Chap. 4, 53–74. Melbourne: ASSH Studies no.19, 2006.

Ohmae, K. *The End of the Nation State: The Rise of Regional Economies.* London: HarperCollins, 1995.

Pollard, Jack. *Australian Rugby Union: The Game and the Players.* Sydney: Angus & Robertson, 1984.

Roberts, Michael, and Alfred James. *Sri Lanka and Australia at Cricket.* Sydney: Walla Walla Press, 1998.

Stell, Marion K. *Half the Race: A History of Australian Women in Sport.* Sydney: Angus & Robertson, 1991.

Watson, Don. *Recollections of a Bleeding Heart: A Portrait of Paul Keating PM.* Sydney: Knopf, 2002.

The importance of prior knowledge: the Australian Olympic Committee and the Sydney 2000 Olympic Games

Stephen Frawley[a] and Kristine Toohey[b]

[a]School of Leisure, Sport and Tourism, University of Technology, Sydney, Australia; [b]Department of Tourism, Leisure, Hotel and Sport Management, Griffith University, Queensland, Australia

This study investigates how the Australian Olympic Committee (AOC) was involved in the formation of the Sports Commission (SSC) within the Sydney Organising Committee for the Olympic Games (SOCOG) and as a critical contributor to the staging of the Sydney 2000 Olympic Games. Using a figurational sociological framework, the intended and unintended consequences of the AOC's strategic and operational involvement are explored. The case shows how important early negotiations were in the case of the Sydney Olympics, when the host governments and Olympic Organizing Committees, in the period immediately following the winning of a bid, were inexperienced in Olympic negotiations and distracted by the euphoria of securing the Games. This left the more knowledgeable Olympic organization, the AOC, well placed to leverage its prior experience and extensive Olympic figurations, in order to gain a strategic advantage over the other Australian Olympic stakeholders. The research makes a contribution to Olympic studies, specifically in relation to the role of the host National Olympic Committee (NOC) in the organizing of an Olympic Games. Furthermore, the research findings have management implications for the International Olympic Committee (IOC) and future host NOCs, particularly in relation to the structuring of Olympic Organizing Committee governance arrangements.

Introduction

This study explores one facet of the organization of the Sydney 2000 Olympic Games, specifically how the power relations between the Australian Olympic Committee (AOC) and the Sydney Organising Committee for the Olympic Games (SOCOG) resulted in the formation of the SOCOG Sports Commission (SSC), the body that had primary responsibility for the organization of sport at the Sydney Games. Using a figurational sociology perspective, it examines how the AOC was able to exploit its relationship with SOCOG because of its prior Olympic knowledge and the particular organizational model adopted for these Games, which involved a number of stakeholders rather than just a single organizing committee. The impact of the SSC is then investigated using information sourced through semi-structured interviews with 22 former SOCOG managers.

The essay is divided into sections, the first of which provides a context to the study. The second discusses the theoretical perspective that informs it. The third section examines the historical development of the AOC's legal position in the staging of the Sydney Games. The fourth section presents and analyses the interview data. The fifth and final section outlines the limitations of the study and presents conclusions.

As is well known, the Summer Olympic Games are a major global sporting event held every four years. For each Games, cities bid to the event's governing body, the International Olympic Committee (IOC), for the right to stage the Games. There are a number of reasons why cities such as Sydney seek to host the Olympics. These revolve around increasing prestige through heightened national pride and sense of shared identity; favourable positioning of the host city and nation in the eyes of the global community; providing an impetus for sport and urban infrastructure development; extracting spin-off economic benefits through tourism and destination marketing; and enhancing the potential for success of the country's Olympic team by competing on home soil.[1]

Despite the lure of such benefits, 'organising the Olympic Games is a huge and complex task which is carried out for each host city largely by people with no previous experience and under the intense scrutiny of local and international media'.[2] The one organization in the host nation that has guaranteed previous Olympic experience is its National Olympic Committee (NOC), which, in the case of Australia, was the Australian Olympic Committee (AOC). The role of both the organizing committee and host NOC (as they relate to the staging of the Olympic Games), is governed by the IOC, and based upon the *Olympic Charter*.[3]

Australia has hosted two summer Olympic Games: Melbourne in 1956 and Sydney in 2000. The Sydney Olympic Games were held in an era where the size, political ramifications, technology and security requirements, and global reach of the Olympics meant these Games required far more organization and budget than their Melbourne counterpart. While both Games were considered successful, the Sydney Games were described by the IOC President, Juan Samaranch, at the Closing Ceremony, as the 'best ever'.[4] The agency given primary responsibility for the organization and staging of these Games was known as the Sydney Organising Committee for the Olympic Games (SOCOG). However, according to Michael Knight, the SOCOG President (from 1995 until 2001) and New South Wales (NSW) Government Olympic Minister (from 1995 until 2001), a major contributing factor for the Games' success, was not necessarily the organizing committee, but emerged from the centrality of the Australian Olympic Committee (AOC) in planning the Sydney Games. In the *Official Report of the Games of the XXVII Olympiad*, he stated:

> While many things contributed to the successful staging of the Olympic Games in Sydney, two things were fundamental to what has come to be called the 'Sydney Model' for organising a Games. Firstly, the Government was central to the process. Not only did the Government of the State of New South Wales underwrite the Olympic Games financially, the public sector played the leading role in delivering the building program … Secondly, the Australian Olympic Committee was closely involved in the organising of the Games. The creation of an autonomous Sports Commission, with strong AOC representation, which had direct control over preparations for the sporting competition and the management of the Athletes Village, was essential to Sydney fulfilling our commitment to put the athletes first.[5]

This organizational model differed to that of the previous summer Games, held in Atlanta. Aligned to this organizational disparity was dissimilarity in financial arrangements. While the 1996 Atlanta Olympics were privately funded, the Sydney Games were fully underwritten by the host state, New South Wales, Government. While the NSW Government was the financial underwriter of the Games it was also legally bound because of contractual arrangements, signed either before Sydney won the right to stage the Games, or immediately thereafter, to include the AOC in all key Olympic decision making. This provided the AOC with a strong foundation by which to leverage this legal arrangement to its advantage, as will be demonstrated by the formation of the SOCOG Sports Commission (SSC), whose remit was to organize the Olympic sport programme at the Sydney Games. The formation of the SSC, with legal authority and with a separate structure to the SOCOG Board, was the result of both intended and unintended consequences and will be examined from a figurational sociological perspective.[6]

Theoretical approach: processes of interdependence

The interdependent and changing relationships of key Sydney 2000 Olympic stakeholders (such as the NSW Government, SOCOG and the AOC), as will be shown through the formation of the SSC, provides a detailed organizational case study, revolving around the use of power, that can inform future Olympic organizers and other mega events conducted in a similar context, as all Olympics now involve a myriad of contractual relationships between governments, OCOGs and NOCs. For example, the IOC now requires each Candidate City to provide financial guarantees issued by either the city itself, or by other relevant local, regional or national public authorities or an appropriate third party before it is even considered for selection as the host of a Games.

Critical organizational theorists such as Clegg, Courpasson and Phillips[7] have suggested that scholars in management research have adopted a generally narrow approach to the study of power relations in organizations and that broader perspectives are needed. Hardy and Clegg[8] argue that a significant portion of organizational management research has focused on the use of authority to overcome conflict, brought about by the illegitimate, rather than the legitimate exercise of power. Thus, they contend that management research has tended to examine power in terms of conflict situations. However, this is not its only exercise. In understanding power and human agency, a figurational (Eliasian) approach brings a different perspective because it examines what are typically shifting power relations between interdependent groups and networks over time, and so this approach is not predicated on what Hardy and Clegg would term the illegitimate use of power.[9] It is this temporal aspect that provides the rationale for the selection of figurational sociology as the most appropriate theoretical framework to examine this Olympic case study.

Using a figurational approach in an Olympic context is appropriate, as Frisby has noted that the Olympic Games can provide an insight into sport organizational research that: 'involves questioning taken-for-granted knowledge and examining the complex relationships between local forms of domination and the broader contexts in which they are situated ... [it] requires an understanding of how material and economic arrangements are enforced by contracts and reward systems'.[10] While a number of management theories, such as stakeholder and agency theories, could be used to examine the role of the AOC in establishing the SSC, the figurational approach, as developed by Elias[11] and utilized by sport sociology scholars and a growing number of organizational management researchers, has been chosen as it can also assist in explaining the dynamics and flow of such power relations in an Olympic context over an extended time period.[12]

Figurational sociology, as developed by Norbert Elias, places importance on interdisciplinary research links, especially between the disciplines of sociology and history.[13] In *The Civilizing Process: The History of Manners* Elias argued that analysis of social experience without history is empty and ambiguous.[14] One principle of a figurational approach is the concept of 'interdependency networks'. Elias conceptualized 'figurations' as structures of mutually oriented and dependent people who operate within historically produced, interdependency networks.[15] Figurations, such as those between organizations, are viewed as dynamic, or 'in process',[16] because power relations between individuals and/or groups are continually in flux, rather than being static or still.[17]

The emphasis on a historical perspective in figurational analysis has the purpose of accentuating how interdependency networks evolve and change over time.

Elias contended that interdependency networks frame the 'underlying regularities by which people … are bound over and over again to particular patterns of conduct and very specific functional chains'.[18] This type of longitudinal approach is necessary for understanding the organizational phenomenon that is being studied.[19]

The notion of interdependence relies on a number of features that also distinguish a figurational approach.[20] Firstly, the approach outlines that humans are interdependent through the figurations and networks that they form with other people over time.[21] Secondly, these figurations are continually in flux, or in process of change, undergoing processes of different orders, some quick, some slow, others more enduring.[22] Thirdly, over time, developments take place in figurations that are generally unplanned or unforeseen.[23] As Elias noted: 'underlying all intended interactions of human beings is their unintended interdependence'.[24] The fourth feature of a figurational approach is the centrality of power to interactions. Power is not viewed as 'a substance or property possessed by particular individuals and groups, but as a characteristic of all human relationships'.[25]

Arnason notes that while Elias' concept of power has been unfavourably compared to that of functionalist theorists, such as Parsons, this comparison is not valid, as Elias does not consider there are systemic instances which circumscribe the dynamics of power. Thus, his concept of power is relational. This aligns it more closely with Foucault's view of power. As figurational analyses conceptualize power as relational, this means that it can be held and wielded unequally. Accordingly, the balance of power between groups in a society (or an organization) is never permanent but rather ever flowing and dynamic.[26] 'From this perspective of chains of interdependence we can begin to understand … the way power relations reflect a complex interweaving of interdependencies amongst people, a "networked agency"'.[27] Weick further explains this in a management specific context: 'interdependence is the crucial element from which a theory of organization is built, interacts rather than acts are the crucial observables that must be specified'.[28] Despite power being viewed as a fluid concept, another figurationalist, Dopson, posits that within every network some individuals or groups have more central functions than others and that these individuals or groups will be most central within a chain of interdependence and thus relied upon more heavily.[29]

In addition to a figurational perspective, our analysis of power relations draws on the work of Flyvbjerg.[30] Flyvbjerg suggests that there cannot be an adequate understanding of planning or organizing without viewing it from within the context of values and power, as he notes: 'rationality without power spells irrelevance'.[31] In line with Flyvbjerg and Elias, this study investigates the outcomes of the AOC's power relations with SOCOG and examines how these relations changed and developed over the course of the organization of the Sydney Games.

Flyvbjerg, building on the work of Dahl,[32] suggests that organizational researchers ought to examine those who govern and manage and those who have strong power relations. Moreover, drawing on Foucault,[33] Flyvbjerg[34] posits that social researchers should also ask: 'what are the governmental rationalities that operate when those who do have power, actually govern?'[35] The contextual emphasis for Flyvbjerg, Hardy and Clegg is therefore not only on power relations, but also their supporting values. For example, when examining the development of large infrastructure projects, Flyvbjerg argues that researchers need to scrutinize the likely beneficiaries of project approval: in other words, a combination of figurations, values and interests.

The following section will now follow Flyvbjerg's theoretical proposition by examining the historical involvement of the AOC in the staging of the Sydney Olympic Games, particularly how the organization's early involvement provided it with a platform that was beneficial for its role as a central stakeholder in organizing the Games as well as providing for its financial future.

Historical context: the development of the AOC relationship with SOCOG

In March 1991, two years before Sydney was awarded the Olympic Games, the AOC, the New South Wales (NSW) Coalition Government (under the leadership of Premier Nick Griener) and the City of Sydney signed a contract that was unique to the Sydney Games and would have a significant impact on the financing and organizing of the 2000 Olympics.[36] Known as the 'Endorsement Contract', this 31-page document was jointly composed by the AOC's President, John Coates, and the AOC's Legal Counsel, Simon Rofe.[37] While its main purpose was to sanction the City of Sydney candidature for the 2000 Olympic Games (necessary for IOC regulations before a city could bid for a Games), it also effectively rendered the NSW Government fully responsible for the cost of staging the Games, whilst committing both parties to further contractual obligations, should Sydney be successful in securing the 2000 Olympic Games.[38]

The central elements that underpinned the Endorsement Contract can be traced back to the mid 1980s. At this time, Coates was the CEO for the City of Brisbane's bid to stage the 1992 Olympics, and IOC member, Kevan Gosper, was the President of the AOC.[39] While the Brisbane bid was unsuccessful, the involvement of Coates in the process proved to be vital for later Australian bids and also for the AOC.[40] Both Coates and Rofe undertook the contract planning for the Brisbane bid and then refined it further with the Melbourne bid to stage the 1996 Games. Although both these bids failed to achieve their goal, they provided valuable insider knowledge on the bid processes that would aid Sydney's chances of securing the Games and also underpin the AOC's strategy in developing its role in the Sydney 2000 bid process and subsequent Olympic planning.[41] Pivotal to the success of this contract planning was the positioning of the AOC, not as a mere token organization, required by IOC regulations to sign relevant approvals, but one which was integral to the planning and organizing of the Sydney Games.[42] Coates noted that:

> Much has been written and spoken in the media about the power and influence of the AOC in the organization and staging of the Games. Without doubt, that power and influence is founded in the Endorsement Contract. Everything that has developed between the AOC, the state of NSW and SOCOG has its roots in that contract.[43]

However, the Endorsement contract would have been meaningless if Sydney did not win the right to host the Games of the XVII Olympiad. This occurred on 23 September 1993 at the 101st IOC Session in Monte Carlo. Another contract, known as the 'Host City' contract, was signed at this Session by representatives of the IOC, the City of Sydney and the AOC. Every successful bid city, its NOC and the IOC is required to sign such a 'Host City' contract. Together with the *Olympic Charter*, this contract determines the obligations and requirements of hosting an Olympic Games. Although the 'Host City' contract had the approval of all three signatory organizations, it was the IOC that had dictated its terms, as it is the IOC that is the main authority of the Olympic Movement. Amongst its many clauses, this contract stipulated that the AOC and the City of Sydney form an Organizing Committee of the Olympic Games (OCOG) within eight months,[44] which was to be charged with the responsibility for staging the Games. According to the *Official Report of the Games of the XXVII Olympiad*:

> It had also been agreed at that time that A$60 million was to be paid to the AOC to fund reasonable costs and expenses during the period 1997–2000, including the preparation and participation of the Australian teams in the 1998 Olympic Winter Games and the 2000

Olympic Games. The A$60 million was negotiated to be paid by the State of NSW as a condition of the AOC endorsing Sydney's candidacy to host the 2000 Olympic Games and, in the event that the candidature was successful, of the AOC entering into a joint marketing program with the Organising Committee wherein the intellectual properties of the AOC were combined with those of SOCOG in a single marketing program. The AOC therefore did not have rights to a separate marketing program.[45]

Thus, while the AOC received a financial reward for its part in the success of Sydney's bid, it also relinquished a degree of independence in regards to its marketing (a primary source of its finance) until the Games. Nevertheless, despite this lack of marketing autonomy, the combination of the Endorsement Contact and the Host City Contract had put the AOC in a powerful position as one of the key stakeholders of the Sydney Olympics.

In 1995, after the election of a new Labor Government (under the leadership of Premier Bob Carr) in the host state of NSW, the incumbent became fully aware of its inherited Olympic Games obligations, as stipulated in the 1991 Endorsement Contract. Through the first months of 1996, the Labor Cabinet became increasingly disturbed with what it considered to be the one-sided nature of the contract, and the potential financial risk that was imposed on the state.[46] As a result, the Minister for the Olympic and Paralympic Games, Michael Knight (who was appointed to this position in March 1995), started arguing through the media with John Coates, now the now AOC President, about the fairness and equity of the Endorsement contract that was originally signed in 1991, and also in regard to an element of the Host City Contract.[47]

The AOC and the NSW Government were primarily in dispute over two particular contract clauses: one clause in the 1991 Endorsement Contract and another clause within the 1993 Host City Contract. The key point of difference within the Host City Contract revolved around the distribution of profits from the Games.[48] The Host City Contract, following accepted IOC process, determined that all profits generated from the Games (if any) would be split between the AOC and the IOC.[49] The AOC was to receive 90% (10% for itself and the other 80% which it would administer for the benefit of sport in Australia) while the IOC was to receive the remaining 10%. One particular clause in the Endorsement Contract also displeased the NSW Government. This clause gave the AOC the power of veto over every single line item in the SOCOG budget. The Government viewed this arrangement as untenable.[50] Not only was it hampering SOCOG's financial planning and dealings, it also posed difficulties in regard to the day-to-day operations of SOCOG.[51]

The extraordinary consequences of the combination of the two contracts meant that the NSW Government would receive no financial return from any Games profit, even though it was providing the overwhelming majority of the capital required for the Games, whilst also underwriting all the financial risk. In addition, SOCOG could be hamstrung in its daily operations and planning if the AOC invoked its veto, resulting in a greater likelihood of little or no profit from the Games.[52] With these problems in mind, the Government examined the possibility of breaking the contracts;[53] however the AOC, wanting to maintain its potential financial legacy from the Games, aggressively warned it against such action. The AOC argued that the contracts were untouchable, that they were embedded in NSW law and, in the case of the 'Host City' Contract, as a further impediment to amendment, in Swiss law as well. Gordon notes that 'Swiss law would not sanction the breaking of contract commitments'.[54]

Independent from Government

This particular battle was not the first time that the AOC had fought with Government. The AOC had long believed that it should be autonomous from Government control.[55]

The resistance stemmed, historically at least, from pressure placed by the Australian Government to prevent the Australian Olympic Team competing in the 1980 Moscow Olympic Games and stipulations regarding the government's financial support when it failed to do so.[56] Since that time, the AOC had embraced an 'independent from Government' approach.[57] This philosophy had influenced, for example, the structure and membership of the early planning for the 2000 Games. The AOC successfully argued that the NSW Coalition Government should establish a private Bid company (the Sydney 2000 Olympic Bid Limited [SOBL]) to run the Bid rather than it being handled by a NSW Government Department. This AOC strategy of seeking independence from Government would continue to cause difficulties with their relationship with the NSW Government. As a lawyer and an Olympic administrator who knew the legal and operational consequences of the contracts, Coates had ensured (with AOC lawyer, Simon Rofe) that the AOC increased its power through the documents, rather than just being an ineffectual but required signatory to relevant Sydney 2000 contracts. Gordon notes that with these early contracts the AOC had outsmarted the NSW Government which was less experienced in Olympic business.[58]

However, as 1996 progressed, the Carr NSW Government, increasingly frustrated by the terms of the two contracts, and noting the Coates' viewpoint about their 'watertight' legal status decided to adopt a new strategy and buy its way out of the contracts.[59] At this point, the former Labor Federal Minister for Sport and SOCOG Board Member, Graham Richardson, stepped in as a dealmaker, a role that he had experienced on numerous occasions as a senior member of the Australian Labor Party. Richardson, who had known both Coates and Knight for many years, suggested independently to both men that they needed to settle their dispute quickly as the public fight between the two was becoming unseemly, and SOCOG was becoming focused on the dispute rather than on the planning necessary for a successful Games.[60] Richardson warned that failure to reach accord would lead to an escalation of organizational crisis.[61] For example, the AOC, if provoked, could activate its opportunity to be the financial gatekeeper of SOCOG, impeding the planning and organization of the Games.[62] Richardson would later suggest: 'The right of veto was hanging like the sword of Damocles over everyone's head … if you were going to progress the Games that had to go. John Coates knew that, he was playing his cards well … he also knew that he had to extract a fair price.'[63]

Richardson decided to organize a dinner meeting between Coates and Knight in an attempt to resolve the dispute. The meeting took place at a regular Labor Party haunt, the House of Guangzhou within Sydney's Chinatown district. While lobster, a house specialty, was ordered, it would be the prawn dish that would be the most apocryphal.[64] The meeting between the three men became known as 'The Knight of the Long Prawns', a suggestion to the food and location, but also a more oblique historical reference, alluding to Knight's political reputation.[65] Richardson was deliberately late to arrive, forcing Coates and Knight to engage in some discourse for approximately thirty minutes.[66] He later claimed that he thought that it would be impossible for both Coates and Knight to sit together in a restaurant and not to begin some discussion.[67]

Knight opened negotiations with Coates by offering the AOC A$24 million in exchange for the AOC forgoing its right of veto over the SOCOG budget, and its 90% share of any potential Games profit.[68] Coates rejected the initial offer. Debate continued for the next couple of hours through a number of dinner courses, until it was agreed that a settlement of A$75 million would be made to the AOC. This A$75 million was tagged in 1993 dollars (the year the Host City Contract was signed). Taking inflation into account, it eventually became an A$90 million payout, when the funds were transferred to the AOC after the completion of the Games. Both new arrangements required the approval of the

IOC. The IOC agreed on the basis that it retained its rights to 10% of any SOCOG surplus, which it would then use for sport development in the Oceania region.[69]

Not satisfied with only the cash component, the AOC also required a further concession from the NSW Government. This was that a commission within SOCOG be formed to organize sport-specific and sport-related activities for the Games. This demand indicated that the AOC was seeking more than just money: it was also following the brief of the Sydney Bid Committee, which had promised to deliver an 'Athletes Games'. Coates later explained that he wanted such a commission because:

> I was concerned that the SOCOG Board wasn't giving any attention to sport ... The sporting side wasn't being reported on, there was no direction, people running the Games at that stage didn't come from a sporting background ... So, I said I wanted a sports commission of SOCOG established under my chairmanship, with AOC majority representation, and for it to be delegated the responsibilities for running sport, with the budget. He [Knight] understood that made good sense, and his first reaction was to say, 'I want someone on the committee'. I said, 'well, Graham's been Minister for Sport'. Richardson became the Knight nominee.[70]

The new agreement, while seemingly expensive, delivered greater financial certainty to the NSW Government and greater operational security to SOCOG, by the removal of the AOC's veto power.[71] It was, nevertheless, still advantageous to the AOC in financial terms. On the day that Coates signed the new agreement, he suggested it was the 'most significant day in the history of the AOC'.[72]

The relationship between the AOC and the NSW Labor Government which, until this point, had been less than harmonious, now began a new, pragmatic chapter. After the conclusion of the contract renegotiation it did not take long for both parties to become strong allies and for the idea of a Sport Commission to be transferred into reality. According to Gordon, the agreement signalled a 'shift in philosophies' and a new sense 'of unity and realism'. What now united Knight and Coates was 'a shared realization that ... each would need the other'.[73] Through the renegotiated contracts, the NSW Government, through Michael Knight's position as Chair of the SOCOG Board, was able to gain financial control of the Games, rather than its previous position of financial liability without the control. The cash payment would enable the AOC to ensure its continued financial independence in an Australian post-Olympic environment. Thus, while it may appear that the AOC again outmanoeuvred the NSW Government, both parties were satisfied with the outcomes and Coates and Knight began to form a strong working partnership.

The SOCOG Board carried the motion to set up the SSC on 5 June 1996. The SSC was chaired by John Coates and established as a permanent commission of SOCOG. Its powers, functions and membership could not be altered or abolished without the prior written consent of both the President of the AOC and the President of SOCOG, the two men who had agreed to renegotiating the Endorsement and Host City contracts. It was made up of representatives from the IOC and the AOC, and also included Graham Richardson, the man who had brokered the deal between Knight and Coates.[74] Thus, all the parties who were present at the Guangzhou dinner had input into the new commission.

Once the SSC was formed it needed to take leadership for the organization of SOCOG's sport responsibilities at the Games. This study now draws on interviews as source material to investigate the impact of the SSC on the organization of sport for the Sydney 2000 Games.

Technique

A qualitative, semi-structured interview methodology was selected as the appropriate approach. First, it allowed the researchers to draw on their detailed insider knowledge of SOCOG, and second, it assisted in collecting richly descriptive interview responses.[75]

With the interviewing of people being central to this study, great care was taken to minimize any ethical concerns that may have arisen. The research design followed the operating procedures for human research as outlined by the Griffith University Human Research Ethics Committee. The confidentiality of the interview respondents was of paramount importance to the researchers. In order to achieve this goal all interview transcripts were coded and then stored separately to the interview tapes in a locked storage cabinet. Secondly, the research was conducted in a manner that did not disrupt or waste the time of the study participants. The following section is divided into two parts. The first part will examine the research informants and type of questions that were posed to them, while the second part will discuss how the qualitative data stemming from this was analysed.

Informants

In-depth interviews were conducted with former SOCOG Sport Division senior and middle managers. The interview sample was selected because of the central sport planning position these managers held within SOCOG. The managers interviewed were all responsible for the competition management of an Olympic sport at the Sydney Games. In addition to competition management, two senior SOCOG Managers were also interviewed. The lead researcher knew all the informants that were interviewed as he had worked with them in the SOCOG Sport Division, from 1998 to 2001.

The subject selection was based on the principle of theoretical sampling, which involves the deliberate selection of individuals within a certain population.[76] This method involves choosing a small number of targeted representatives to provide insight to a specific case. The interviews with the sample group took place in the second half of 2002 and the first half of 2003. The managers interviewed had each worked for SOCOG for an average period of four years. From a group of 30 possible respondents, 26 were contactable. From this group of 26, 22 people agreed to participate in the study. Nineteen of the respondents were male, while three were female. Sixteen of the interviews were conducted in person, while three interviews were conducted by phone due to geographical and logistical limitations. The face-to-face and phone interviews conducted ranged from 45 minutes to two and a half hours in length. These particular interviews were all tape recorded and then transcribed. Three additional interviews were conducted via e-mail, due to either health or geographic reasons. These electronic interviewees were sent a list of questions with responses sent back via e-mail. Follow-up correspondence took place if further data was deemed necessary from these three respondents.

The analysis of the qualitative data consisted of a three main stages. These included data reduction, data coding and data verification.[77] After a close reading of the interview transcripts, data that was deemed to be outside the scope of the study was excluded.[78] Themes emerged through careful and repeated reading of the interview transcripts.[79] The collected data was then coded into identified themes. Coding assisted the management of the raw data through the creation of thematic categories.[80] Each piece of data was placed in a code category. Codes were assigned to key words, phrases and sentences.

Gratton and Jones argue that validity is an important consideration in determining codes, that codes: 'should be valid … they should accurately reflect what is being researched, they should be mutually exclusive, in that codes should be distinct, with no overlap, and they should be exhaustive … all relevant data should fit into a code'.[81] This process was initially conducted manually, followed by a second round of analysis, using the software package Nvivo 7. Within the codes, the researchers looked for examples to describe situations that were of interest to the study and its objectives. The researchers looked for statements that confirmed as well as refuted the research aims, in order to build a strong picture for the study.[82]

In summary, coding was undertaken to highlight the emerging themes and to assist the analysis of approximately 100,000 words of interview transcripts. However, as Dey[83] argues, researchers need to be aware of the mechanistic nature of qualitative data analysis when using specific software packages. This problem was minimized by spending time manually reviewing the data output for context, something that can be easily lost when using software like Nvivo 7 alone.[84]

Results and analysis: the SSC and the organization of sport

As a trained attorney, Coates and, *ipso facto* the AOC, through his position as President, understood the importance of the law in utilizing organizational power. The establishment of the SSC, with its responsibilities entrenched in NSW Parliamentary Legislation, meant that this body had the power to determine much of the SOCOG specific organization of sport at the Games, not the Directors of the SOCOG Board.[85] Within SOCOG itself, the SSC had responsibility for management of the Sport Division and all its sport-specific functional areas (known in SOCOG as Programmes). These Programmes included: Sport Operations; Sport Competition (including pre-Games training and test events); International Sport Federation Relations; National Olympic Committee Relations; Sports Equipment and Freight; Games and Competition Scheduling; and International Olympic Committee Sport Relations, including the IOC Coordination Commission.[86]

The SSC was also responsible for a number of other sport-related functions within non-sport SOCOG Divisions. Part of the SSC's responsibility was to ensure that various (non-sport) programmes delivered the specifications and requirements of the Sport Division in accordance with its commitments to SOCOG and the IOC.[87] Such programmes included: Human Resources (sport competition volunteers); Marketing (test events and sports equipment sponsorship); Facilities (the field of play and training venues); Villages (athletes and officials); Medical (athletes and officials); Transport (athletes and officials); Accreditation (athletes and officials); Accommodation (athletes and officials and test events); Security (with regard to athletes and officials), ticketing (with regard to the scheduling of competition); Technology (with regard to scoring, timing and results systems); Broadcasting (with regard to the field of play and athlete press conferences); Ceremonies (with regard to athletes); and, Olympic Family (with regard to language services and customs).[88] Thus, the SSC's responsibilities included key functions across the organizing committee, not just sport.

Although the SSC was an innovation in OCOG organization and planning, some previous OCOGs had put in place dedicated sport sub-committees (such as the case with the 1992 Barcelona Olympics), whose remit related specifically to the organization of sport. However, no previous OCOG had a structure with such broad and legitimized powers as the SSC. Indeed, the SSC had its authority enshrined in legislation.[89] According to a former senior SOCOG official, the SSC had:

> total power, because the [SOCOG] Sports Commission was an autonomous body having full control over all decisions relating to the organization and conduct of sport and athletes under an agreed charter of responsibility. With the only exception being with the budget and that the overall budget for sport had to be approved by the SOCOG Board. After that the Sports Commission had the right to use that budget as it wished without exceeding it and it had total autonomy, so I think it was a first in that regard.[90]

Five key themes emerge from analysis of the interview data: the impact of the SSC; people and knowledge; power and legitimacy of the SSC; and the decisions made by the SSC. These themes are each discussed in turn.

Impact of the SSC

The majority of the respondents stated that the SSC had a significant impact on the organization of sport at the Sydney 2000 Olympic Games. Twenty of the 22 respondents also viewed the AOC's involvement in SOCOG as a positive organizational feature. They suggested that because the responsibility for sport was taken away from the SOCOG Board, decisions could be made quickly by people who possessed the appropriate sport management expertise. According to a SOCOG official, the SSC 'had a major bearing on moving everything through that needed to be'.[91] Additionally, another respondent suggested that the SSC was 'politically well positioned' containing 'several heavy hitters amongst its hierarchy'.[92]

Supporting the above points, a number of respondents suggested that OCOGs and their boards tend to get overwhelmed in a range of unrelated sport issues, ranging from budgetary difficulties to protocol disputes. For example, one respondent argued that the SSC 'was particularly important ... in that it managed all the requirements for the athlete, it took control of those budget areas, it took control of decision making, the turnaround on decision making was immediate'.[93] In an OCOG, with many competing functional areas, many of which (for example, technology, marketing, broadcasting, ticketing, ceremonies etc.) are integral to a successful Games, the organization of sport is not often seen as a high priority until late in the project cycle. One respondent suggested that the SSC provided certainty that sport would be highly thought of in the planning process: 'I do not think anyone could underestimate or exaggerate the extent to which the SSC provided a huge weight ... an authority that you knew you could place confidence in making a decision'.[94]

Only two of the 22 respondents believed that the formation of the SSC resulted in negative consequences for the organization of sport at the Games. One of these respondents suggested that the SSC should have been more diverse in its representation. For example, it contained no women. Additionally, there was no Paralympic representation on the SSC, even though the SOCOG Sport Division was also largely responsible for the delivery of sport at the Sydney 2000 Paralympic Games. A further view was that the SSC extended its influence into matters that were beyond its brief: 'I had a bit of a problem with the Sports Commission; with some of the people on it ... [they] delved into too many other things ... If you get off side with [the SSC] ... you're in big time trouble, and I was never off side ... but I think I could have been if I wasn't careful, because I didn't agree with some of the things'.[95]

People and knowledge

It was also noted that the composition of OCOG boards often has minimal sport management knowledge and expertise. One respondent argued that, 'with John Coates in charge and with his influence on the SOCOG Board, you could be sure that decisions taken were in the best interests of the sport'.[96] The interview data also outlined that the SSC provided support where the SOCOG Board was lacking in sport organizational skills. As one respondent noted, 'I think [the SSC] had a significant impact ... it took away from the Board ... the responsibilities of sport, because inevitably, history shows that the organizing committee itself never finds time to spend on sport'.[97] Host organizing committees, it was argued, are forever focusing on 'political matters, raising revenue, marketing, IOC related issues etc, etc. Sport tends to be forgotten because there isn't time and secondly, often because of the composition of the Board ... is not necessarily made up with people with sport expertise'.[98]

Legitimacy and power of the SSC

Those interviewed argued that the main strength of the SSC came from the power and legitimacy it possessed within SOCOG. It was argued that the establishment of the SSC showed a real commitment to sport from both SOCOG (which transferred power from the board to the SSC) and the NSW Government (which had agreed to the AOC's proposal that it be formed). Additionally, it was noted in the interview data that the power to determine the place of sport within SOCOG resided with the individuals who sat on the SSC:

> The members of the [SOCOG] Sports Commission understood [the Olympic] Sport [Programme] ... a few of the SOCOG Board didn't ... they were more interested in the dollar ... Whereas, for Coatesy [SSC Chairmen John Coates], in particular the dollar wasn't part of it. If you had a genuine case it happened and it happened ... much quicker.[99]

The SSC had legitimacy in the eyes of the respondents because it was specifically dedicated to sport and policy issues and it consisted of high-profile people with sport management knowledge and expertise. The SSC membership included the President of the AOC and SOCOG Board member as Chairperson (John Coates); the Secretary-General of the AOC and SOCOG Board member (Craig McLatchey); the senior Australian member of the AOC and SOCOG Board member (Kevan Gosper); two representatives from the SOCOG Board who had sport management experience (Graham Richardson and Graham Lovett); and the Chief Executive Officer of SOCOG (Mal Hemmerling, followed by Sandy Hollway).

A number of the respondents interviewed believed that the Sydney Games would still have been successful without the SSC, but they argued that this success would have been much more difficult to achieve. For example, the respondents argued that the SOCOG Sport Division would have struggled to stage the range and number of test events without the influence of the SSC: 'the Games would still have been successful ... but it would have been much more difficult. I can see for example, that we may have struggled to be able to achieve the number of test events we wanted to pursue, because a lot of people [in non-sport SOCOG Divisions] thought test events were a waste of money and a waste of time.'[100]

Decisions made by the SSC

The interview data highlighted a number of key sport-related decisions that were advocated and championed by the SSC. These decisions were viewed as important to the success of the Sydney 2000 Olympic Games. For instance, key decisions that were made by the SSC included: supporting the inclusion of the Canoe/Kayak Slalom on to the competition schedule for the Sydney Games, which necessitated the construction of the new white water facility at Penrith Lakes; Beach Volleyball remaining at Bondi Beach, despite local protests; supporting the introduction of women's Water Polo onto the Sydney sport competition schedule; and supporting extra athlete places for women's diving and women's shooting. As one respondent noted,

Without [the SSC] ... pushing the athlete and the sport side of [the Games] ... I am sure the sports would not of had the facilities for the athletes, for the spectators, and the whole lot that we had. They made sure for me that the Olympic Games ... [that] SOCOG didn't lose focus on what the hell it was there for, which was the sport and the athletes.[101]

Discussion

The staging of an Olympic Games involves a large number of stakeholders. The formation and structure of the SSC, as an autonomous decision-making body within SOCOG, strengthened the bond between two of these stakeholders, and allowed the Sport Division an unprecedented level of operational legitimacy and financial autonomy within the OCOG.[102] The SSC also provided a forum for the AOC, through its representatives on the SSC, to ensure that the planning and delivery of sport was central to, and not a secondary consideration for, the SOCOG Board. Because of this cooperation the place of the AOC in the organization of the Games became more central, rather than just ceremonial, and the bonds between Knight and Coates, two Australian Olympic powerbrokers, were transformed from antagonistic to supportive.[103] They were both political realists and pragmatists.

A figurational approach to this research has encouraged the analysis of organizational development and change from a temporal perspective. Organizational developments 'represent the product of generations of interwoven, interdependency ties and do not suddenly appear fully formed as often is assumed'.[104] The changing relationship between AOC and the NSW Government (which itself changed hands) is an example of this dynamic organizational development. The formation of the SSC was an unplanned outcome of an AOC and NSW Government disagreement, highlighting the complex historical interactions between two of the stakeholders involved in the organization of the Sydney Games.

When examining planned or unplanned organizational development, Flyvbjerg, drawing on Foucault, suggests the study of power should take place from a strategic perspective.[105] Flyvbjerg argues that it is not only important to understand who has organizational power, but also to examine the rationalities at play when those with power govern or organize.[106] Both the AOC and the NSW Government benefited from the successful staging of the Sydney 2000 Olympic Games. The AOC extracted a significant financial legacy whilst the NSW Government basked in the reflected glory of its role in a successful Games and, at least publicly, claimed to be happy with the financial arrangements. For example, the NSW Government's *Report on the Financial Contribution by the New South Wales Government to the Sydney 2000 Olympic Games* states:

The Games have left important legacies, including the economic benefits, which have flowed to the State as a result of the Games. In addition, Sydney has gained world class entertainment, sporting and recreational facilities as well as the expertise and capacity to attract a growing number of world-class events.[107]

Both Coates and Knight rationalized their involvement in the Games as benefiting either the athletes of the world or the people of NSW. However, both individuals also gained significantly from the successful staging of the Olympic Games. Each was awarded the IOC Gold Olympic Order at the Games Closing Ceremony and have continued working within the Olympic Movement (although they have continued to be criticized for their confrontational approach to management). Coates was also made an IOC member, while Knight left the NSW Parliament shortly after the Games and has acted as a consultant to the IOC and the Athens Olympic Organizing Committee (ATHOC).

After the infamous 'Knight of the Long Prawns' the two men, through the SSC, worked together resourcefully and pragmatically to help deliver a very successful Sydney 2000 Olympic Games sport competition programme. Yet they continued to be involved in controversy in other aspects of SOCOG and Olympic planning and organization, such as the marketing of Olympic tickets and the use of American marching bands for the Opening Ceremony.

The fluid and changing interdependent relationships between the AOC, the NSW government and SOCOG, and the resultant formation of the SSC, can be viewed by using Elias's notion of figurations. From the beginning of planning for the Sydney Games, the AOC positioned itself to be central to the 2000 Olympic Games. In terms of 'having power', this authority certainly increased. New configurations continued to develop and change over the life of SOCOG as contracts were renegotiated and new state governments were formed.

The case of the Sydney Olympics shows how important early negotiations can be in Olympic matters. Host governments and OCOGs are relatively lacking in experience in the period immediately following the winning of a bid and may be distracted by the euphoria of securing the Games. This can leave the more experienced Olympic organizations, such as the NOCs, well placed in the early stages of preparations to leverage their prior experience and extensive Olympic figurations to gain an advantage at a time when contracts need to be signed. The results of this can endure long after the OCOG has been disbanded, because of the financial benefit that the NOC could negotiate. For example, the British Olympic Association, the host NOC for the London 2012 Games, notes that:

> The 2012 Olympic Project presents a greater opportunity to ensure that sport not only remains high on the political agenda, but begins to impact on the social landscape of the entire United Kingdom. That is the real legacy behind the BOA's dream, and all must take advantage of this opportunity to ensure a legacy for sport for generations to come.[108]

While the final outcome of the AOC's involvement was positive for the planning and delivery of the Sydney Olympics, it was also beneficial for the financial legacy of the Australian Olympic movement. The funds that the AOC received, from signing over its veto rights in the Endorsement contract and from the monies it received with the renegotiation of the Host City Contract, were used to create the Australian Olympic Foundation. In 2005, this had assets of about A$112.9 million. The investment objectives for the Australian Olympic Foundation[109] are to 'protect and grow the capital base' through careful investment strategies while 'providing sufficient income and liquidity to provide a base distribution to the Australian Olympic Committee … towards its known commitments'.[110]

Limitations and conclusion

There are a number of limitations associated with this research that must be acknowledged. Firstly, consistent with Australian law, there is a 30-year embargo on some internal SOCOG documentation, for example, the SOCOG Board minutes. Access to these documents would have made this study more complete. Secondly, there was a time lag factor associated with this study. For example, the qualitative interviews were conducted in 2002 and 2003, some time after the completion of the Sydney Olympics. Ideally, it would have been preferable to complete these interviews just after the completion of the Games.[111] Thirdly, as outlined earlier, the lead researcher was personally involved in the organization of sport at the Sydney 2000 Olympic Games. Some organizational scholars may argue that this is a negative feature of the study, in that the researchers are too close to the subject at hand, while others scholars may consider this internal knowledge a strong feature of the research.[112]

In conclusion, this study examined one aspect of the role played by the AOC in the organization of the Sydney 2000 Olympic Games. The study examined the impact that formation of the SSC had on the AOC, with regard to its operational and financial autonomy within SOCOG. The research highlighted the significant impact that the SSC had on the organization of sport at the Sydney Games, establishing that the AOC had significant legal authority within SOCOG and that the formation of the SSC gave the SOCOG Sport Division a very high level of importance within SOCOG.

Historically and contextually, the longer-term contest for power involving the AOC and the NSW Government was central to this study. The fluid relations and network interdependency involving SOCOG, the AOC and two NSW state Governments, can be viewed and analysed using Elias's concept of figurations. Rather than considering organizational development in static terms, Elias' framework recognizes that historical context is interconnected to the past as well as to the present.[113] Both the intended strategies of the AOC and the NSW Government produced unplanned consequences that impacted on how SOCOG organised sport at the Sydney Games.

This study, while Sydney specific, has relevance to future Games. The 'Sydney model' of having more than one organization with responsibility for Games organization has been replicated for the 2012 Games. These are to be are delivered by two key organizations: the London 2012 Organizing Committee and the Olympic Delivery Authority. Government involvement is led by the Department for Culture, Media & Sport (DCMS). This organization is:

> responsible for the London Olympic Games and Paralympic Games Act 2006, the overall finances of the Games, and sponsorship of the Olympic Delivery Authority. DCMS also works closely with other key stakeholders – the LOCOG, Mayor of London, the British Olympic Association, the British Paralympic Association and other Government departments and relevant bodies – on preparations for the Games.[114]

It is hoped that this research will contribute to the sport event management body of literature, specifically in relation to knowledge development for staging the Olympic Games. The research has management implications for both the IOC and future host NOCs, particularly in relation to the structuring of OCOG governance arrangements. In the past, very little research has been conducted on the role of the host NOC in the staging of an Olympic Games. The present study has started to fill that gap.

Notes

[1] Barney, Wenn and Martyn, *Selling the Five Rings*; Booth, 'Gifts or Corruption'; Cashman, *The Bitter-Sweet Awakening*; Cashman and Hughes, *Staging the Olympics*; Hill, *Olympic Politics*; Lenskyi, *Inside the Olympic Industry*; Lucas, *The Future of the Olympic Games*; MacAloon, *This Great Symbol*; McGeoch and Korporaal, *The Bid*; Preuss, *Economics of the Olympic Games*; Toohey and Veal, *The Olympic Games*; Tomlinson, 'The Commercialisation of the Olympics'; Balmer, Nevill and Williams, 'Home Advantage in the Winter Olympics'. An abridged version of this study was published in Adair, Coe and Gouth, *Beyond the Torch*.
[2] Young and Wamsley, *Global Olympics*; Toohey, *Official Report of the XXVII Olympiad*, 2.
[3] Toohey and Veal, *The Olympic Games*
[4] Toohey, *Official Report of the XXVII Olympiad*.
[5] Ibid., 97.
[6] Elias, *The Civilizing Process*.
[7] Clegg, Courpasson, and Phillips, *Power and Organizations*.
[8] Hardy and Clegg, 'Some Dare Call It Power'.
[9] Newton, 'Power, Subjectivity and British Industrial and Organizational Sociology'.
[10] Frisby, 'The Good, the Bad, and the Ugly', 7.
[11] Elias, *The Civilizing Process*.

[12] Dopson, 'The Diffusion of Medical Innovations'; Dopson, 'Applying an Eliasian Approach'; Dopson, 'Managing Ambiguity and Change'; Dunning, *Sport Matters*; Dunning, 'Culture, "Civilization" and the Sociology of Sport'; Dunning and Malcolm, *Sport*; Dunning, Malcolm and Waddington, *Sport Histories*; Dunning and Sheard, *Barbarians, Gentlemen and Players*; Elias, *The Civilizing Process*; Elias, *State-Formation and Civilization*; Elias, *Time*; Elias, *What is Sociology*; Elias and Dunning, *Quest for Excitement*; Franklin, 'On Fox-Hunting and Angling'; Hutchins, 'Analysing Sporting Violence'; Maguire *et al.*, *Sports Worlds*; Murphy, Sheard and Waddington, 'Figurational Sociology'; Newton, 'From Freemasons to the Employee'; Newton, 'Organization'; Newton, 'Power, Subjectivity and British Industrial and Organizational Sociology'.

[13] Abrams, *Historical Sociology*; Jarvie and Maguire, *Sport and Leisure in Social Thought*; Mandalios, 'Historical Sociology'.

[14] Elias, *The Civilizing Process*.

[15] Maguire *et al.*, *Sports Worlds*.

[16] Elias, *The Civilizing Process*.

[17] Dopson, 'Applying an Eliasian Approach to Organizational Analysis'; Newton, 'Organization'.

[18] Elias, *Time*, 489.

[19] Dopson, 'Applying an Eliasian Approach to Organizational Analysis'; Newton, 'Organization'.

[20] Elias, *The Civilizing Process*; Van Krieken, *Norbert Elias*.

[21] Elias, *The Civilizing Process*; Van Krieken, *Norbert Elias*.

[22] Elias, *The Civilizing Process*; Van Krieken, *Norbert Elias*.

[23] Elias, *The Civilizing Process*; Van Krieken, *Norbert Elias*.

[24] Newton, 'Power, Subjectivity and British Industrial and Organizational Sociology', 417.

[25] Murphy, Sheard and Waddington, 'Figurational Sociology', 93.

[26] Armason, 'Figurational Sociology as a Counter Paradigm'; Murphy, Sheard and Waddington, 'Figurational Sociology'.

[27] Newton, 'Power, Subjectivity and British Industrial and Organizational Sociology', 420.

[28] Weick, *The Social Psychology of Organizing*, 330.

[29] Dopson, 'The Diffusion of Medical Innovations'.

[30] Flyvbjerg, *Rationality and Power*; Flyvbjerg, *Making Social Science Matter*; Flyvbjerg, 'Phronetic Planning Research'.

[31] Flyvbjerg, 'Phronetic Planning Research', 292.

[32] Dahl, *Who Governs?*

[33] Foucault, 'Governmentality'.

[34] Flyvbjerg, *Rationality and Power*; Flyvbjerg, *Making Social Science Matter*; Flyvbjerg, 'Phronetic Planning Research'.

[35] Flyvbjerg, 'Machiavellian Megaprojects', 18.

[36] Booth and Tatz, 'Swimming with the Big Boys?'; Brabazon, 'The Legal Structure of the Sydney Olympic Games'.

[37] Gordon, *The Time of Our Lives*.

[38] Brabazon, 'The Legal Structure of the Sydney Olympic Games'.

[39] Gordon, *Australia and the Olympic Games*.

[40] McGeoch and Korporaal, *The Bid*.

[41] Gordon, *The Time of Our Lives*.

[42] Cashman and Hughes, *Staging the Olympics*.

[43] Gordon, *The Time of Our Lives*, 67.

[44] International Olympic Committee, *1993 Host City Contract*; Cashman and Hughes, *Staging the Olympics*; Gordon, *The Time of Our Lives*.

[45] Toohey, *Official Report of the XXVII Olympiad*, 28.

[46] Ibid.

[47] Australian Broadcasting Corporation, *Blood Sport*.

[48] Gordon, *The Time of Our Lives*.

[49] Brabazon, 'The Legal Structure of the Sydney Olympic Games'; Jobling, 'Bidding for the Olympics'.

[50] Brabazon, 'The Legal Structure of the Sydney Olympic Games'.

[51] Ibid.

[52] Ibid.

[53] Webb, *The Collaborative Games*; Gordon, *The Time of Our Lives*, 58.

54 Brabazon, 'The Legal Structure of the Sydney Olympic Games'; Gordon, *The Time of Our Lives*, 54.
55 Gordon, *The Time of Our Lives*.
56 Toohey, 'The Politics of Australian Elite Sport'; McGeoch and Korporaal, *The Bid*.
57 McGeoch and Korporaal, *The Bid*.
58 Gordon, *The Time of Our Lives*.
59 Australian Broadcasting Corporation, *Blood Sport*.
60 Ibid.
61 Ibid.
62 Gordon, *The Time of Our Lives*.
63 Australian Broadcasting Corporation, *Blood Sport*.
64 Gordon, *The Time of Our Lives*.
65 Publishing and Broadcasting Limited, *Blood on the Rings*.
66 Australian Broadcasting Corporation, *Blood Sport*.
67 Ibid.
68 Ibid.
69 Bloomfield, *Australia's Sporting Success*; Toohey, *Official Report of the XXVII Olympiad*.
70 Gordon, *The Time of Our Lives*, 62–3.
71 Ibid.
72 Ibid., 64.
73 Ibid. For further reading on this crisis see Cashman *et al.*, 'When the Carnival is Over'.
74 Toohey, *Official Report of the XXVII Olympiad*.
75 Bremmer, Brown and Canter, 'Introduction'.
76 Minichiello *et al.*, *In Depth Interviewing*.
77 Miles and Huberman, *Qualitative Data Analysis*.
78 Ibid.; Punch, *Introduction to Social Research*.
79 Gratton and Jones, *Research Methods for Sport Studies*.
80 Ibid.
81 Ibid., 219.
82 Ibid.
83 Dey, *Creating Categories*.
84 Gratton and Jones, *Research Methods for Sport Studies*.
85 Toohey, *Official Report of the XXVII Olympiad*.
86 Ibid.
87 Ibid.
88 Langton, *Australian Olympic Committee – Internal Report*.
89 Toohey, *Official Report of the XXVII Olympiad*.
90 Frawley and Toohey, 'Shaping Sport Competition', 17.
91 Ibid.
92 Interview respondent 07.
93 Interview respondent 08.
94 Interview respondent 05.
95 Interview respondent 09.
96 Interview respondent 10.
97 Interview respondent 01.
98 Ibid.
99 Interview respondent 04.
100 Interview respondent 01.
101 Interview respondent 06.
102 Toohey, *Official Report of the XXVII Olympiad*.
103 Gordon, *The Time of Our Lives*.
104 Dopson, 'The Diffusion of Medical Innovations', 1141.
105 Flyvbjerg, *Rationality and Power*.
106 Ibid.
107 New South Wales Government, *Report on Financial Contribution*, 3.
108 British Olympic Association, 'Our Role in 2012'. 2007. www.olympics.org.uk/contentpage.aspx?no=269.
109 Australian Olympic Foundation, 'Chairmans' Report', 2.

[110] Ibid., 2.
[111] Veal, *Research Methods for Leisure and Tourism*.
[112] Dandelion, 'Insider Dealing'.
[113] Elias, *The Civilizing Process*.
[114] London Organizing Committee for the Olympic Games, http://www.London2012.Com/About/the-People-Delivering-the-Games/Stakeholders/Index.Php.

References

Abrams, P. *Historical Sociology*. Somerset: Open Books, 1982.
Adair, D., B. Coe, and N. Gouth. *Beyond the Torch: Olympics and Australian Culture*. Melbourne: ASSH, 2005.
Armason, J. 'Figurational Sociology as a Counter Paradigm'. *Theory, Society and Culture* 4 (1987): 429–56.
Australian Broadcasting Corporation. *Blood Sport*. Sydney: ABC Television, 1999. Video recording.
Australian Olympic Foundation. 'Chairman's' Report to the Board of the Australian Olympic Foundation'. Sydney, 2005.
Balmer, N., A. Nevill, and A. Williams. 'Home Advantage in the Winter Olympics'. *Journal of Sport Sciences* 19, no. 2 (2001): 129–39.
Barney, R.K., S.R. Wenn, and S.G. Martyn. *Selling the Five Rings: The International Olympic Committee and the Rise of Olympic Commercialism*. Salt Lake City, UT: The University of Utah Press, 2002.
Bloomfield, John. *Australia's Sporting Success: The Inside Story*. Sydney: University of New South Wales Press, 2003.
Booth, D. 'Gifts or Corruption? Ambiguities of Obligation in the Olympic Movement'. *Olympika* 8 (1999): 43–68.
Booth, D., and C. Tatz. '"Swimming with the Big Boys"? The Politics of Sydney's Olympic Bid'. *Sporting Traditions* 11, no. 1 (1994): 3–23.
Brabazon, M. 'The Legal Structure of the Sydney Olympic Games'. *UNSW Law Journal* 22, no. 3 (1999): 662–90.
Bremmer, M., J. Brown, and D. Canter. *The Research Interview: Uses and Approaches*. Orlando, FL: Academic Press, 1985.
Cashman, R. *The Bitter-Sweet Awakening: The Legacy of the Sydney 2000 Olympic Games*. Sydney: Walla Walla Press, 2006.
Cashman, R., and A. Hughes. *Staging the Olympics: The Event and Its Impacts*. Sydney: University of New South Wales Press, 1999.
Cashman, R., K. Toohey, S. Darcy, C. Symons, and B. Stewart. 'When the Carnival Is Over: Evaluating the Outcomes of Mega Sporting Events in Australia'. *Sporting Traditions* 21, no. 1 (2004): 1–32.
Clegg, S., C. Hardy, and W. Nord. *Handbook of Organization Studies*. London: Sage, 1996.
Clegg, S., D. Courpasson, and N. Phillips. *Power and Organizations*. London: Sage, 2006.
Dahl, R.A. *Who Governs? Democracy and Power in an American City*. New Haven, CT: Yale University Press, 1961.
Dandelion, B.P. 'Insider Dealing: Researching Your Own Private World'. In *Ethics, Sport and Leisure*, edited by A. Tomlinson and S. Fleming. Aachen: Meyer and Meyer, 1997.
Dey, I. *Creating Categories: Qualitative Data Analysis*. London: Routledge, 1993.
Dopson, S. *Managing Ambiguity and Change: The Case of the NHS*. Basingstoke: Macmillan Press, 1997.
Dopson, S. 'Applying an Eliasian Approach to Organizational Analysis'. *Organization* 8, no. 3 (2001): 515–35.
Dopson, S. 'The Diffusion of Medical Innovations: Can Figurational Sociology Contribute?' *Organization Studies* 26, no. 8 (2005): 1125–44.
Dunning, E. 'Culture, "Civilization" and the Sociology of Sport'. *The European Journal of Social Sciences* 5, no. 4 (1992): 7–19.
Dunning, E. *Sport Matters: Sociological Studies of Sport, Violence and Civilization*. London: Routledge, 1999.
Dunning, E., and D. Malcolm. *Sport: Critical Concepts in Sociology: Approaches to the Study of Sport*. Vol. 1. London: Routledge, 2003.

Dunning, E., and K. Sheard. *Barbarians, Gentlemen and Players: A Sociological Study of the Development of Modern Rugby Football*. Oxford: Martin Robertson & Company, 1979.

Dunning, E., D. Malcolm, and I. Waddington. *Sport Histories: Figurational Studies in the Development of Modern Sport*. New York: Routledge, 2004.

Elias, N. *The Civilizing Process: The History of Manners*. Oxford: Basil Blackwell, 1978.

Elias, N. *What Is Sociology?* Translated by G. Morrissey. London: Hutchinson, 1978.

Elias, N. *The Civilizing Process: State-Formation and Civilization*. Oxford: Basil Blackwell, 1982.

Elias, N. *Time: An Essay*. Oxford: Basil Blackwell, 1994.

Elias, N., and E. Dunning. *Quest for Excitement: Sport and Leisure in the Civilizing Process*. Oxford: Basil Blackwell, 1986.

Flyvbjerg, B. *Rationality and Power: Democracy in Practice*. London: University of Chicago Press, 1998.

Flyvbjerg, B. *Making Social Science Matter: Why Social Inquiry Fails and How It Can Succeed Again*. Cambridge: Cambridge University Press, 2001.

Flyvbjerg, B. 'Phronetic Planning Research: Theoretical and Methodological Reflections'. *Planning Theory & Practice* 5, no. 3 (2004): 283–306.

Flyvbjerg, B. 'Machiavellian Megaprojects'. *Antipode* 1, no. 37 (2005): 18–22.

Foucault, M. 'Governmentality'. *Ideology and Consciousness* 6 (1979): 5–21.

Franklin, A. 'On Fox-Hunting and Angling: Norbert Elias and the "Sportisation" Process'. *Journal of Historical Sociology* 9, no. 4 (1996): 432–55.

Frawley, S., and K. Toohey. 'Shaping Sport Competition: The SOCOG Sports Commission and the Planning and Delivery of Sport at the Sydney 2000 Olympic Games'. In *Beyond the Torch: Olympics and Australian Culture*, 15–28. Melbourne: ASSH, 2005.

Frisby, W. 'The Good, the Bad, and the Ugly: Critical Sport Management Research'. *Journal of Sport Management* 19, no. 1 (2005): 1–12.

Gordon, H. *Australia and the Olympic Games*. St Lucia: Queensland University Press, 1994.

Gordon, H. *The Time of Our Lives: Inside the Sydney Olympics*. St Lucia: Queensland University Press, 2003.

Gratton, C., and I. Jones. *Research Methods for Sport Studies*. London: Routledge, 2004.

Hardy, C., and S. Clegg. 'Some Dare Call It Power'. In *Handbook of Organization Studies*, edited by S. Clegg, C. Hardy, and W. Nord, 622–42. London: Sage, 1996.

Hill, C.R. *Olympic Politics*. Manchester: Manchester University Press, 1992.

Hutchins, B. 'Analysing Sporting Violence'. In *All Part of the Game: Violence and Australian Sport*, edited by D. Hemphill, 19–39. Melbourne: Walla Walla Press, 1998.

International Olympic Committee. *1993 Host City Contract for the Games of the Xxvii Olympiad in the Year 2000*. Lausanne: International Olympic Committee, 1993.

International Olympic Committee. *Olympic Charter*. Lausanne: International Olympic Committee, 1997.

Jarvie, G., and J. Maguire. *Sport and Leisure in Social Thought*. London: Routledge, 1994.

Jobling, I. 'Bidding for the Olympics: Site Selection and Sydney 2000'. In *The Olympics at the Millennium: Power, Politics, and the Games*, edited by K. Schaffer and S. Smith, 258–71. New Brunswick, NJ: Rutgers University Press, 2000.

Langton, W. *Australian Olympic Committee – Internal Report*. Sydney: Sydney Organising Committee for the Olympic Games (SOCOG), 2000.

Lenskyj, H.J. *Inside the Olympic Industry: Power, Politics and Activism*. Albany, NY: State University of New York Press, 2000.

Lucas, J.A. *The Future of the Olympic Games*. Champaign, IL: Human Kinetics, 1992.

MacAloon, J.J. *This Great Symbol: Pierre De Coubertin and the Origins of the Modern Olympic Games*. Chicago, IL: Chicago University Press, 1981.

Maguire, J. G. Jarvie, L. Mansfield, and J. Bradley. *Sports Worlds: A Sociological Perspective*. Champaign, IL: Human Kinetics, 2002.

Mandalios, J. 'Historical Sociology'. In *Blackwell Companion to Social Theory*, edited by B. Turner, 278–302. Oxford: Blackwell, 1996.

McGeoch, R., and G. Korporaal. *The Bid: How Australia Won the 2000 Olympics*. Melbourne: William Heinemann Australia, 1994.

Miles, M.B., and A.M. Huberman. *Qualitative Data Analysis: An Expanded Sourcebook*. 2nd ed. Thousand Oaks, CA: Sage Publications, 1994.

Minichiello, V., R. Aroni, E. Timewell, and L. Alexander. *In Depth Interviewing: Principles, Techniques, Analysis*. 2nd ed. Sydney: Longman, 1995.

Murphy, P., K. Sheard, and I. Waddington. 'Figurational Sociology'. In *The Handbook of Sport Studies*, edited by E. Dunning and J. Coakley, 92–105. London: Sage, 2002.

New South Wales Government. *Report on the Financial Contribution by the New South Wales Government to the Sydney 2000 Olympic Games*. Sydney: New South Wales Government, 2002.

Newton, T. 'Power, Subjectivity and British Industrial and Organizational Sociology: The Relevance of the Work of Norbert Elias'. *Sociology* 33, no. 2 (1999): 411–40.

Newton, T. 'Organization: The Relevance and the Limitations of Elias'. *Organization* 8, no. 3 (2001): 467–95.

Newton, T. 'From Freemasons to the Employee: Organization, History and Subjectivity'. *Organization Studies* 25, no. 8 (2004): 1363–87.

Preuss, H. *Economics of the Olympic Games: Hosting the Games 1972–2000*. Sydney: Walla Walla Press, 2000.

Publishing and Broadcasting Limited. *Blood on the Rings*. Sydney: Channel Nine, 2001. Video recording.

Punch, K.F. *Introduction to Social Research: Quantitative and Qualitative*. London: Sage Publications, 2001.

Tomlinson, A. 'The Commercialisation of the Olympics: Cities, Corporations, and the Olympic Commodity'. In *Global Olympics: Historical and Sociological Studies of the Modern Games*, edited by K. Young and K. Wamsley. Oxford: Elsevier, 2005.

Toohey, K. 'The Politics of Australian Elite Sport: 1949–1983'. PhD diss., Pennsylvania State University, 1990.

Toohey, K. *Official Report of the XXVII Olympiad*. Sydney: SOCOG, 2001.

Toohey, K., and A.J. Veal. *The Olympic Games: A Social Science Perspective*. Wallingford, UK: CABI Publishing, 2000.

van Krieken, R. *Norbert Elias*. New York: Routledge, 1998.

Veal, A.J. *Research Methods for Leisure and Tourism: A Practical Guide*. Sydney: Prentice Hall, 2006.

Webb, T. *The Collaborative Games: The Story Behind the Spectacle*. Sydney: Pluto Press, 2001.

Weick, K. *The Social Psychology of Organizing*. Reading, MA: Addison-Wesley Publishing Company, 1969.

Young, K., and K. Wamsley. *Global Olympics: Historical and Sociological Studies of the Modern Games*. Oxford: Elsevier, 2005.

Rugby union football in Australian society: an unintended consequence of intended actions[1]

Peter Horton

School of Education, James Cook University, Queensland, Australia

The place of rugby union football in Australian society presents a rich context to play and display critical social issues, particularly, identity formations and contestations. This essay examines the development of elite rugby union in Australia from its inception to professionalization. In its amateur development, the processes of colonization and cultural impositions created its culture and legacy. With the overlapping of sporting and economic networks, rugby union entered the professional era. This essay argues that the development from amateurism to 'shamateurism' to professionalism was uneven and contested on various levels. Whilst the development of rugby union in Australia was both a reflection and manifestation of globalization it did not totally parallel the globalization of sport in general, indeed rugby union football remains a particularly 'glocal' game. The points of resistance and departure, this essay concludes, distinguish the identity of rugby union from other sporting institutions and their wider social contexts.

In Britain in 1895, as a consequence of the process of class-distancing, the sport of rugby split into rugby union and rugby league.[2] The division of rugby in the Antipodes lagged just 12 years behind that and, despite its colonial context the determining social dynamics were very similar. In Australia each of these sports maintained its social distance until sport, per se, began to become increasingly intertwined with a growing number of aspects and layers of social activity. Australian rugby union football at the elite (professional) level is now penetrated and supported by an array of professionals from various fields including: medicine, media, management, economics, advertising, personal management, sports administration, stadium management, sports psychology, exercise physiology, sports analysis and coaching. This extension of the figuration that constitutes rugby union is demonstrated by the extent of the team that supports the Australian national team, the Wallabies. During the Rugby World Cup (RWC) in France in 2007 the 'team' that represented Australia included a playing squad of 30, supported by a non-playing staff of over 20.

Contemporary rugby matches at the elite level are commodities characterized by the collective efforts and influences of both the producers (the players and their support staff, the administrators and the officials) and the consumers, both the live spectators and the television audience. The consumers are very demanding and, as a corollary, so are the game's commercial sponsors that support the sport through the various levels of sponsorship, advertising and purchase of corporate boxes and entertainment suites at the major venues. The major direct revenue source for the Australian Rugby Union (ARU) and the State Rugby Unions and the Super 14 franchises in New South Wales (NSW) (Waratahs), Queensland (Reds), ACT (Brumbies) and WA (Force) however, comes from the allocation of funds from the television broadcasting rights.[3]

This largely linear-historical analysis considers the process of the development of rugby union football in Australia as a feature of the emergence of the global sports formation.[4] The diffusion of sport and its later globalization has travelled a very distinct temporal-historical pathway[5] and the development of rugby union football demonstrates this process. Yet, consistent with Roland Robertson's assertions that, although globalization is about the creation of a 'single place', it is not about the development of a homogeneous global culture,[6] this analysis of Australia's rugby union culture will demonstrate both sameness and difference from other 'glocal' forms of the game.[7] Arjun Apparadurai suggested that a series of unpredictable global flows or 'scapes' that interact with each other are the virtual structures along which people, technologies, beliefs, capital and mediated images are globalized.[8] This discussion of the development of the culture of rugby union football in Australia, particularly at the elite level, will focus upon the changes in the nature of the relationships the players have had with the game at significant nodal points and how they have contributed to the current nature of rugby union football in Australian society.

The culture of the game emerges

Football, in the generic sense,[9] was part of the cultural hegemony of British imperialism, and it became a central element of the cultural fabric of the dominant social groups in colonial Australia.[10] The first rugby club formally established in Australia was Sydney University Rugby football club, circa 1865. Then the game was played by various 'Gentlemen's' clubs and later at The King's School and other leading educational institutions.[11] The founding in 1874 of the Southern Rugby Football Union, which became the New South Wales Rugby Union (NSWRU), saw the real beginnings of the institutionalized form of the game in Australia. The first inter-colonial rugby match, played in 1882 in Sydney between NSW and Queensland, not only provided an avenue for the promotion of the game in the colony of Queensland, it also offered a focus for rugby football in New South Wales and may well have offset the further encroachment of Australian football and Association football in New South Wales.[12]

In Australia, the development of modern sport, a product of the colonial British middle class,[13] developed its own character partly as a pragmatic response to the competitive and rugged nature of the colonial environment. It was thus consistent that colonial rugby players and supporters could accept what is now common as the modern corporatized sport concepts of competition, premierships, gate money, training and coaching (some coaches/trainers were even paid), without any resultant loss of the game's amateur status and image. It was this practical philosophy of the early directors of rugby football that established its character in the colonies, and indeed, many of these attitudes have persisted.

Central among the features of Australian rugby union football are the associated social mores and the belief system players, administrators and supporters subscribed to,[14] and even though today it has become a professional sport, the ARU's current mission statement still zealously advocates the game's unique culture.[15] Rugby union has distinct origins and throughout its history it has been the players that have created and reproduced the game's culture. Their displays and efforts were and still are the major elements in the game's discourse. Rugby's unique form, its uncompromisingly violent nature, its highly complex set of 'laws' and its subtext of heroism, selflessness and camaraderie have made it a game that only the 'committed' could appreciate. This still describes the game as it is played today. Significantly, in the professional arena, its traditions, passion, pride and 'camaraderie' are elements even the most instrumental technically rational coaches would never completely expunge from their coaching rationale.

Prior to its recent professionalization the critical moment in the history of the rugby union was when it split into league and union. The bifurcation, precipitated, superficially at least, by player demands regarding loss of earnings and match payments, was more about the uneven distribution of power that existed in the game. In the 1900s officials of the NSWRU, supposedly the guardians of the game,[16] assumed the position of 'owners' and 'controllers'. In metropolitan Sydney, the heartland of the Australian game, tensions emerged between the largely working-class player-base and the NSWRU officials who had ignored the players' demands.[17]

The democratization of rugby in Australia

As the founding rugby union in Australia, the officials of the NSWRU had naturally assumed the mantle of controllers, of the game. This meant that the NSWRU was the *de facto* national rugby union and this is exactly what it was until the formal establishment of the Australian Rugby Football Union (ARFU) in 1949. Thus, it could be said that a direct link in sporting ethos, attitude, beliefs and culture can be drawn from the original committee of the SRFU (est. 1874) to the founding of the ARFU in 1949. The custodians of the game in Australia or, to use Carling's irreverent expression, the 'old farts'[18] (the amateur voluntary administrators and officials), were for the Australian game's first 75 years, New South Welshmen.

The split of rugby football into union and league in Australia in 1908 was largely due to the fact that the NSWRU refused to accept proposed changes to the rules under which the game was played and governed, particularly in regard to match payments.[19] The tensions surrounding the split[20] emanated from deep-lying beliefs and prejudices that further exacerbated the growing class divide that had developed in many Australian cities by 1908.[21] Fuelled with a good deal of anti-English sentiment and the sense of alienation from the 'mother country', the working class in Sydney readily adopted rugby league football, viewing it as a symbol of their struggle for nationhood; as the union game so apparently reeked of English imperialism.[22]

Although the quest for political autonomy was achieved and the nation of Australia being declared in 1901, the declaration of war in 1914 saw Australian society again divided, this time on grounds of loyalty, religion and parochialism. This division extended into the sporting community, and various administrative bodies became embroiled in the question of whether or not to continue to play competitively during the war years. To continue to play was viewed by the Protestant Empire loyalists as being tantamount to treason. To discontinue and thus support the British was viewed, by those of Irish Catholic origin, as condoning Britain's 'occupation' of Ireland, particularly after the Dublin massacres in 1916.[23] The upshot of the divergence in the decisions made by the administrators of the two rugby codes, at this time, coupled with tensions emanating from the Great Strike in 1916 and the largely sectarian-based positions in the national debate over the introduction of conscription in the same year, positioned rugby union and rugby league at opposite ends of what, in effect, became a debate about loyalty. The rift further assumed a class basis, with the rugby league fixtures being heavily supported by the working class. This polarization established the ground rules for the future relationship between the two codes.

Following the war, rugby union in Queensland was in a parlous state. During the 1919 season, in the state capital Brisbane, player numbers were so low that the teams played with no breakaways and, when the Brothers and the University of Queensland clubs switched to rugby league, the game appeared to have died in Brisbane. In the NSW capital Sydney, after competitive play had been suspended during the war, rugby union football had been swamped by rugby league football, as this code in Sydney had continued to be played throughout the war.[24] Thus, the war widened the schism between league and union, with each code being seen to be the champion and vehicle of disparate political, social, religious, economic and even moral groups in Australian society.[25]

Issues of national loyalty, political affiliation, class, sectarianism, parochialism, sporting ethos, as well as amateurism, generated how the players, administrators and supporters of each rugby code viewed each other. The cultural identity and the underpinning motivating philosophy of those playing and administering rugby union football in Australia, up to the professional era, were shaped by the loyalties established during and immediately after the First World War. The two rugby codes were to remain ardent rivals, diametrically opposed in philosophy, based largely on the dichotomy of amateur versus professional sport, but amplified into and through class, or a perceived sense of class, education (private v state schools), occupation, and surprisingly on issues relating to sporting conduct. The mutual disaffection was not, however, simplistically founded; many working-class men played union and some rugby union clubs were based in working-class suburbs or towns, and, ironically, many clubs had strong links to the Catholic church and colleges whilst others, though not exclusively, were Public School (GPS) old boys clubs. However, union was viewed commonly as the preserve of the middle and upper middle classes.[26] The sport itself was referred to as the game played by the 'rah rahs'.[27]

The Second World War, Wallabies and the ARFU

Rugby union continued to be affected administratively, financially and in regard to its support base due to the dislocation it suffered because of the virtually complete cessation of play during the First World War. The game struggled to gain viability for the next 20 years and, just as the Second Wallabies[28] arrived in the UK to begin their tour in 1939, the Second World War was declared, and the tour was cancelled. Again war was to become a modelling force in the process of rugby union's development in Australia. However, unlike during the First World War, rugby union continued to be played, albeit in a seriously limited manner, at club and school levels, in both NSW and Queensland, throughout the course of the Second World War.[29]

Immediately the war ended, play, at the elite level, resumed with interstate and international matches being played in 1946.[30] Again, it was hardly a case of 'normal play' being resumed. At this time that sport began a metamorphosis as the fourth phase of global sportization began to emerge.[31] Sport became intertwined with post-war industrialization, and gained greater commercial and political currency. The resultant shape of global sport, and the changes that later occurred in rugby union in Australia, demonstrate that the nature of globalization and its outcomes may well have been both uncontrollable and unintended, but they certainly sowed the seeds for future power struggles that emerged during the third phase of Australian rugby union's evolution, as it moved from a quasi professional ('shamateur') state to full professionalism.[32]

The establishment of the Australian Rugby Football Union (ARFU) in 1949 was an outcome of the struggles and rivalries between the NSWRU and all other states' rugby unions, particularly Queensland's.[33] However, much of the momentum came directly from the International Rugby Football Board (IRFB),[34] as global controllers of the game.[35] In 1949, Australia, New Zealand and South Africa became full members of the IRFB.[36] This recognition of the allied ex-colonial territories was expedient and necessary, as collectively they had already become very powerful and internationally successful rugby playing nations. The 'shift' in power and the recognition of southern hemisphere rugby also illustrates the implicit regionalization and polyculturalism that are central dimensions of globalization.[37] This was particularly apparent with regard to the game's growing popularization in the Pacific island nations, which illustrated the emergence of an increasing variety in the number of forms of rugby union football. The impact of Pacific Island rugby players, their physical attributes, flair and power has in recent years been particularly significant.[38] Indeed, the 'Pacificization' of rugby union football in Australia is currently well under-way.[39]

'Doing it tough': the very amateur years

The period from 1950 to 1980 was characterized by a sense of 'business as usual' with the hegemonic control based in Sydney: NSW dominating on and off the field as it had during the previous 50 years. Its power manifested itself most precipitously in 1962 when NSW refused to play Queensland on the grounds that the northern state players were just not competitive enough: the previous season they had lost heavily to NSW in Brisbane and in both clashes in Sydney. Even more embarrassingly, Queensland had been defeated by the rugby union minnow state of Victoria (14-9). The NSWRU attempted to justify its decision by citing Queensland's poor results from 1949 to 1961; they had won just four of the 43 matches played against NSW during this period. Queensland rugby union not only struggled for viability in its rivalry with NSW but also within the state against an energetic rugby league, particularly in Brisbane. By 1959 there were only 16 clubs playing union in the whole of the state.[40] Although the clubs' support was enthusiastic and their supporters loyal, the QRU was virtually bankrupt.[41] The QRU had no ground of its own, renting an oval, at a pepper-corn rent, from the Brisbane Grammar School, and it was only the windfalls it received from the Fijian tours in 1952 and 1954 that allowed the QRU to begin to develop the game in the state's clubs and schools.

Even with an increase in loyalty, intensity and parochialism of rugby union in Queensland, its state team could not match the power of NSW until the late 1970s; Sydney remained the rugby union capital of Australia. NSW continued to dominate the interstate contests and the Australian national team selections from 1950 to 1979. The turning of the tide was heralded with Queensland's historic 42-4 victory against NSW at Ballymore in 1976. The win was seen by die-hard Queensland supporters and the long-suffering QRU administrators as assuaging 34 years of bile resulting from the 1962 snub. Interestingly NSW did not beat Queensland again until 1980.[42]

Prior to the late twentieth century's increasing commercialization and finally the professionalization of rugby union football, the dominant driving and directional influence of the game unquestionably came from Sydney. All centres of the game in Australia fiercely clung to the game's amateur ethos, even though many flagrant contradictions, such as, 'boot money'[43] and 'under the table' expenses, emerged in elite international sport, particularly in Europe.[44] The appeal of amateur rugby was sustained by its implicit cultural history which Gruneau argues was 'beyond mere amusement or crass commerce'.[45] The tensions evoked by this were rapidly assuaged as the twentieth century closed.

The television-union synergy: the demise of the dockyard brawl

In the last 20 years global rugby union football has gained a higher level of marketability and attractiveness to television and sponsors by improving the product.[46] The massive strides in coaching and administration that occurred in the 1970s throughout the world, combined with the growth in televised coverage, meant that technically better and far more attractive spectacles became available not only to wider domestic audiences but globally.[47] The advance in technical, scientific and medical aspects of the game was intertwined with the deeper penetration of the sport by economics, management and communications. Essentially rugby union shifted from being a player-centred activity to a market-centred one. Even the laws of the game were adjusted to make it more accessible to a wider audience. The relationship between players and supporters (the audience) changed as it became primarily based upon commercial functions rather than on mere support. The higher level of skill and the improved power of players, combined with the adoption of more expansive playing styles, produced a far more marketable product for television broadcasters and sponsors. Critics of contact sports, notably in the 1970s by neo-Marxists, such as Brohm, reinforced the view of rugby football as the most 'uncivilized'[48] of football codes; 'a perfect illustration of the fascistic delirium ... a case book of the deliberate cultivation of brutality'.[49] The untamed, or so it was thought, mayhem of the 'traditional' rucks and mauls; the dangerous impacts of the unrestrained scrum contacts; lineouts that were viewed by critics as being nothing short of 'dockyard brawls'; and the tolerance of the dispensing of swift, heavy and violent justice, meant the game still had a foot firmly planted in its mob-football origins.[50] Prior to its shift into the entertainment sector, the entire sub-culture of rugby union was very much the domain of the players; it was characterized as the players' game.[51] Central to this was the fact that the vast majority of administrators, officials and coaches were predominantly ex-players. Management support thus came from those steeped in the culture of the game and tolerant of its uncompromising physical nature, largely manifested in tight-forward dominated and dour contests. The spectators were an integral part of the game's sub-culture. They came largely from the rugby community and the games were not, in essence, about entertainment but rather were about identity, loyalty and parochialism. In Australia any series win against a leading nation, irrespective of the quality of play, was heralded. The national broadcasting authorities generally begrudgingly televised such matches, and the rugby unions involved did not receive a fee of any kind from them.[52] By comparison, the combined global television rights to the Rugby World Cup (RWC) in 2003, which was watched in over 200 countries, by an audience of 3.4 billion people, cost the broadcasters hundreds of millions of dollars.[53]

End of the game or end of a phase?

The growing level of television exposure, driven by the emergence of satellite broadcasting in the 1980s, meant matches could be seen live from around the world, and thus the economic capital of test rugby union increased. The live television broadcasts of the Wallabies' 'Grand Slam'[54] winning tour of the UK in 1984 not only besotted committed Australian supporters, but also the success also created a new body of fans. As the game became truly professional in name and practice in 1995, the demands of television and the commercial exigencies of mediasport became even more dominant.[55] The professionalization of rugby union football emerged as an outcome of the intersection of various wider social, cultural, ideological and global forces. Pragmatic economic decisions were made by the game's administrators in reaction to an irrepressible climate for change; rugby union had moved inexorably into the next phase of its development The game that once had been the staunchest amateur football code embraced the 'filthy lucre' with almost indecent haste in 1995 The relatively large offers from the media barons and the sponsors were just too good to turn down.

The diaspora of postmodernism and globalization unlocked the institution of rugby union football as it had so many other sports. The consequences are manifest and, for the rugby traditionalists, have been lamentable.[56] Skinner, Stewart and Edwards contend that the emergence of professional rugby union represents the collapse of the traditional game. The result of the assault of the ravaging forces of commercialism, have 'undermined'[57] the 'traditional sport values, practices and structures' of rugby union football.[58] However, Maguire[59] departs from an essentialist perspective. He argues that this phase is part of the on-going process of the game's development with the continued commodification, democratization and further politicization of the game being features. Amidst the globalization of sport and a commingling of rugby cultures in the game, the fundamental game-form still remains distinguishable from other sports although the superstructure is quite similar.[60] Rugby's emergence from 'shamateurism'[61] is not some insidious link to consumer capitalism but a part of a tightening of the social interdependency and overlapping of functions as an outcome of the game's development. It should not be viewed as an invasion; rather it places rugby union football as being interconnected with sport per se and the wider society, and not as a separate splendid cultural island.

Professionalism has altered the game in many ways, not least by the very demands and constraints it puts on the players, not only those at the top but those approaching the elite representative levels. It is suggested that the early contractual agreements young players enter and the concomitant obligations may well stunt their social, academic, professional, even their spiritual, development. By way of criticism, those looking back nostalgically to the amateur elite era always talk of the characters, the camaraderie, the sacrifices, the enduring friendships and the fun that emerged.[62] The intensity of the physical, psychological, temporal and travel demands and the single-mindeness required of playing a game as a job, as opposed to engaging in it, albeit obsessively, as a pastime, has thrust the modern elite players very clearly into the world of economic rationalism, accountancy and marketing. Elite Australian rugby players are now celebrities and have become significant elements in contemporary popular culture which, though offering 'Hollywood scales of reward'[63] and the implicit cultural power, also comes with a heavy burden of being in the public gaze and under constant scrutiny both on and off the playing field.[64]

Financescape, mediascape, rugby

The game of rugby union football is now firmly instituted as a major feature of hyper-commercialized corporate sport. The Rugby World Cup (RWC) competition, as a global media-driven sports festival, ranks third (albeit distantly) behind the Olympic Games and the Football World Cup, with regard to the size of the global television audiences, which for the 2003 RWC, held in Australia, was 3.4 billion.[65] The 2003 RWC directly contributed an additional A$289 million to the country's GDP and another A$494 million in additional roll-on industry sales.[66] The consequent tax-take to the Australian government was estimated to be in the vicinity of A$100 million. Over 1.8 million spectators attended the matches and the festival brought an additional 65 000 international visitors to Australia.[67] The true significance of the sport's penetration of the market in Australia can be gleaned from the fact that in the World Cup year, 2003, Australian sport businesses contributed close to A\$8 billion to the GDP, which equalled the individual areas of 'printing, motor vehicles, investment and insurance'.[68]

At the elite level rugby union football in Australia is now a feature of global mediasport which is part of the corporate cultural capitalism.[69] Media oligopolies now morph, market and deliver televised sport to the billions of fans on both pay-TV and free-to-air networks. The top flight of matches played in Australia is now defined by three televised competitions: the RWC, which, as a concept and a commercial entity is literally owned and organized by the International Rugby Board (IRB) and staged in an Olympiad-like manner every four years; the annually-contested Super 14 competition, which involves 14 teams drawn from New Zealand and South Africa with five teams each and Australia which has four; and, the follow-on Tri-Nations competition which consists of home and away fixtures between the national sides from these three nations.

The crescendo effect of the growing intensity of the rivalry built up in the 13 rounds and finals of the Super 14 competition, screened entirely on Rupert Murdoch's Fox Sports network, serves as an entrée for the annual Tri-Nations competition, also broadcast by Fox Sports and various free to air channels. The extent of the advance of the relationship between the game and television is indicated by the fact that, in December 2004, the ARU signed a five year A\$421 million broadcasting rights deal with News Ltd., compared to 1995 when the ARU's contract with Channel 10 was only A\$2 million. The free-to-air rights for the 2007 RWC, successfully gained in Australia by the Network Ten group, for a reported A\$10 million, is potentially more significant when the make-up of the rugby union audience, 'a strong "AB" demographic [high-end professionals]'[70] is considered. David White, Ten's general manager, suggested that this deal is expected to produce 'some solid commercial returns'.[71] The commodity, international rugby union football in its various forms, comes not only as a product itself, but with an array of advertised merchandise and sponsors' products. However, in Australia this is a recent development. The process, of which this is a part, obviously has its origins, as has been discussed previously, in the earliest days of the game's history in colonial Australia. Following a somewhat sterile period in terms of development after the Second World War the game took a significant step forward in the mid-1970s with the emergence of new approaches to the game's administration, management and coaching; a new breed of players also emerged.

The success of the Australian teams that followed in the 1980s, particularly the 'Grand Slam' winning Wallabies of 1984, saw rugby union begin to become a serious commercial target. The inaugural Rugby World Cup (RWC) in 1987 and Australia's victory in the final of the second Rugby World Cup against England at Twickenham in 1991, and the concomitant financial spin-offs from sponsorships and the expansion of television coverage were changing the image of the previously conservative game. It was becoming a very attractive commercial product. In 1993, the introduction of South African sides, Natal, Transvaal and Northern Transvaal, plus Western Samoa, in to the Trans-Tasman 'Super 6' competition played between NSW, Queensland and four New Zealand provinces,[72] further expanded the commercial potential of southern hemisphere rugby union football and the journey into the professional era was well under way. NSW became known as the 'Waratahs', Queensland as the 'Reds', and the latter team went on to win the 'Super 10' final against Natal in Durban by 21-10. This result, in the main, was the consequence of the total training regime introduced in 1991 by the coach John Connolly. Preceding home matches, the team trained four nights a week from 6.00pm to 9.00pm. They did weight sessions at 6.00am for an hour three mornings a week, had a light run on Saturday afternoons and played on Sundays.[73] The same level of intensity in training and playing was undoubtedly a feature of all the franchises taking part in the Super 10 competition. However, taking Robertson's advance of his five-phase model of globalization into consideration, it is suggested that the game in each of the participant countries had become glocalized,[74] with the local rugby union cultures forming part of the global game yet simultaneously creating definitive local varieties. Rugby union football in all three nations demonstrated the intensification of the 'interpenetration'[75] of local traits, playing styles, social characteristics with the global elements of governance, media, commercial obligations and demands, and cultural homogenization.

The number of international games was increasing. During the 1994 home season six tests were also played with Ireland touring in May, the Italians in June and Western Samoa in August; the highlight of the season was the one-off Bledisloe Cup test match (v NZ), which Australia won by 20-16. A total of 171,198[76] spectators attended the tests and millions more watched them on television. The demands on the players, who, in the main, had also to maintain full-time careers, were tremendous. The attraction of accepting a 'contract' to play in Europe, or to switch to rugby league, had become even more tempting as rugby union players were training more and playing more frequently than their professional colleagues in rugby league. Union players were not being financially rewarded, whilst the game was becoming more and more profitable for the IRB, the national unions, and the individual state and provincial unions. In an attempt to reduce the defections, Queensland introduced an element of pseudo-professionalism with the institution of a Players' Trust in 1991.[77] This saw a proportion of sponsorship monies and allocated funds from the ARU being divided amongst the players on the basis of the number of games played. This was a critical event in the game's move to full-professionalism. Though players were not being actually paid to play, there was recognition that they should be rewarded for their efforts and compensated for the additional demands the game at the elite level now made. By using the Players' Trust as they did they were able to circumvent the IRB's regulations regarding amateurism. Being able to 'compensate' its elite players the ARU could stem the tide of players taking lucrative contracts to play union in Europe and, of course, of switching to rugby league.[78] Initially vilified by the IRB, the model was adopted by the Five Nations Unions in 1994 as an intermediary stage prior to the advent of full-professionalism a year later.

'Full-on' professionals emerge

In 1994 rugby union football was moving inexorably to full professionalism. Media moguls Kerry Packer and Rupert Murdoch went into battle for sport-content for their respective television networks with rugby league, initially, being the primary football target. Union was soon drawn into the contest. The audacious and very nearly successful effort by Ross Turnbull and Geoff Levy to launch the World Rugby Corporation (WRC) in 1995, with Kerry Packer's backing via his PBL Corporation, proved to be the catalyst which thrust the rugby unions of South Africa, New Zealand and Australia, as the newly formed collective: 'South Africa, New Zealand, Australia Rugby' (SANZAR) into a defining media agreement with Murdoch's News Ltd..[79] This agreement placed the southern hemisphere unions firmly into the professional era, giving them an assured level of funding and administrative control of the game at the elite level in the southern hemisphere.[80] The three unions realized that they had all but lost control of the sport with the WRC nearly becoming the company that 'owned' rugby union. Though the southern hemisphere rugby unions retained administrative control, the players had demonstrated that they were key producers, and that the product, rugby union, could not continue without them. The unions may have won this battle, but rugby would never be the same.[81]

In a unique move the elite, now essentially professional, players in Australia, immediately assumed the high ground in employment relationships with the ARU. This emerged with the signing of an agreement penned by ARU director, Ian Ferrier, which was designed, through massive financial incentives, to keep the top players in union. The Ferrier agreement, signed on 16 August 1995, not only directed the majority of the monies from News Ltd to the players in the three Australian franchises (the Waratahs, the Reds and the Brumbies), it also gave the players representation on the states/territories unions' boards and on the board of the ARU. A players' association, the Rugby Union Players' Association (RUPA) was established to protect and control the professional rugby players' interests.[82] The formalization of professionalization, globally, came with the signing of the Paris Declaration on 25 August 1995. This was ratified by the IRB in September that year. The declaration stated that rugby union players could openly receive financial payment for playing. The line had now been crossed. The last great bastion of amateurism in all football had fallen.[83] The game had now to respond to commercial needs, at the elite level at least, and would further morph as it moved into the next phase of its development.

External restraints

Currently television now dictates much of the image of elite rugby union football, and how it is played in terms of both manner and the laws. Many technical modifications have been made to the laws to either make the game more attractive to spectators by taking out the more turgid phases of the play, or to take out the open displays of gratuitous violence, which are now viewed as being unacceptable. Typical of the technical manipulation of the laws are the major changes made to those governing the lineouts. The previously acceptable displays of 'manly' violence so typical in lineouts are no longer tolerated by society. As Elias would argue, this is a consequence of the effect of the civilizing process[84] of society.[85] Other changes in the laws that now allow the lifting and support of jumpers at the lineout were purportedly made to speed up the transition from the restart. However, this change also proved to be a marketing miracle for the game's promoters, for the sight of jumpers soaring into the air was very attractive to the new wave of supporters being drawn to the game, particularly the younger spectators.[86]

On-field regulation of the game has also moved into the professional era as witnessed by the adoption of a card system (red and yellow). Cards are issued in football, (soccer, as it is known in Australia), to players who are deemed to have seriously violated the laws. However, in rugby union both cards evoke dismissal from the field, though for the yellow it only represents a suspension of 10 minutes. The red, as in football, means the player will not return to the game and will have to face a judiciary hearing, at which he or she may (as the game is now also played by a growing number of women) will receive a further penalty of a fine and/or a period of suspension, which now is far more imposing with the loss of earnings (for the elite male players), enormous fines and potentially the cancellation of playing contracts being possible outcomes.

The control and sanitization of all Australian football codes, including rugby union, is evidenced by the fact that players who have committed an offence unseen by on-field match officials face being cited post-match on the basis of video evidence, initiated either by the opposition's management or, in the case of an international rugby union matches, the IRB Match Commissioner. The emergence of this form of censure is further evidence of the 'game-play' of rugby union becoming increasingly bureaucratized with the previously standard external regulation of the play by referees now becoming policed and regulated. Offences are classified in terms of their seriousness or level of cynicism (professional fouls). The full coterie of match officials: referees, touch-judges and television match officials (TMOs) are all involved in deciding the necessary action needed to be taken when individual transgressions occur. The presentation of a card to a player, done in a very deliberate manner, adds a deal of 'theatre' to the referee's performance and is an explicit demonstration of the regulation and accountability of not only the players but also of the match officials. In televised sporting contests match officials are now under heavy scrutiny, as evidenced by the video refereeing, as are the actions of the players.

This altering of laws to diminish violence and injuries is not unique to rugby contemporaries. It has been an on-going process. Almost as soon as the major football codes became institutionalized they came under the influence of societal demands to curb the violent tenor of the games.[87] This process continued with rugby union throughout the twentieth century and continues in the twenty-first century. Not unexpectedly, the movement gained pace and judicial teeth with professionalization in 1995. To gain a wider supporter-base and obviously a bigger television audience, the new 'owners' of the game, the alliance of media and corporate capital advertisers, had to increase the excitement to 'spectacularize' the proceedings, in effect to 'sex up' the whole thing. On the one hand they had to offer better skills, more scoring, more speed, more power and more collisions to attract audiences and sponsors alike, but on the other they could not tolerate the previous levels of gratuitous violence typical for Australia which was most apparent in the traditional international clashes with England, Wales and New Zealand. Nor could they condone the low scoring arm-wrestling type, attritional clashes that such 'battles' often produced, hence the lineout and scrum law modifications plus the almost total banning of rucking, particularly of players. The professional era meant that the whole game including administrators, players, coaches and officials were required to become better prepared, more compliant and, thus, better units of production.[88]

Conclusion or new beginning?

In the final of the RWC 2003 the Wallabies came very close to achieving what would have been for them the ultimate sporting success, victory in the final of a 'home' Rugby World Cup final. The fairy story ending did not eventuate; in fact, the final against England turned into a horror story with the home team losing to England in extra-time to the 99th minute drop goal by Jonny Wilkinson in front of 82,957 spectators with the rest of the rugby union world looking-on through one of Rupert Murdoch's affiliated television stations.[89] Tough rugby, great theatre and even better entertainment: for this is how the new owners of rugby rate success. Although Australia was defeated, the success of the RWC itself in 2003 was a massive financial coup for the ARU. As a mega-sporting festival, the tournament demonstrated the game's global economic efficacy. The impact on the Australian economy of hosting the 2003 RWC was estimated at producing an increase of over A$1 billion,[90] whilst the IRB, through its subsidiary company IRB Ltd, which owns the RWC and all marketing, advertising and television rights, made a profit of £44 million (approximately A$111 million). The ARU as host national union was estimated to have made a profit of A$87 million.[91] Record global television audiences for rugby watched the RWC 2003 whilst the associated roll-on effect for the sponsors and advertisers around the world would have been immense. Thus, the tournament was clearly a financial success for the ARU; the product of effective sports administration, event management, stadium presentation and the delivery of the event.

The changing face of Australian rugby union football over the course of the history of the RWC very closely matches the modernization of Australia's economy, which in itself has been metamorphosed since the late 1980s.[92] Both have been significantly affected by global forces and both are axiomatically linked. The professionalization of rugby union was not solely hastened by the attitude shift that flowed on the global ideoscape,[93] which saw a sudden change in the system of amateur rugby union players and administrators globally. Instead the professionalization of rugby union, and the emergence and development of the culture of the game in Australia were the unintended consequences of a host of direct and very conscious decisions at all levels of the game. These decisions, made throughout the sport's history in Australia, were never designed with any sense of social engineering in mind, though very specific social consequences were intended. As was apparent at the time of the First World War, while the bifurcation of rugby was intended, the cultural spilt was not, although it was manifestly accepted by both sub-cultures. Reflecting upon the colonial days of rugby's history in Australia, it can be seen from Galtung's[94] suggestion, that even an imperfect (or amateurish) form of imperialism (hegemony) can achieve ideological, economic and political dominance. This was evident in the case of the emergence of rugby in both NSW and finally Queensland, when, almost by accident, rugby football achieved a competitive position in the battle for football supremacy.[95] The global flow of cultural ideas, including a belief in valuing participation in sport for leisure and later profit, was an important ideoscape and a central dimension of the cultural imposition of British Imperialism: it was, as Charles Tennyson said, the Victorian British that taught the World to play.[96] Imperialism was a forceful form of globalization. This cultural diffusion, of which sport was a central feature,[97] was one of the most vigorous global movements that emerged in the nineteenth century and has continued apace ever since. The global movement that embraced sports also conveyed ideological and philosophical belief systems regarding the ethos of sport and the merits of physical activity per se.

The first point of departure for the two forms of rugby during the take-off phase of the globalization of sport[98] was the split into league and union which created the initial form of professional rugby. The penetration of elite rugby union in the late twentieth century by global market capitalism, was, to all intents and purposes, the final chapter in the solidification of the symbiotic relationship between major sport and the 'financescapes'[99] and, as has been shown, this relationship was so powerful that it easily unpicked the ideological fabric of the last bastion of football amateurism, rugby union. Once the media moguls started to covet rugby union in 1995 it became embedded as part of the 'media-leisure/sport-capital nexus'.[100] Its culture, its community, along with the very manner and style in which it was played, were to change forever. The laws of the game were modified to cater for non-devotee fans and the most fundamental cultural artefacts of the game and the tone were reshaped so that the new fans, attracted to the new mediated televised form of rugby union, could tolerate it. The question now became – would the fans stay loyal?

Current state of play

The 2007 Super 14 series was categorically a disaster for the Australian franchises and the responses from the corporate sector and the 'new' fans and, perhaps some of the old. If the poor sales for the 2007 home test series were anything to go by, the situation is somewhat alarming. The inept performance against Wales in the first test in 2007, in front of a record-low crowd of 40,872[101] for the Telstra Stadium in Sydney, demonstrated the market sensitivity that has become a feature of what is now just another one of an increasing number of top-level sports entertainment product available to the 'new' fans. Perhaps what should be of greater concern to the ARU is that many of the empty seats were those normally filled by the traditional fans from the rugby community who were also disenchanted with the product, although for more esoteric reasons? In the second test against Wales, in which the Wallabies produced another indifferent performance, they were booed from the field at half-time. The new fans were clearly not pleased; nor perhaps were the traditional ones.

In reaction to the apparent impending doom facing Australian rugby union the ARU board, still made up of amateur sport administrators and volunteers, did not turn to its traditional power base for a solution but (back) to the ultimate professional sports administrator, John O'Neill. O'Neill was previously CEO of the ARU from 1995–2003 and it was he who guided Australian rugby union through the turbulent waters of the advent of professionalism and then so successfully to and through the RWC in 2003. O'Neill was waved goodbye to by the Australian 'old farts' of the ARU who believed they could reclaim 'custody' of *their* game after the enormous success he had just delivered to them. However, in 2007 the amateurs conceded; the game is now unquestionably the domain of the professional. As RUPA chief executive Tony Dempsey reflected, 'The game as an industry has matured'.[102]

The concern now is that elite Australian rugby union, as part of Rupert Murdoch's media stable, must score well in television ratings. Defeats and poor performances do not help the cause. Australia's insipid performance in the RWC 2007, with its very disappointing defeat against the team in the quarter final, did little to advance the game's marketability in Australia. The good news is that, community, schools and junior rugby union were all thriving before the RWC in 2007, as witnessed by an overall increase in participation rates from 148,750 in 2002, just before the RWC in Australia, to 193,382 in 2006.[103] Concern must exist at the ARU that rugby union football's popularity may have plateaued in 2006.[104] With football continuing its rise in popularity, rugby union as a product may falter compared with football, as well as Australian Rules football and rugby league, in the popularity stakes, which would have very serious economic repercussions for the ARU.

The quest for a new Wallabies' coach in late 2007 was unprecedented as, for the first time foreign coaches were considered for the post, with Robbie Deans being the successful candidate. This could be viewed as an indication that rugby union in Australia has possibly become less xenophobic and more, albeit thinly, cosmopolitan.[105] However, as the coach is in fact a New Zealander,[106] heralding this 'shift' may be excessive. Before Deans was interviewed for the position, the news of this precipitated a number of parochial comments, though legendary Wallaby captain John Eales openly supported the inclusion of the New Zealander in the list of candidates.[107] On the 14 December Robbie Deans was appointed as the Wallaby coach for a three-year period. He will be paid $1 million a year and, very significantly, he will have the freedom to personally select his own coaching staff.[108] In light of the Wallabies' indifferent effort in the RWC 2007 and the economic consequences this is likely to have with sponsors and the fans, Deans' selection suggests that a major overhaul of the whole ARU philosophy, particularly at the elite level, is about to occur. In terms of this analysis, however, these events are indicative of the extent to which rugby union football is now immersed in global mediasport. There is a ready exchange of knowledge and personnel between sports locally and globally, which is exemplified by the career moves of the ARU's chief executive officer John O'Neill who is now faced by the market threat posed to rugby union in Australia by football, which is a 'monster' of his own making. After being ignominiously 'released' by the ARU in 2003 O'Neill was engaged by the Frank Lowy-backed Football Federation of Australia in 2004 on the basis that he was the country's top sports administrator.[109] In 2004 O'Neill reinvented football in Australia; he created the 'A' League and then in 2006 saw Australia, the 'Socceroos', qualify for the Football World Cup finals for the first time in 30 years.[110]

Even though elite rugby union in Australia operates in a globalized context, it remains culturally distinct, which supports the rejection of the idea that globalization completely annihilates local cultures.[111] The development of rugby union football's culture and its place in the wider Australian sports culture attests to the notion that, although symbiotic relationships between local and global sport cultures exist, the impact of an individual cultural context is still the dominant influence in such relationships.[112] Rugby union football's development in Australia and the various points of resistance and departure that have framed this process will, it is suggested, ensure that rugby union in Australia will remain definitively Australian; whether this will bring it continued success remains problematic.

Notes

[1] Maguire, *Global Sport*, 215.
[2] Dunning and Sheard, *Barbarians, Gentlemen and Players.*
[3] ARU, *Annual Report (Financial Statement)*, 2006, 6.
[4] Maguire, *Global Sport*, 54–94.
[5] Robertson, *Globalization*, 58.
[6] Ibid., 133–5.
[7] Giulianotti and Robertson, 'Recovering the Social', 168.
[8] Apparadurai, 'Disjuncture and Difference', 295–311.
[9] Throughout the rest of the paper 'football' will be used in reference to Association football (soccer).
[10] Cashman, *Paradise of Sport.*
[11] Hickie, *They Ran with Ball*, 38–119.
[12] Horton, 'Football Identity, Place'.
[13] Horton, 'Dominant Ideologies'.
[14] Horton, 'A History of Rugby Union Football'; Hickie, *They Ran with the Ball*; Moran, *Viewless Winds*; Howell, Wilkes and Xie, *Wallabies*; Mulford, *Guardians of the Game*; Marples, *History of Football*; Dunning and Sheard, *Barbarians, Gentlemen and Players*; Starmer-Smith, *The Barbarians*; Wyatt and Herridge, *Rugby Revolution.*
[15] The ARU express these sentiments in its mission statement thus:
Rugby Union is a game that develops leadership, team spirit, courage, sportsmanship, and friendship. These values and traditions develop from the first time a young player shakes hands with their opposite number, leading to a life long passion for and involvement with the game at all levels. Foremost, the game of Rugby embodies the best Australian values and the nation's indomitable spirit. The key values of the game of rugby consist of Australian pride, team work and camaraderie, love of the game, and tradition and heritage.

Australian Pride – Rugby embodies the best Australian values and the nation's unyielding spirit. Through it's success on the International stage, rugby provides all Australians with a sense of pride, affiliation and belonging.

Teamwork and Camaraderie – Rugby is unselfish and focused on team play achievement. Its rugged nature is balanced by the concepts of fair play, sportsmanship, fun and ultimately mateship. This can be experienced at any age, any level and anywhere – on the field, in the stands or in the pub.

Love of the Game – Rugby engenders an abiding passion – an intensely personal pleasure in playing or watching. It creates an unaffected joy.

Tradition and Heritage – The ethos of rugby has shaped a code of behaviour that has transcended generations since 1823. It's time-honoured legacy creates a broader social environment.
[16] Mulford, *Guardians of the Game.*

[17] Fagan, *Rugby Rebellion*; Howell and Howell, *Greatest Game*, 2–25; Lester, *Story of Australian Rugby League*.

[18] Wyatt and Herridge, *Rugby Revolution*, 84.

[19] Fagan, *Rugby Rebellion*, 21–37.

[20] Fagan, *Rugby Rebellion*; Howell and Howell, *Greatest Game*, 2–25; Lester, *Story of Australian Rugby League*.

[21] Horton, 'The "Green" and the "Gold"', 77–8.

[22] Phillips, 'Football, Class and War'.

[23] O'Farrell, *The Irish in Australia*, 253.

[24] Howell and Howell, *Greatest Game*, 35–42.

[25] Phillips, 'Football, Class, War'.

[26] Parsons, 'Capitalism, Class and Community'.

[27] This epithet, used somewhat disparagingly by working-class footballers in Britain and later in Australia, stems from the cheers of encouragement, 'hoorah', used at sporting events of the upper and middle classes, such as, rugby union games, cricket matches and particularly rowing regattas.

[28] Until the game became commercialized the title 'Wallabies' was generally only used with reference to the Australian teams that made the full British Isles tour involving tests against all four home countries and a complete itinerary of other matches against regional, county, club and university sides, following in the footsteps of the First Wallabies captained by Herbert Moran in 1908–09, who Pollard suggested favoured this exclusivity (Pollard, *Australian Rugby Union*, 860). The marketing potential of the tag 'Wallabies' or 'Wallaby' is immense and its adoption for all products and matches involving the Australian rugby union team is indicative of the extent of the game's penetration by corporate cultural capitalism and its emergence as a feature of mediasport. The last full Wallaby tour took place in 1984 when the Eighth Wallabies completed the 'grand slam' against all four Home countries. The term 'grand slam' refers to beating all the four home countries on a Wallaby tour to the UK.

[29] Mulford, *Guardians of the Game*; Diehm, *Red, Red, Red*.

[30] In 1946 all interstate and international football was reinstated with NSW winning the traditional interstate series against Queensland three matches to nil. The entrenched (sibling) rivalry between New Zealand and Australia continued in 1946 when Australia toured New Zealand and the challenge for the Bledisloe Cup resumed. New Zealand toured Australia the following year and played two tests; over 53,000 spectators attended the matches in Brisbane and Sydney.

[31] Maguire, *Global Sport*, 84–6.

[32] Zakus and Horton, 'A Professional Game for Gentlemen', 163–73.

[33] Queensland, traditionally seen as the Premier state's most serious rival had lost so much ground, in player strength and, naturally financially since its post-First World War 'hibernation', that it could only muster enough credibility or power to gain more than three votes of the ten on offer.

[34] Pollard, *Australian Rugby Union*, 48–9.

[35] It was in 1997, when the game had become fully professional and the international governing body made a political economic decision to move it headquarters to Dublin, that it became the IRB.

[36] Australia as a full member of the IRFB was able to play with special dispensation for several years with regards to the laws governing kicking into touch on full and the use of time-keepers; both have since been universally accepted. Australia also promoted the change to the point-value of a try, up from 3 to 4pts and the introduction, internationally, of replacements.

[37] Maguire, *Global Sports*, 21.

[38] The impact now extends to both rugby codes with players with a Pacific Island heritage being prominent at the elite level of both league and union. The New Zealand All Blacks, the Wallabies and all the Super 14 teams from both nations have many players with a Pacific Island background whilst in the National Rugby League (NRL) it is estimated 'that 33% of the 375 players in the top 25-man squads at the 15 clubs are Pacific Islanders and the number is closer to half at the junior representative level' (B. Walter, 'Islanders in the Sun'. *Sydney Morning Herald*, March 25, 2006).

[39] The Wallaby squad for the home international series in 2007 has five players with a Pacific Islander heritage and the Australia 'A' squad has a similar number. 29.5% of the current squads from the three Australian Super 14 teams and the Victorian State squad are of Pacific Island descent. 55% of the Victorian squad, which does not play in the 'Super 14' competition, is

Pacific Islanders. The Wallaroos (women's national team) have seven Pacific Islanders in their squad of 26 players. The growing trend nationally is indicated by the fact that the latest figures, provided by the Geoff Shaw, General Manager of Community Rugby at the ARU, indicate that players with a Pacific Island heritage make up over 40% of the Australian U/16 representative squads.

[40] Diehm, *Red, Red, Red*, 169.

[41] Bickley, *Maroon*, 96–8.

[42] Diehm, *Red, Red, Red*; Mulford, *Guardians of the Game*; Pollard, *Australian Rugby Union*.

[43] Wyatt and Herridge, *Rugby Revolution*, 53.

[44] Gruneau, 'Amateurism as a Sociological Problem', 575.

[45] Ibid.

[46] Wyatt and Herridge, *The Rugby Revolution*, 239–50.

[47] Potential global television audiences for the next RWC are assessed to be over 3 billion people. See http://www.imgworld.com/sports/team_sports/default.sps.

[48] This expression is used in a strict sense regarding violence, its restraint and the acceptance of violent behaviour in general, as well as in the sporting context.

[49] Brohm, *Sport, a Prison of Measured Time*, 17.

[50] Horton, 'A History of Rugby Union Football', 9–51.

[51] Dunning and Sheard, *Barbarians, Gentlemen and Players*.

[52] Zakus and Horton, 'A Professional Game'.

[53] Department of Industry, Tourism and Resources, *Economic Impact of RWC* 2003, 9.

[54] In Australian rugby union, 'Grand Slam' refers to defeating all the four home unions, England, Scotland, Wales and Ireland on a single British Islands tour.

[55] Wenner, 'Playing the Mediasport Game'.

[56] Hickie, 'The Amateur Ideal'.

[57] Skinner, Stewart and Edwards, 'The Postmodernisation of Rugby Union', 51.

[58] Ibid., 60.

[59] Maguire, *Global Sport*

[60] Ibid.

[61] Dunning and Sheard, *Barbarians, Gentlemen and Players*, 226.

[62] Howell, Wilkes and Xie, *The Wallabies* and Howell and Xie, *Wallaby Greats*.

[63] Rojek, 'Sports Celebrity', 683.

[64] O'Regan, 'Another Side of the Rugby World Cup'.

[65] URS, 'Economic Impact of the RWC, 2003'.

[66] Ibid.

[67] Ibid.

[68] P. Switzer, 'Scoring Big Time'. http://www.charteredaccountants.com.au/index.cfm?su=/charter/charter_archive/2003/june_2003.

[69] Wenner, 'Playing the Mediasport Game'.

[70] AAP, 'Ten secures Rugby World Cup rights'. http://www.rugbyheaven.smh.com.au/articles/2006/11/15/1163266614941.html.

[71] Ibid.

[72] Mulford, *Guardians of the Game*, 217–20; Diehm, *Red, Red, Red*, 259–62.

[73] Diehm, *Red, Red, Red*, 264.

[74] Giulianotti and Robertson, 'Recovering the Social', 167–70.

[75] Ibid., 169.

[76] Zakus and Horton, 'A Professional game', 172–3.

[77] Diehm, *Red, Red, Red*, 264–5.

[78] Ibid.

[79] Fitzsimons, *Rugby War* for a complete outline of the whole process of battle for Rugby Union football in the southern hemisphere.

[80] Zakus and Horton, 'A Professional Game', 166–7.

[81] Ibid.

[82] Dabscheck, 'Paying for Professionalism', 1–9.

[83] Allison, *Amateurism in Sport*, 49.

[84] Elias, *Civilizing Process*.

[85] In their sociological study of the development of Rugby union football Dunning and Sheard discussed, historically, this notion of the growing intolerance of gratuitous violence in Rugby

union football featured in their study entitled *Barbarians, Gentlemen and Players* which utilized Elias' theory of the civilizing processes to analyse the development of the game from its earliest folk origins (the barbarian phase) to the game that evolved at Rugby School and promoted to other English Public Schools and the universities, thus played and controlled by 'gentlemen', and to the bifurcation of the rugby code and the emergence of rugby league football in 1895 which along with the development of amateur rugby union as a 'modern' sport marked their 'players' phase. The current phase, which, since 1995 has seen the formal sanctioning of professional rugby union, should possibly be tagged the 'superstar' phase?

86 G. Shaw, Personal Communication – conversation with author, October 23, 2003, Townsville.
87 Dunning and Sheard, *Barbarians, Gentlemen and Players*.
88 Zakus and Horton, 'A Professional Game'.
89 Ibid., 184.
90 URS, 'Economic Impact of the RWC, 2003'.
91 ARU, *Annual Report*, 2004.
92 Harcourt, 'The Game they Play in Heaven'.
93 Apparadurai, 'Disjuncture and Difference'.
94 Galtung, 'A Structural Theory of Imperialism', 81-94.
95 Horton, 'Football, Identity, Place', 1362.
96 Tennyson, 'They Taught the World'.
97 Mangan, *Cultural Bond*, and Mangan, *Games Ethic*.
98 Robertson, *Globalization*.
99 Apparadurai, 'Disjuncture and Difference'.
100 Jarvie and Maguire, *Sport and Leisure*, 234.
101 A. McBride, 'Wallabies Snatch Unlikely Victory Off Wales'. SportsAustralia.com. http://sportsaustralia.com/articles/news.php?id=1389.
102 *The Australian*, June 7, 2007, 16.
103 ARU, *Annual Report, 'Community Rugby'*, 2006. However, a circumspect analysis of these figures does reveal that the largest sectional rise is in the schools that played only irregularly in one off gala days or in 'knock-out' competitions. The current, apparently strong, figures demonstrated in comparison with other sports at junior levels of 8% are flattering as these include a massive new population of junior rugby union players (22%) in Western Australia, courtesy of the new Super 14 franchise, the Western Force. A dimension of these statistics which is very significant, culturally, is the continued increase in the number of registered senior players in women's rugby, to 1,915 in 2006. The Australian women's national team, the Wallaroos, placed 5th in the finals in 2002 and 7th in 2006.
104 Sweeney Sports Report, 2006.
105 Beck, 'Rooted Cosmopolitanism'.
106 R. Guinness, 'ARU Ready to Offer Deans Triple the Going Rate to Tackle Wallabies Job'. http://www.rugbyheaven.com.au/news/news/deans-could-get-triple/2007/11/28/1196036984356.html#.
107 John Eales, 'Interview'.
108 M. Hinton, 'Deans is the New Wallabies Coach'. http://www.rugbyheaven.com.au/news/news/deans-gets-wallabies-job/2007/12/14/1197568227944.html.
109 Frank Lowy, a post-Second World War migrant, Australia's second richest man, is founder and major share holder of the Westfield Group. He was instrumental in the complete restructuring of Australian football (soccer) in 2003, when he assumed control. He is Chairman of the Football Federation of Australia and has personally financially backed football's redevelopment. Securing John O'Neill's services in 2004 has been attributed solely to Lowy.
110 O'Neill, *It's Only a Game*.
111 Giulianotti and Robertson, 'Recovering the Social', 168.
112 Robertson, 'Glocalization', 27.

References

Allison, L. *Amateurism in Sport: An Analysis and a Defence*. London: Frank Cass, 2001.
Apparadurai, A. 'Disjuncture and Difference in the Global Cultural Economy'. *Theory, Culture and Society* 7 (1990): 295–310.
ARU. *Annual Report, (Financial Report and Analysis)*. Sydney: ARU, 2004.
ARU. *Annual Report (Financial Statement)*. Sydney: ARU, 2006.

ARU. *Annual Report, 'Community Rugby'*. Sydney: ARU, 2006.
Beck, U. 'Rooted Cosmopolitanism: Emerging from Rivalry of Distinctions'. In *Global America? The Cultural Consequences of Globalization*, edited by U. Beck, N. Sznaider, and R. Winter, 15–29. Liverpool: Liverpool University Press, 2004.
Bickley, W.H., ed. *Maroon: Highlights of One Hundred Years of Rugby in Queensland, 1882–1982*. Brisbane: QRU, 1982.
Brohm, J.M. *Sport, a Prison of Measured Time: Essays*. London: Ink Links Ltd., 1978.
Cashman, R. *Paradise of Sport: The Rise of Organised Sport in Australia*. Melbourne: Oxford University Press, 1995.
Dabscheck, B. 'Paying for Professionalism: Industrial Relations in Australian Rugby Union', The Montague Burton Visiting Professor in Industrial Relations Lecture, Cardiff Business School, Cardiff University, 2002.
Diehm, I. *Red, Red, Red: The Story of Queensland Rugby*. Sydney: Playright Publishing, 1997.
Dunning, E., and K. Sheard. *Barbarians, Gentlemen and Players: A Sociological Study of the Development of Rugby Football*. Oxford: Martin Robertson, 1979.
Eales, J. 'Interview'. Foxsports, December 13, 2007. http://www.foxsports.com.au/rugby/video/0,24537,1834-5607,00.html.
Elias, N. *The Civilizing Process*. Trans. E. Jephcott. 2 vols. Vol. 2: State Formation and Civilization. Oxford: Basil Blackwell, 1982.
Fagan, S. *The Rugby Rebellion: The Divide of League and Union*. Sydney: RL 1908, 2005.
Fitzsimons, P. *The Rugby War*. Sydney: HarperSports, 1996.
Galtung, J. 'A Structural Theory of Imperialism'. *Journal of Peace Research* 8, no. 2 (1971): 81–117.
Giulianotti, R., and R. Robertson. 'Recovering the Social: Globalization, Football and Transnationalism'. *Global Networks* 7, no. 2 (2007): 166–86.
Gruneau, R. 'Amateurism as a Sociological Problem: Some Reflections Inspired by Eric Dunning'. *Sport in Society* 9, no. 4 (2006): 559–82.
Harcourt, T. 'The Game they Play in Heaven Meets the Dismal Science – An Economist's Guide to the Rugby World Cup 2003'. A speech to the Australian Business Economists, October 8, 2003, Sydney. http://www.abe.org.su/papers/Tim%252.
Hickie, T. *They Ran with the Ball: How Rugby Football Began in Australia*. Melbourne: Longman Cheshire, 1993.
Hickie, T. 'The Amateur Ideal in the Era of Professional Rugby'. In *Rugby History: The Remaking of the Class Game*, edited by M. Bushby and T.V. Hickie, 17–50. ASSH Studies, 22, 2007.
Horton, P.A. 'A History of Rugby Union Football in Queensland 1882–1891'. PhD diss., University of Queensland, 1989.
Horton, P.A. 'Dominant Ideologies and Their Role in the Establishment of Rugby Union Football in Victorian Brisbane'. *The International Journal of the History of Sport* 11, no. 1 (1994): 115–28.
Horton, P.A. '"Scapes" and "Phases": An Overview of Two Approaches to Sport and Globalisation'. *Social Alternatives* 15, no. 1 (1996): 53–62.
Horton, P.A. 'The "Green" and the "Gold": The Irish Australians and Their Role in the Emergence of an Australian Sports Culture'. *Sport in Global Society Series – The International Journal of the History of Sport, 'Sport in Australasian Society: Past and Present'* 17, no. 2/3 (2000): 65–92.
Horton, P.A. 'Football, Identity, Place: The Emergence of Rugby Football in Brisbane'. *The International Journal of the History of Sport* 23, no. 8 (2006): 1341–68.
Howell, M.L., and R.A. Howell. *The Greatest Game under the Sun: The History of Rugby League in Queensland*. Brisbane: Leon Bedington for the Queensland Rugby Football League Ltd, 1989.
Howell, M.L., and L. Xie. *Wallaby Greats*. Auckland: Rugby Publishing Ltd, 1996.
Howell, M.L., B. Wilkes, and L. Xie. *The Wallabies: A Definitive History of Australian Test Rugby*. Norman Park, QLD: GAP Publishing, 2000.
Jarvie, G., and J. Maguire. *Sport and Leisure in Social Thought*. London: Routledge, 1994.
Lester, G. *The Story of Australian Rugby League*. Sydney: Lester-Townsend, 1988.
Maguire, J. *Global Sport: Identities, Societies, Civilizations*. Cambridge: Polity Press, 1999.
Mangan, J.A. *The Games Ethic and Imperialism*. Harmondsworth; New York; Ringwood, Vic.: Penguin, 1985.
Mangan, J.A. *The Cultural Bond: Sport, Empire and Society*. London: Frank Cass, 1992.
Marples, M. *The History of Football*. London: Secker and Warburg, 1954.
Moran, H.M. *Viewless Winds*. London: Peter Davies, 1939.

Mulford, J.G. *Guardians of the Game: The History of the New South Wales Rugby Union 1874–2004*. Sydney: ABC Books, 2005.

O'Farrell, P. *The Irish in Australia*. Kensington, NSW: New South Wales University Press, 1993.

O'Neill, J. *It's Only a Game: The Autobiography of John O'Neill*. Sydney: Random House, 2007.

O'Regan, M. 'Another Side of the Rugby World Cup'. In *The Media Report*. Australia: ABC Radio, October 9, 2003.

Phillips, M. 'Football, Class and War: The Rugby Codes in New South Wales, 1907–1918'. In *Making Men: Rugby and Masculine Identity*, edited by J. Nauright and T. Chandler, 158–80. London: Frank Cass, 1996.

Pollard, J. *Australian Rugby Union: The Game and the Players*. Sydney: Angus & Robertson, 1985.

Robertson, R. *Globalization: Social Theory and Global Culture*. London: Sage, 1992.

Robertson, R. 'Glocalization: Time-Space and Homogeneity-Heterogeneity'. In *Global Modernities*, edited by M. Featherstone, S. Lash, and R. Roberson, 25–44. London: Sage, 1995.

Rojek, C. 'Sports Celebrity and the Civilizing Process'. *Sport in Society* 9, no. 4 (2006): 674–90.

Skinner, J., B. Stewart, and A. Edwards. 'The Postmodernisation of Rugby Union in Australia'. *Football Studies* 6, no. 1 (2003): 51–69.

Starmer-Smith, N. *The Barbarians: The Official History of the Barbarians Football Club*. London: Macdonald and Jane's, 1977.

Sweeney Sports Report. Melbourne: Sweeney Research Consultants, 2006.

Tennyson, C. 'They Taught the World to Play'. *Victorian Studies* March (1959): 211–22.

URS. *Economic Impact of the Rugby World Cup 2003 on the Australian Economy – Post Analysis*. Prepared for the Department of Industry, Tourism and Resources, 2004.

Wenner, L.A. 'Playing the Mediasport Game'. In *Mediasport*, edited by L.A. Wenner, 3–26. London: Routledge, 1998.

Wyatt, D., and C. Herridge. *The Rugby Revolution*. London: Metro, 2003.

Zakus, D., and P.A. Horton. 'A Professional Game for Gentlemen: Rugby Union's Transformation'. In *The Games Are Not the Same: The Political Economy of Football in Australia*, edited by Bob Stewart, 142–98. Melbourne: Melbourne University Press, 2007.

Social capital in Australian sport

Dwight Zakus[a], James Skinner[b] and Allan Edwards[b]

[a]Department of Tourism, Leisure, Hotel and Sport Management, Griffith University, Queensland, Australia; [b]School of Education and Professional Studies, Griffith University, Queensland, Australia

Socio-cultural studies of sport in society have employed various conceptual categories from a variety of theoretical perspectives, with the latest to gain wide currency being 'social capital'. While there is much general debate on the concept and its measurement in the study of society, the number of studies using social capital has grown remarkably. Of the research using social capital as a central concept, little of this work focuses on understanding sport's position and role in society. This study adds to this new focus by linking recent empirical work and published papers on sport and social capital in Australian society. Social capital is seen to add many positive features to life in society, to provide positive development for individuals, and for building community capacity.

Introduction

Sport in Australian society is seen as one of the central defining characteristics of the population, along with the Sydney Harbour Bridge and Opera House, koalas and kangaroos, beer, sun, and surf.[1] While sport is an important cultural element of the country, its centrality and actual significance has, to date, not been thoroughly and empirically tested. However, several recent studies have begun to address this situation.[2]

While sport may define important cultural and identity characteristics for the nation's population,[3] sport's role in wider community projects, such as contributing to social capital and development, has not been systematically studied. Yet, sport is credited with adding many positive developmental elements to individuals in Australian society.[4] While this often overlooks the negative aspects that occur within and around sport, sport is, nonetheless, believed to add to the quality of communitarian life and socialization of individuals. While debate continues in the popular and academic media about the benefits of engagement with sport, there is limited research on how engagement with sport contributes to the development of social capital. Moreover, to date this has not been directly tested in Australia.

In this essay we briefly discuss the concept of social capital, its use in sport studies, and data from a number of recent studies on the connection between it and sport. The goal is to establish if there is evidence for sport's contribution to social capital in what is argued to be a 'sport mad' nation. This demands some discussion on social capital, sport social capital, and empirical evidence for sport's contribution to the development (both positive and negative) of social capital in Australian society. While we do not take a position on policy initiatives that link sport with social capital generation, many current comments and studies seek to identify ways in which sport can contribute to a number of social panaceas through its use as a policy tool. To make some preliminary links material is provided from several sources. These sources include surveys used in a market research project for Basketball Australia and the National Basketball League; a survey used in a study for the Australian Football League (AFL, also known as Australian rules football), which sought to determine one community's interest in and support for this sport code, as well as to understanding sport's role in generating community identity of a rapidly growing regional Australian city.

Added to this, is material from the few existing studies on sport's relationship to social capital generation. This includes material from rural sport studies in Western Australia and from studies on volunteers, which give an integrated, fuller picture of how sport contributes to the generation of social capital in Australian communities.

All of this aims to provide a more precise definition and identification of composite elements of the concept of social capital within the Australian context[5] and to provide a basis for further empirical studies of the role sport and sport clubs play in building social capital and community capacity.[6] It is through a discussion of these studies that we hope to reduce a void identified by Coalter who suggested that to overcome this: 'more research is required to explore the processes of social capital formation in sport clubs'.[7] Sport clubs are the key delivery point for sport in Australia and thus have the greatest potential for the generation of social capital and building of community capacity.

Social capital in current thought: a brief overview of the concept

Over the last ten years, the concept of social capital gained salience as a means of understanding how communities might operate to become safer and more productive places where positive identities and lifestyles might be forged. While the concept of social capital has a long history,[8] in the last two decades it has gained greater cache with social researchers, government agencies, think-tanks and other bodies. Much of this debate takes varying theoretical positions and empirical analysis of the concepts.

As a basic definition we use The World Health Organisation's statement that 'social capital represents the degree of social cohesion which exists in communities'.[9] How this social cohesion is facilitated is a point of debate. In social capital terms it is suggested that bridging social capital is more likely to assist in this social cohesion process. Bridging social capital applies to broader overlapping networks that produce wider identities and reciprocity, such as associations between people from other social groups which can vary in religion and ethnicity, or socio economic status. By contrast, bonding social capital applies to trust and reciprocity contained in dense or closed networks and is apparent when individuals who know each other are brought closer together.[10] Despite its fluidity as a concept, Australia has followed other countries in taking up the idea of the importance of social capital. The concept is now widely used in government policy and research, NGO (non-government organization) research, and in various types of social research. For example, in the Productivity Commission Paper, 'Social Capital: Reviewing the Concept and its Policy Implications', the authors state:

> At present, there is limited understanding of the social capital and how different policies interact with it, and measurement is difficult. Further, research, coupled with small scale policy experimentation, may be warranted to provide better knowledge and tools for incorporating social capital considerations in policy analysis where appropriate.[11]

While this paper does not delve into the policy implications of social capital, it provides examples of small scale studies that sought to provide better knowledge and tools of the concept's salience in understanding sport in Australian society.

Essentially the concept of social capital embraces four important integrated elements: networks, trust, reciprocity and social norms. Social capital is seen as a way of expanding empowerment, well-being and community development: all of which are geared toward an improved civil society. As Spies-Butcher writes, following Portes, 'social capital theory is little more than the long standing acknowledgement that civic involvement and social networks can have positive implications for individuals and society as a whole'.[12] A number of studies from the Australian Family Studies Institute,[13] centres such as the Centre for Australian Community Organisations and Management[14] at the University of Technology Sydney, and government organizations such as the Productivity Commission make major contributions to the literature, definitions and techniques to measure and make sense of the concept in the Australian context. The Australian Bureau of Statistics (ABS) has also contributed major studies to both the conceptual development and the methodological analysis of social capital. These documents provide the basis for the work presented here.[15]

Despite a growing recognition of the social and economic benefits of social capital and increased number of studies using the concept, conceptual and methodological debates persist. Calls continue for more work on clearer definitions and for the identification of the composite elements and techniques used to measure the concept.[16] The concept's use widely varies in academic and policy applications.[17] In local community studies and neighbourhood organization contexts it adopts ideological perspectives ranging from communitarianism to neo-liberalism, and is present in materials published by global organizations such as the World Bank and the United Nations.

The third sector: volunteers and civic engagement

A key area in the current discourse on social capital relates to the third, non-profit, or voluntary, sector. Much of the social capital discourse in this domain relates to its potential for increasing civic engagement or active citizenship. Here the sport delivery system is the focus. This raises the question, 'How do people contribute to the sport and sport club communities and activities?' Moreover, at the more basic level of sport, it could be asked, 'What ways do people become engaged in civic responsibilities and how does citizenship move beyond the formal level of voting and tax-paying?' As sport has always been a part of this type of engagement and citizenship, is social capital only a new label to identify the relationships and networks?

A number of research papers on volunteers in sport[18] indicate that we know the importance of volunteering to sport organizations and clubs. However, in these studies, it was found that it can no longer be assumed that volunteers are committed only by the desire to volunteer. There is a pressing need for sport managers in community-based sport to understand that the nature of the relationship between volunteers and their organizations is complex and it is undergoing dramatic change due to pressing economic and emerging social forces.[19]

Australia has long been characterized by a strong tradition of volunteering. Australian Bureau of Statistics figures show that over five million (5.2 million) people volunteered during the year 2006.[20] Sport and recreation organizations attract, after the community welfare sector, the largest numbers of volunteers.[21] In 2006 187 million volunteer hours were given to sport and recreation organisations, or 26% of the total volunteer hours provided by all Australians that year.[22] The significance of volunteering in the sport sector is noteworthy.

This is highlighted by the fact that of all 'highly committed volunteers' (those who contribute more than 300 hours per year, or an average of six hours per week) nearly 53%

volunteer in sport organizations.[23] Despite these seemingly impressive figures there is a marked decline in the number of volunteer hours given to sporting organizations. This decline in the volunteer component, not only of sport, but across the national community, has been compared to the decline in civil society.[24] Although sport volunteering has not been proven to have a direct correlation to social capital, the third sector does play a key role in the development of sustainable social capital and community capacity.[25] Although community sport organizations and clubs are core components of this third sector activity, the importance of volunteers in this key role should not be over-estimated and requires ongoing analysis.

It is clear that Australian sport at any level cannot function without volunteers. Whether they are local club coaches, managers, or administrators or volunteers for major international sport events, if people do not engage in these civic activities many, if not most, sports would not be able occur. An ABS document provides further indication of the importance of voluntary work as it 'meets needs, expands opportunities for democratic participation, personal development and recreation within a community and helps to develop and reinforce social networks and cohesion'.[26] Similarly, Talbot, in her examination of the UK system, suggests that sport provides an exemplar for governments in active citizenship and volunteering. Moreover, she notes that the European Commission has referred to sport as the largest citizenship movement in Europe.[27]

Despite government enthusiasm for social capital to be developed through volunteering and sport,[28] Seippel notes that there are several problems with the present social capital discourse if it is used to assess the contribution of the voluntary sector. The first problem is that the voluntary sector as a whole, in spite of its obvious internal differences, is often treated as one with respect to both its internal structures and external effects. Second, even when studies distinguish between the different kinds of voluntary community organizations, methodological approaches to understanding and measuring social capital do not reflect the specific particularities of voluntary community sport organizations. Finally, there is a lack of studies investigating sport as a specific component of community life.[29]

The above suggests there is a need for a more detailed understanding of the unique place of community sport organizations within the voluntary sector[30] and the role of sport in the development of community capacity.[31] Further research is needed that highlights the various aspects of voluntary community sport organizations that make them unique within their community and the roles they potentially play in building bridging social capital and enhancing community capacity.

Does sport contribute to the social capital 'glue' of Australian society?

We noted in the introduction that much is made of centrality of sport in the lives of Australians; in fact, the popular mythology views Australia as sport mad or obsessed with its successful sport accomplishments.[32] How widespread and valid this claim is, and how the interest in sport, both in active and vicarious participation, pertains to the overall Australian population, is not well measured. While this study does not claim to fully provide a complete answer, results from the following studies indicate that sport is important to daily life and a regular focus of attention in Australia.

A study for the Australian Football League[33] (AFL) sought empirical data that could begin to answer the importance of sport in Australian society. Over 300 surveys were completed across five shopping centres in the Gold Coast City located in South East Queensland. One hundred and thirty-seven females (44%) and 172 males (56%)

completed a survey using a mall intercept convenience sampling strategy. The following age groups comprised the sample: 18–25 year olds, 25%; 26–35, 20%; 36–45, 21%; 45–65, 22%; over 65, 7% (5% of respondents did not indicate their age group). Over 58% had lived on the Gold Coast for more than five years, dispelling the notion of this city being highly transient, and 85% were born in Australia. Basic descriptive statistical frequencies are provided here as they overwhelmingly paint a picture of the sample population's position on sport.

Responses to two statements are especially pertinent. The first was, 'Sport is important to the Australian way of life'. The second, 'Sport is an important part of my daily life'. In response to the first question, an overwhelming majority of respondents (97%) strongly agreed or agreed that sport is an important part of the Australian way of life, confirming that sport appears to be a significant part of Australian cultural identity and national self-concept.

In response to the second question of whether sport was important to the personal lives of Australians, 69% of respondents strongly agreed or agreed that sport was an important way of life to them, while approximately 25% disagreed or strongly disagreed.

What is interesting to note is that 72 of the respondents who said that sport was *not* important to their personal way of life still strongly agreed or agreed that sport was important to the Australian way of life [χ^2 (16, N 299) = 90.283, p = .000]. In other words, a significant number of respondents felt sport was important to the Australian way

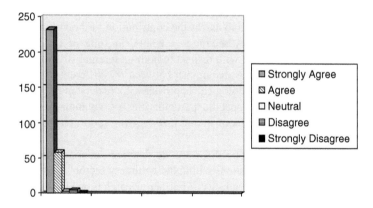

Figure 1.   Frequencies of responses for statement 'Sport is important to the Australian way of life'.

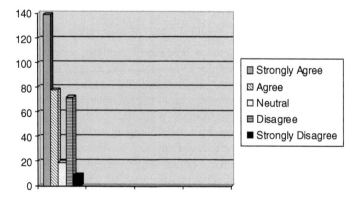

Figure 2.   Frequencies for responses to statement 'Sport is an important part of my daily life'.

of life if not to their own personal lives. This provides an interesting insight to the cultural identity of Australians.

In terms of active participation, this survey did not differentiate between direct and indirect types of involvement. Respondents could reply that their involvement was as either direct participants or volunteers, or that they were involved indirectly as spectators. Results in Table 1 indicate that approximately 75% of respondents had some involvement in sport.

Two further statements delved more deeply into this data. First, those surveyed were asked to respond to a statement on whether they were 'actively' involved in sport. Sixty per cent responded that they strongly agreed or agreed to this statement, with 5% strongly disagreeing and 25% disagreeing. The second statement focussed on data on attendance at sport. Here respondents were asked to indicate their weekly attendance at sport. Over 60% strongly agreed or agreed, 9% were neutral, and 35% strongly disagreed or disagreed that they attended a sport match each week. From this there is strong indication that sport plays an important part of regular life amongst Australians either through direct participation or as spectators.

A final set of statements related to how respondents perceived sport's contribution to life in their home city. The first line of inquiry, 'sport is important for building community life', resulted in a strong response in the positive (see Table 2).

The second statement probed whether 'professional sport teams give cities a feeling of being a real city'. Only 25.5% of respondents strongly disagreed or disagreed with this idea. Over 56% felt that this is a defining characteristic of a 'real' Australian city. From this we can surmise that sport franchises help to identify a city and its civic import.

The final statement, 'having an AFL (Australian Football League) or NRL (National Rugby League) team on the Gold Coast will benefit the city', focussed on having actual specific sport franchises in the Gold Coast City. Table 3 shows that most felt this would benefit the city.

From the above findings it is clear that sport has an important function in Australian lives, for both active and passive participants. It also provides some indication that sport plays an important role in defining Australian cultural identity and a sense of community belonging, and provides communities with a real sense of presence. In this light sport has the potential to assist in the development of positive social capital outcomes.

In other Australian specific research in this vein, conducted in rural areas, Tonts reported on a similar line of questioning in his study of sport social capital in rural Western Australia. Two survey statements, 'sport is an important way of keeping in touch with friends and family' and 'sport is important in promoting a sense of community in this area', each received 'agree' responses at the low 90% level.[34] Atherley similarly found 'that local sporting clubs are a main focus of community life and participation in, or

Table 1. Response frequency for statement 'I am actively involved in sport as either a participant, volunteer, spectator (at community level and/or professional level sport)'.

Response category	Frequency	Percentage
Strongly Agree	141	44.3
Agree	91	28.6
Neutral	11	3.5
Disagree	65	20.4
Strongly Disagree	10	3.1
Total	318	100.0

Table 2. Response frequencies for survey statement 'sport is important for building community life'.

Response category	Frequency	Percentage
Strongly Agree	188	59.1
Agree	87	27.4
Neutral	9	2.8
Disagree	14	4.4
Strongly Disagree	1	.3
Total	299	94.0
Missing	19	6.0
Total	318	100.0

exclusion from, [and] such groups affects residents' daily life, social networks, community integration and flow of information'.[35] Both of these authors offer other references to support the contention that in Australia 'sporting clubs in particular are often regarded as a central element of rural life'.[36] We argue that results from these studies further locate sport and sport clubs as key elements in community life and in the building of social capital in Australian communities.

In another Australian study, Pooley, Cohen and Pike make the case for a psychometric concept of 'sense of community', adding further salience to the concept of social capital. They report on four other studies. Each of these adds an important element to the general literature on social capital.[37] These authors provide further evidence of the role sport plays in developing social capital and a sense of community. For example, in his study Tonts reported that nearly 45% (44.7%) of all responses and nearly 82% (81.8%) of household survey responses saw 'the most important aspect of local sport' being social interaction. This survey response was corroborated by the one-on-one interviews he conducted.[38]

Other recent empirical findings

Finally, a second research project conducted for Basketball Australia, State basketball associations, and the National Basketball League also sought to gain empirical evidence regarding the relationship of sport and social capital in Australia. One aspect of data collection in this study was to complete a survey, again using a mall intercept convenience sampling strategy. In this study, shopping centres across metropolitan and regional cities of Australia (Adelaide, Brisbane, Canberra, Cairns, Coffs Harbour, Gold Coast, Melbourne, Perth, Sydney, Townsville, West Sydney and Wollongong) were sites for data

Table 3. Response frequencies for survey statement 'having an AFL or NRL team at the Gold Coast will benefit the city'.

Response category	Frequency	Percentage
Strongly Agree	180	56.6
Agree	86	27.0
Neutral	16	5.0
Disagree	15	4.7
Strongly Disagree	1	.3
Total	298	93.7
Missing	20	6.3
Total	318	100.0

Table 4.   Respond frequencies for the statement 'what best describes your participation/interest in sport?'.

Response category	Frequency	Percentage
Active participant (play sport formally on a regular basis)	295	36.2
Recreational participant (play sport as a recreation/leisure)	186	22.8
I have children regularly involved in sport	107	13.1
I am a coach/volunteer/official	44	5.4
I attend sport or watch it on TV regularly	94	11.5
I attend sport or watch it on TV occasionally	80	9.8
Total	806	98.9
Missing	9	1.1
Total	815	100.0

collection. A total of 815 surveys were completed, with 326 females (40%) and 464 males (57%; 25 did not identify their gender) in the sample. The following age groups comprised the sample: 15–24 year olds, 60%; 25–34, 25%; 35–44, 10%; 45–54, 5%. Respondents were from urban, regional and country locations in the following states and territories: 20% Victoria, 19% New South Wales, 3% Australian Capital Territory, 34% Queensland, 13% South Australia, 6% West Australia, 4% Tasmania, and 1% Northern Territory. Again, participation rates were high in the active and participant sport activity categories with 60% of people indicating some involvement in sport (see Table 4).

People were also asked whether they would have or had their children (or future children) involved in organized sport. As shown in Table 5 over 95% indicated they would encourage their children to participate in organized sport. From this finding it is very clear that sport is seen as an important element of Australian family life. The respondents were not questioned about their specific reasons for wanting their children to be active in sport. As sport, however, creates opportunities for social interactions that can facilitate outcomes such as mutuality and trust between participants, it could be suggested that parents encourage their children to play sport as they consider the social aspects of sport important. Moreover, as mutuality and trust are key elements of social capital, it adds salience to the argument for the role sport can play in its generation of social capital.

The surveys also sought to ascertain whether people identified themselves as sport fans. The following table (Table 6) indicates that many Australians consider themselves to be sport enthusiasts. This data asked respondents to self-identify how strongly they consider themselves to be a fan. By looking at the results in quintiles, 32% are in the top end of the scale (9–10 range), 38.5% were in the next quintile (7–8 range), and 19% were in the upper middle quintile (5–6 range). In other words; over 89.5% of respondents claimed to be strong sport fans.

Table 5.   Response frequencies for statement 'If I had children/I have children, I would actively encourage them to participate in sport'.

Response category	Frequency	Percentage
Yes	779	95.6
No	17	2.1
Total	796	97.7
Missing	19	2.3
Total	815	100.0

Table 6.   Response frequencies for the statement 'On a scale of 1–10, how strongly do you consider yourself to be a sports fan?'

Response category	Frequency	Percentage
1	12	1.5
2	16	2.0
3	22	2.7
4	36	4.4
5	73	9.0
6	81	9.9
7	128	15.7
8	186	22.8
9	118	14.5
10	141	17.3
Total	813	99.8
Missing	2	0.2
Total	815	100.0

Results from this study again provided support for social capital being seen as the 'social fabric or glue' that ties community members together and that sport has a role in this process.

People must have some level of trust with teammates, opponents, coaches, referees and administrators for sport to occur. It is widely accepted that sport is a normative institution in society. That is, we are taught how to behave and interact within sport and societal bounds (notwithstanding the negative behaviour of athletes or the downside of sport – sexism, drugs, racism, etc.). The notion that sport builds networks is fairly self-evident. Sport teams are networks, competitions are networks, and leagues are networks. It is often claimed that one builds lifelong important networks through sport.[39] Finally, the need for working together to achieve goals, of expecting in return what one puts into the sporting effort, builds reciprocal relationships. Sport inherently holds and can develop the key common elements of social capital.

Conclusion

From the above findings, it can be argued that sport is a key element in the Australian social, national and cultural landscape. Sport, sport clubs and other organizations comprising the sport delivery system play an important role in building local and national social capital thereby enhancing life in Australia. As Elkington noted, 'sport in small country towns is an important ingredient in providing people with a sense of community'[40] and can play a key role in the formation of positive social capital.

The perception held by Australians is that sport has some role in their daily lives and is something in which they regularly and directly or indirectly participate. It is also something they see as important for their children, and as something that helps define community and nation. Therefore it could be argued that well-managed sport can play a role in generating social capital as it can facilitate the building of networks of trust, safety and mutuality within a community. Sport also provides an outlet for civic engagement and active citizenship as evidenced from recent ABS statistics and research into volunteer roles and target of participation.

The role sport plays in the generation of social capital requires greater investigation; in particular, two key areas require much more research. The first of these surrounds the need to understand how 'sport is often a site of social exclusion and marginalisation'.[41]

Exclusion takes on many social, economic and cultural elements, but exclusion often is also based on racial, ethnic, gender, ability and place (community) lines. In this light, some researchers have argued that in Australia sport and recreation spaces are sites of conflict and contestation between different ethnic groups. For example, Macdonald and Skinner note the latent ethnic tensions between rival soccer clubs in Australia.[42] The traditional organization of these soccer clubs along ethnic lines has also served to marginalize the game from the mainstream Australian sporting consciousness.[43]

By contrast and as previously suggested, Seippel notes that social networks developed through sport strengthen communities, further various individual and social competencies, and generate social integration.[44] These claims however, require more study and analysis as the evidence to support these claims to date is limited. This evidence is even more essential if sport is to be a policy instrument of government. Potentially, sport has many positive attributes for government as it lends itself to realizing civic outcomes including: participating as volunteers; the development of organizational skills (running activities; setting up clubs; seeking sponsorship; developing expertise in governance; strategic planning; budgeting); and gaining confidence to play an active role in local communities.

Sport is therefore a two-edged sword. It has been a tool 'of both imperial con-solidation and disintegration simultaneously'.[45] This is because sport is a cultural vehicle for thinking nationally and supra-nationally via its languages, symbols and rules. Sport shapes and cements national, gendered and cultural identities.[46] The cultural centrality of sport in Australia means it carries a heavy political and symbolic significance.[47] As such, it is clear that further research into the social capital implications of sport in Australia is necessary.

Notes

[1] Toohey, *Politics of Australian Elite Sport*; Cashman, *Sport in the National Imagination*.
[2] These include Zakus *et al.*, *Basketball Market Research Report*; Zakus, Bird and Roobottom, *Report for the Australian Football League*; and Zakus, Skinner and Edwards, 'Identifying and Measuring Social Capital'.
[3] Cashman, *Paradise of Sport*.
[4] Coalter, 'Sports Clubs', 538.
[5] For additional information see Rowland, *Is the Club Really a Better Place?*
[6] Zakus, Skinner and Edwards, 'Identifying and Measuring Social Capital'.
[7] Coalter, 'Sports Clubs', 537.
[8] For additional information on the history of social capital, see Field, *Social Capital*; Putnam, *Bowling Alone*; and Spies-Butcher, 'Understanding the Concept of Social Capital'.
[9] Productivity Commission, *Social Capital*, 8.
[10] See Tonts, 'Competitive Sport'; and Atherley, 'Sport, Localism'.
[11] Productivity Commission, *Social Capital*, viii.
[12] Spies-Butcher, 'Understanding the Concept of Social Capital', 6.
[13] See Stone and Hughes, *Social Capital*.
[14] See Onyx and Bullen, *Measuring Social Capital*; Onyx and Leonard, *Social Capital*.
[15] ABS, 'Aspects of Social Capital'; ABS, 'Measuring Social Capital'.
[16] Edwards, in *Measuring Social Capital*, and Coalter, in 'Sports Clubs' have been strong advocates for more work in this area.
[17] For additional discussions of these disciplines see Spies-Butcher, 'Understanding the Concept of Social Capital'; Woolcook, 'Social Capital'; Quibria, *The Puzzle of Social Capital*.
[18] See Engelberg, Zakus and Skinner, 'Volunteer Commitment'; Engelberg, Skinner and Zakus, 'The Commitment of Volunteers'.
[19] Cuskelly, Hoye and Auld, *Working with Volunteers*.
[20] ABS, 'Voluntary Work, Australia'.

21 Cuskelly, Harrington and Stebbins, 'Changing Levels of Organizational Commitment'.
22 ABS, 'Voluntary Work, Australia, 2006'.
23 Lyons and Hocking, 'Australia's Highly Committed Volunteers'.
24 Putnam, *Bowling Alone*.
25 Nichols, 'Pressures on Volunteers'.
26 ABS, 'Voluntary Work, Australia, 2006', 1.
27 Talbot, 'Voluntary Sector Sport'.
28 Coalter, 'Sports Clubs'.
29 Seippel, 'Sport and Social Capital'.
30 Coalter, 'Sports Clubs'.
31 Tonts, 'Competitive Sport', 137.
32 Stoddart, *Saturday Afternoon Fever*.
33 Zakus, Bird and Roobottom, *Report for the Australian Football League*.
34 Tonts, 'Competitive Sport'.
35 Atherley, 'Sport, Localism', 349.
36 See Tonts and Atherley, 'Rural Restructuring', 126–8.
37 Pooley, Cohen and Pike, 'Can Sense of Community Inform Social Capital?' Their findings augment those found by Zakus, 'The Saskatchewan Roughriders'. In a similar vein Zakus and Chalip, 'Fanship and Identity', using similar scales to Pooley, Cohen and Pike, found that a professional sport franchise added to the psychological sense of community.
38 Tonts, 'Competitive Sport'.
39 Skinner, Zakus and Edwards, 'Football Communities'.
40 Elkington, 'Country Communities', 75.
41 Tonts and Atherley, 'Rural Restructuring', 127. Also see Collins and Kay, *Sport and Social Exclusion*.
42 Macdonald and Skinner, 'The Long and Winding Road'.
43 Skinner, Zakus and Edwards, *Football Communities*.
44 Seippel, 'Sport and Social Capital'.
45 A. Timms, 'Winning. Why Sport Means So Much'. *The Sydney Morning Herald, SuperSport Magazine*, January 20, 2007, 6.
46 Giulianotti, *Football*.
47 Ibid., 1–24.

References

Atherley, K. 'Sport, Localism and Social Capital in Rural Western Australia'. *Geographical Research* 44, no. 4 (2006): 348–60.
Australian Bureau of Statistics. 'Aspects of Social Capital'. http://www.abs.gov.au/AUSSTATS/abs.
Australian Bureau of Statistics. 'Voluntary Work, Australia, 2006'. http://www.abs.gov.au/ausstats/ABS@.nsg/Latestproducts/444.1.
Australian Bureau of Statistics. 'Voluntary Work, Australia, 4441'. http://www.abs.gov.au/Ausstats/abs@.nsf.
Australian Bureau of Statistics. 'Measuring Social Capital; Current Collections and Future Directions'. http://abs.gov.au/websitedbs/D3110122.nsf.
Cashman, R. *Paradise of Sport: The Rise of Organised Sport in Australia*. Oxford: Oxford University Press, 1995.
Cashman, R. *Sport in the National Imagination: Australian Sport in the Federation Decades*. Sydney: Walla Walla Press, 2002.
Coalter, F. 'Sports Clubs, Social Capital and Social Regeneration: Ill Defined Interventions with Hard to Follow Outcomes'. *Sport in Society* 10, no. 4 (July 2007): 537–59.
Collins, M.F., and T. Kay. *Sport and Social Exclusion*. London: Routledge, 2003.
Cuskelly, G., M. Harrington, and R.A. Stebbins. 'Changing Levels of Organizational Commitment amongst Sport Volunteers: A Serious Leisure Approach'. *Loisir/Leisure Special Issue: Volunteerism and Leisure* 27, nos. 3–4 (2003): 191–212.
Cuskelly, G., R. Hoye, and C. Auld. *Working with Volunteers in Sport: Theory and Practice*. London: Routledge, 2006.
Edwards, R.W. *Measuring Social Capital: An Australian Framework and Indicators*. Canberra: ABS, 2004.

Elkington, S. 'Country Communities: Sport and Recreation'. In *Country Communities: Responding to Change*, 151–208. Wodonga: Clyde Cameron College, Australian Institute of Agricultural Science, Northern Victorian Sub-Branch Australian Farm Management Society, and Department of Planning, 1982.

Engelberg, T., D.H. Zakus, and J. Skinner. 'Volunteer Commitment: Theory, Research, and Emerging Issues'. *Australian Journal of Volunteering* 12, no. 1 (2007): 26–34.

Engelberg, T., J. Skinner, and D.H. Zakus. 'The Commitment of Volunteers in Community-based Sport: A Research Review and Agenda'. *Third Sector Review* 12, no. 2 (2006): 81–96.

Giulianotti, R. *Football: A Sociology of the Global Game*. Cambridge: Polity Press, 1999.

Lyons, M., and S. Hocking. 'Australia's Highly Committed Volunteers'. In *Volunteers and Volunteering*, edited by J. Warburton and M. Oppenheimer, 44–55. Leichhardt, NSW: Federation Press, 2000.

Macdonald, R., and J. Skinner. 'The Long and Winding Road'. *The Sport Management Association of Australia and New Zealand Newsletter* 2, no. 2 (2001): 21–2.

Nichols, G. 'Pressures on Volunteers in the UK'. In *Volunteering as Leisure/Leisure as Volunteering: An International Assessment*, edited by R.A. Stebbins and M. Graham, 197–207. Wallingford, Oxford: CABI Publishing, 2004.

Onyx, J., and P. Bullen. *Measuring Social Capital in Five Communities in NSW: An Analysis*. Lindfield, NSW: Centre for Australian Community Organisations and Management, UTS, Sydney, 1997.

Onyx, J., and R. Leonard. *Social Capital: The Relative Use of Strong and Loose Network Ties*. Lindfield, NSW: Centre for Australian Community Organisations and Management, UTS, Sydney, 2001.

Pooley, J.A., L. Cohen, and L.T. Pike. 'Can Sense of Community Inform Social Capital?'. *The Social Science Journal* 42 (2005): 71–9.

Productivity Commission. *Social Capital: Reviewing the Concept and its Implications*. Canberra: AusInfo, 2003.

Putnam, R. *Bowling Alone: The Collapse and Revival of American Community*. New York: Simon and Schuster, 2000.

Quibria, M.G. *The Puzzle of Social Capital: A Critical Review*. Manila, Philippines: Asian Development Bank, 2003.

Rowland, B. *Is the Club Really a Better Place?* Melbourne: Centre for Youth Drug Studies, Australian Drug Foundation, 2006.

Seippel, Ø. 'Sport and Social Capital'. *Acta Sociologica* 49, no. 2 (2006): 169–83.

Skinner, J., D. Zakus, and A. Edwards. *Football Communities: Research Report*. Sydney: Football Federation of Australia, 2005.

Spies-Butcher, B. 'Understanding the Concept of Social Capital: Neoliberalism, Social Theory or Neoliberal Social Theory?'. Ph.D. diss., University of Sydney, 2006.

Stoddart, B. *Saturday Afternoon Fever: Sport in Australian Culture*. Sydney: Angus and Robertson, 1986.

Stone, W., and J. Hughes. *Social Capital: Empirical Meaning and Measurement Validity*. Melbourne: AIFS, 2002.

Talbot, M. 'Voluntary Sector Sport: A Case of Human Wealth and Structural Poverty'. Keynote Paper presented at the European Association of Sport Management Congress, Gateshead, Newcastle, 7–10 September, 2005.

Tonts, M. 'Competitive Sport and Social Capital in Rural Australia'. *Journal of Rural Studies* 21 (2005): 137–49.

Tonts, M. and K. Atherley. 'Rural Restructuring and the Changing Geography of Competitive Sport'. *Australian Geographer* 36, no. 2 (2005): 125–44.

Toohey, K.M. 'The Politics of Australian Elite Sport: 1949–1983'. PhD. diss., Pennsylvania State University, 1990.

Woolcock, M. 'Social Capital and Economic Development: Toward a Theoretical Synthesis and Policy Framework'. *Theory and Society* 27 (1998): 151–208.

Zakus, D.H. 'The Saskatchewan Roughriders and the Construction of Identity and Regional Resistance in Saskatchewan, Canada'. *Football Studies* 2, no. 2 (1997): 57–76.

Zakus, D.H., and L. Chalip. 'Fanship and Identity: Does Sport Add to Community and Fan Identity?'. Paper presented at the Sport Management Association of Australia and New Zealand Conference, Gold Coast, Australia, 26–28 November, 1998.

Zakus, D.H., M. Bird, and H. Roobottom. *Report for the Australian Football League: Survey of the Gold Coast.* Brisbane: Velocity Sports, 2006.

Zakus, D.H., J. Skinner, and A. Edwards. 'Identifying and Measuring Social Capital in Australian Sport'. Paper presented at the European Association for Sport Management Congress, Nicosia, Cyprus, 6–9 September, 2006.

Zakus, D.H., M. Bird, T. Briggs, H. Perkins, and S. Meadows. *Basketball Market Research Report.* Brisbane: Velocity Sports, 2007.

Index

Page numbers in *Italics* represent tables.
Page numbers in **Bold** represent figures.

For Product Safety Concerns and Information please contact our EU representative GPSR@taylorandfrancis.com Taylor & Francis Verlag GmbH, Kaufingerstraße 24, 80331 München, Germany

Batch number: 08158219

Printed by Printforce, the Netherlands